Theology, Horror and Fiction

Theology, Horror and Fiction
A Reading of the Gothic Nineteenth Century

Jonathan Greenaway

BLOOMSBURY ACADEMIC
NEW YORK • LONDON • OXFORD • NEW DELHI • SYDNEY

BLOOMSBURY ACADEMIC
Bloomsbury Publishing Inc
1385 Broadway, New York, NY 10018, USA
50 Bedford Square, London, WC1B 3DP, UK

BLOOMSBURY, BLOOMSBURY ACADEMIC and the Diana logo are trademarks of
Bloomsbury Publishing Plc

First published in the United States of America 2021
This paperback edition published 2022

Copyright © Jonathan Greenaway, 2021

Cover design by Eleanor Rose
Cover image: *Saturn Devouring one of his Sons*, 1821–23 (mural transferred to canvas)
by Francisco Jose de Goya y Lucientes, (1746–1828) © Bridgeman Images

All rights reserved. No part of this publication may be reproduced or transmitted
in any form or by any means, electronic or mechanical, including photocopying,
recording, or any information storage or retrieval system, without prior
permission in writing from the publishers.

Bloomsbury Publishing Inc does not have any control over, or responsibility for, any third-
party websites referred to or in this book. All internet addresses given in this book were
correct at the time of going to press. The author and publisher regret any inconvenience
caused if addresses have changed or sites have ceased to exist, but can accept no
responsibility for any such changes.

A catalog record for this book is available from the Library of Congress.

ISBN: HB: 978-1-5013-5178-5
PB: 978-1-5013-7135-6
ePDF: 978-1-5013-5180-8
eBook: 978-1-5013-5179-2

Typeset by Deanta Global Publishing Services, Chennai, India

To find out more about our authors and books visit www.bloomsbury.com
and sign up for our newsletters.

Contents

Acknowledgements — vi

Introduction: Gothic ~~and religion~~ and theology — 1

1 Monstrosity and the problem of evil: A theologico-literary understanding of personhood in *Frankenstein* and *Paradise Lost* — 25

2 'Sinners in the hands of an angry God': Gothic revelation and monstrous theology in the Gothic's Calvinist legacy — 55

3 Gothic writing and political theology: *Wuthering Heights* and *Jane Eyre* as theological texts — 75

4 'Through a glass darkly': Reading the Victorian ghost story theologically — 111

5 The limitations of materialism: Fin-de-siècle Gothic, sin and subjectivity and the insufficiency of degeneration — 125

Conclusion: Through the Gothic castle, back to theology — 175

Bibliography — 181
Index — 191

Acknowledgements

The vast majority of this book was written while a part of the Manchester Centre for Gothic Studies at Manchester Metropolitan University. I would like to acknowledge specifically the formative influence and collegial support of Dr Linnie Blake, Dr Xavier Aldana Reyes, Dr Elle Beal, Dr Sorcha Ni Fhlainn and Dr Matt Foley. I am deeply grateful to Dr Simon Marsden for his mentorship and encouragement to keep thinking about theology and the Gothic and to Dr Alison Milbank for her insightful critique, which has consistently challenged and inspired my ways of thinking.

Much thanks to the entire team at Bloomsbury for their help and support in preparing the book through the COVID-19 outbreak. I'd particularly like to thank the anonymous reader who reviewed the manuscript, understood what this book is trying to do and made insightful, critical and encouraging comments throughout the whole process.

Finally, this book would never have existed without the help, encouragement and support of my wife, Emma.

Introduction

Gothic ~~and religion~~ and theology

The cause and effect of the horror experience in English culture is a form of theological uncertainty, an anxiety which is recognizable at many different levels of consciousness.

Victor Sage, Horror Fiction in the Protestant Tradition (1988)

If belief is absolutely necessary, let it be in a religion that doesn't make you feel guilty. A religion out of joint, fuming, subterranean, without an end. Like a novel, not like a theology.

Umberto Eco, Foucault's Pendulum (1988)

Ruined churches, crucifixes, mysterious priests and closed orders of nuns – these are hugely familiar tropes within the early Gothic, yet this book argues that the nineteenth-century Gothic has just as much by way of theological content. To begin with, before turning to the primary texts, this chapter will provide some wider background for discussing nineteenth-century Gothic writing alongside theology, as well as the ways in which contemporary Gothic criticism has marginalized the theological aspect of the texts in question. From there, the chapter moves on to the theological methodology used and the outline of the argument as whole. Throughout this book, the Gothic novel is positioned as a form that expresses and challenges theological truths, and, furthermore, it is argued that reading the Gothic in conjunction with imaginative approaches to theology can contribute to both Gothic studies and theology more widely.

To pre-empt an immediate objection, it should be stated clearly from the start that the aim here is not to argue that the Gothic novel is some sort of Bible in disguise, neither does this book aim to retrospectively baptize the Gothic novels of the nineteenth century. The purpose of the argument here is to avoid the kind of hermeneutic reductionism that would seek to add the Gothic novel to the body of Christian writing or reduce theological complexity down to a set pattern of religious tropes. It is not that the Gothic is 'really' or 'underneath it all' a religious or even Christian body of work. A more nuanced position requires an awareness that the relationship between Gothic literature and theology has been fraught at best and, at worst, often hostile. Rather than resort to an all-too-common kind of disciplinary one-upmanship, which would subsume Gothic literature into theology without question,[1] what is required is both a degree of theological humility and a willingness to take the suppositions and commitments of theology seriously. Following Milbank, Imfeld and Hampson, who build on the work of Luke Bretherton with regard to theological hospitality, the aim here will be to attempt to draw both Gothic literature and theology to the same discursive table, to create a space within which both Gothic literary criticism and theological ideas may be placed into productive dialogue.[2]

Such a bringing together as a strategy does not involve a passive toleration of each discipline but must rather involve a concerted attempt to maintain a critical tension in which both Gothic literature and theology may mutually enrich and enliven one another despite the undeniably contentious relationship between the two fields. As Milbank, Hampson and Imfeld write, framing the matter as one of hospitable debate:

> Hospitable debate can and at times must be carried out agonistically, as a lively debate between friends, but never in a dismissive, cynical, or *ad hominem* fashion. Never, that is, if it is to be productive.[3]

The theological antagonism, or ambivalent secularism, that runs throughout the Gothic does not oppose theological ideas to Gothic writing but rather serves as a spur for theology to re-evaluate and reconsider key doctrinal and theological ideas in creative and imaginative ways. Rather than seek to claim that the texts are some form of Bible in disguise, the readings in the chapters that follow show that the Gothic text, while undeniably influenced by theological language, tropes and themes of Christian theology, has a deeply ambiguous and often hostile relationship with the theological ideas from which it draws. The Gothic

---

[1] This is most striking in the formative work of Montague Summers, in contrast to the more contemporary alternative strategy that seeks to expunge the inconvenient theology from Gothic writing altogether. (This is discussed in detail in the introduction).
[2] See Zoë Lehmann Imfeld, Peter Hampson and Alison Milbank's editor's introduction to *Theology and Literature after Postmodernity* (London: Bloomsbury Press, 2015) and Luke Bretherton, *Hospitality as Holiness: Christian Witness amid Moral Diversity* (London: Ashgate, 2009).
[3] Imfeld, Hampson and Milbank, *Theology and Literature*, 4.

novel, then, not only links to the historical and theological context of the time in which the text was produced but can serve as a spur in the present, challenging the reader to re-evaluate and rethink theological ideas and concepts. In short, then, the Gothic novel serves as a site of particular contestation to theological thinking, presenting *theo-logos* or talk of God in provocative, challenging and hostile ways.

As such, the Gothic novel chimes with the model of secularization offered by Charles Taylor in the landmark study *A Secular Age*. As Taylor claims, in place of a move from faith and piety to non-belief, the movement of modernity is instead presented as a shift from an age of faith to 'one in which it [faith] is understood to be one option among others, and frequently not the easiest to embrace'.[4] As some landmark critical work has compellingly proven, the idea of a slow collapse of faith into atheism is one that neither sociological nor historical or literary evidence would corroborate.[5] Zoë Lehmann Imfeld, in her study of the Victorian ghost story and theology, argues that the crisis of faith, such as it was, 'was not over the existence, necessarily, of God, but of how to know such a God within the limits of human knowledge'.[6] Mediated, contested and often ambiguous, the Gothic novel functions as a space in which this struggle to know something of the divine finds cultural outworking.

However, before proceeding too much further, it is perhaps useful to offer some general comments on the wider issue of theology and literature and a brief overview on the various approaches and methods used. As Mark Knight points out, it is almost impossible to think of much English literature without the heritage of a particular religious way of life. Harold Bloom saw the King James Bible as an aesthetic and literary feat matched only by the works of Shakespeare.[7] An initial first approach then might well be a kind of literary detective work – uncovering and exploring the religious and theological themes, language and imagery used in the texts. In their book on nineteenth-century literature, Mark Knight and Emma Mason go further, linking the work of writers to the religious and theological debates of the time, and examining how shifts in religious

---

[4] Charles Taylor, *A Secular Age* (London: Harvard University Press, 2007), 3.
[5] For more on this see Taylor (2003) as well as K. S. Inglis, *Churches and the Working Class in Victorian England* (London: Routledge, 2007) and Callum G. Brown, *The Death of Christian Britain: Understanding Secularisation 1800-2000*, 2nd edn (London: Routledge, 2009).
[6] Zoë Lehmann Imfeld, *The Victorian Ghost Story and Theology: From Le Fanu to James* (London: Palgrave Macmillan, 2016), 2.
[7] See Harold Bloom, *The Shadow of a Great Rock: A Literary Appreciation of the King James Bible* (New Haven: Yale University Press, 2012).

attitudes find outworking and expression in the works of the time.[8] For David Jasper, a rediscovery of theology is 'essential to contemporary reflections on philosophy, literature and culture, and that second, theology must be prepared to be reinvigorated by these radical reflections'.[9] Understood thusly, literature and theology cannot be subordinated, neither one to the other, and a theological reading of literature generally does not require simply reading the texts in moral or didactic terms, nor does it require only a focus on self-professed religious writers. Simon Marsden's pioneering book on contemporary Gothic fiction places the theological nature of horror fiction in the context of the haunting absence of religious belief in the contemporary world – a point which is both timely and hugely persuasive.[10]

What this critical argument connects to is the theological notion of 'imaginative apologetics'. Rather than traditional apologia, which depends upon giving a reasoned defence of the faith, through philosophy, in order to convince the nonbeliever, imaginative apologetics does not rely solely on reason. Imaginative apologetics is, as Andrew Davison argues, imaginative twice over: first, by using imagination as a crucial component of theological argument in order to convince, and second to make the argument that human reason and imagination cannot be easily separated.[11] In this sense, then, imaginative apologetics both allows for theological readings of fictional or imaginative works and makes the claim that these fictional works allow for a greater understanding of both the texts in question and theology itself. Thus, this book takes a contemporary or presentist view – the aim here is not principally to explore theological debates around the texts at the time of their production but rather to make the case that these historical texts have much to offer contemporary theological and religious discussion. While the arguments which follow do pay heed to the historical theological elements that may be found within the texts, this is not the principal area under consideration. As Marsden's book has argued that the contemporary Gothic is connected to contemporary theology, my own position is that nineteenth-century Gothic has much to offer here too. With this as some general context, the next section goes on to examine Gothic criticism in

---

[8] See Mark Knight and Emma Mason, *Nineteenth Century Religion and Literature: An Introduction* (Oxford: Oxford University Press, 2006).
[9] David Jasper, *The Study of Religion and Literature: An Introduction* (London: Palgrave Macmillan, 1992), 3.
[10] Simon Marsden, *The Theological Turn in Contemporary Gothic Fiction: Holy Ghosts* (London: Palgrave Macmillan, 2018).
[11] Andrew Davison, ed., *Imaginative Apologetics: Theology, Philosophy and the Catholic Tradition* (London: SCM Press, 2011), xxv.

more detail, exploring some of the reasons why Gothic criticism has frequently not given the theological and religious elements of the Gothic sufficient critical attention, and laying out the method of the readings undertaken in the course of this book in more detail.

The absence of the theological in Gothic criticism

The Gothic horror text has, as Victor Sage argued, always appeared as something to be explained, a provocation for which readers must account.[12] This is perhaps true if the role of the literary critic is essentially expository and politically conservative. In *that* case, the Gothic novel appears as an aesthetic aberration for the critic to explain or excuse – a position that few, if any, of the standard texts on Gothic criticism would seek to take up in the wake of the huge popularity of the Gothic in terms of both scholarship and students. While an outdated view on the Gothic, it does seem undeniable that the Gothic preoccupation with deviance, transgression, violence and heterodox spirituality has quite reliably seen it placed in opposition to the normative standards of morality generally enforced by the religious figures of the day – alongside cultural figures who decried both its poor taste and seeming political radicalism. As Carol Margaret Davison points out,

> In an era when over seventy per cent of the books borrowed from circulating libraries were novels and less than one per cent were religious in nature . . . 'gothomania' was a guilty pleasure for many and a social concern for some.[13]

Many of the early moral concerns often shifted onto aesthetic or technical grounds rather than the explicitly theological or religious. In her discussion of the early Gothic and the history of reading, Katie Halsey notes that the early critical responses to Gothic writing, many of which focused upon the aesthetic (often drawing from Burke's ideas of the sublime), had, by the turn of the century, shifted focus in response to new political conditions:

> In the 1790s, such discussions continued, but critics turned their attention to the moral dangers of the Gothic, and particularly to its perceived political

---

[12] See Sage, *Horror Fiction in the Protestant Tradition*, particularly the preface.
[13] Carol Margaret Davison, *Gothic Literature 1764-1824* (Cardiff: University of Wales Press, 2009), 2.

dimensions and effects. In the polarized political conditions of the 1790s, Gothic novels were often associated with the ideas and principles of the French Revolution. Conservative journals such as the *Anti-Jacobin Review* characterized these fictions as politically dangerous.[14]

What Halsey notes, but does not develop further, is that even though the critical move from aesthetic debate to political concern is very clear, what remains latent are issues of faith. The early aesthetic debates of the 1700s were, in essence, a discussion around a kind of indirect natural theology, which saw, in the splendour and power of nature, a more sure and rational way of navigating 'up' towards the divine befitting of an age of reason. Burke, for example, uses the encounter between Job and God from scripture as an example of something which is 'amazingly sublime, and this sublimity is principally due to the terrible uncertainty of the thing described'.[15] However, in the wake of the French Revolution and the emergent anxieties of political and national identity, there arose a deep suspicion that the Gothic novel could exert a dangerous corrupting influence in its ability to stimulate the imagination. As the Reverends F. Prevost and F. Blagdon wrote in their introduction to the 1801–2 *Flowers of Literature* anthology, 'Happy would it be, for the welfare of the present generation, if those ridiculous fabrications, of weak minds and often depraved hearts, which constitute the enchantment of circulating libraries, could be entirely annihilated.'[16] The conservative writer Hannah More in her *Strictures on the Modern System of Female Education* (1799) argued that the Gothic was a threat to the Christian virtue of the female reader, as the novels were the 'modern apostles of infidelity and immorality' that dispersed 'pernicious doctrines'.[17] Other examples of criticism that saw the Gothic as a specifically theological threat include Coleridge, who, in his review of *The Monk*, attacks the novel as dangerous explicitly on the grounds of how the text uses scripture:

> If it be possible that the author of these blasphemies is a Christian, should he not have reflexed that the only passage in the scriptures [Ezekiel XXIII], which could give a shadow of plausibility to the weakest of these expressions, is represented as being spoken by the Almighty himself? But if he be an infidel, he has acted

---

[14] Katie Halsey, 'Gothic and the History of Reading, 1764-1830', in *The Gothic World*, ed. Glennis Byron and Dale Townshend (London: Routledge, 2013), 172.
[15] Edmund Burke, 'A Philosophical Enquiry into the Origins of Our Ideas of the Sublime and Beautiful 1757', in *Gothic Documents: A Sourcebook*, ed. E. J Clery and Robert Miles (Manchester: Manchester University Press, 2000), 115.
[16] Quoted in Halsey, 'Gothic and the History of Reading', 173.
[17] Ibid., 173.

consistently enough with that character, in his endeavours first to influence the fleshly appetites, and then to pour contempt on the only book which would be adequate to the task of becalming them.[18]

What is striking about Coleridge's review is the fact that the text's theological ambiguity is clearly a cause of a deep anxiety. Of course, while this ambivalence is what makes the Gothic so dangerous for Coleridge it would be something he himself would later make use of in 'The Rime of the Ancient Mariner' (1798). Furthermore, it is this incongruity, which Coleridge saw as so concerning, which makes the Gothic so potentially productive for theology more widely.

Even with this theological context, in terms of the critical response to the Gothic, there has been a notable tendency to focus upon the religious content of the texts removed from the theological issues that surround and underpin them. There are two reasons for such a separation, one of which is key to the development of Gothic criticism, the other to do with the development of criticism more generally. First, twentieth-century criticism on the Gothic novel and its religious elements is greatly indebted to the eccentric bibliophile Montague Summers and, a decade later, Devandra Varma. For Summers, as a somewhat heterodox Catholic, it was essential to downplay the clear Protestantism (and accompanying anti-Catholicism) of the early Gothic novels and insist that 'there is no true Romanticism apart from Catholic influence and feeling'.[19] The insistence upon Catholic feeling as the root of early Gothic writing was joined with an assertion that the early Gothic novel was, in some way, a link back to the great age of faith and the Gothic cathedrals of the twelfth century. Therefore, the rather abstract and immaterial notions of faith become linked to the more concrete particulars of religious practice and institution in the guise of the Roman Catholic Church.[20] Varma's *The Gothic Flame* follows this – even in his reading of *Melmoth the Wanderer*, Varma claims that there are no 'direct theological attacks upon' the Roman Catholic Church and that it is only 'the

---

[18] Samuel Taylor Coleridge, 'Review of Matthew G Lewis' *The Monk*', *The Critical Review*, February 1797, 194–200, http://www.english.upenn.edu/~mgamer/Etexts/coleridge.reviews, Online, first accessed 24 July 2017.

[19] Montague Summers, *The Gothic Quest, A History of the Gothic Novel* (London: Fortune Press, 1938), 390.

[20] Graham Ward makes a similar argument with regard to the postmodern Gothic, arguing that it essentially liquidizes religious iconography and symbol, dividing it from specific religious traditions and practices, thus substituting authenticity for a cheap thrill and imitation transcendence. See Graham Ward, *True Religion* (London: Blackwell, 2003).

vestments, not the doctrines of Catholicism that serve as a source of terror'.[21] As the rather 'more-historicist-than-thou' Mighall and Baldick point out, such a failure of theological comprehension 'would have been regarded by Anne Radcliffe and most of her readers as a disqualification from understanding Gothic novels'.[22] From there, Gothic criticism was principally preoccupied with the understanding of the Gothic as concerned with reflecting the cultural anxieties of the day or manifesting political or psychoanalytic depth with little attention being given to the religious signifiers present in the Gothic.[23] Mishra, seeking to move away from the vague spiritualisms of Varna, rejects any theological notion of the Gothic. The 'Gothic sublime is . . . a version of the Lacanian Real . . . a non-transcendent aesthetics',[24] yet this Lacanian retreat into negativity both ignores the theological tradition of writing on negation and, more importantly, transposes religious and theological ideas into a psychoanalytic register without acknowledging the intellectual underpinnings of theology which give these things meaning and ultimate coherence. Rather than engage with theological ideas, the critical strategy generally falls into two categories. The Gothic text is either critically praised for its depth and insight into subjectivity and psychology, or, in an alternative strategy, is seen as reflecting the cultural fears of a particular historical moment.[25] After the work of Summers and Varma, perhaps the most formative work in the development of Gothic scholarship is David Punter's two-volume work *The Literature of Terror*. While broadly historicist in tone and content, the book once again elides the theological content of the Gothic, in this case through psychoanalysis. This is most glaring in the treatment of Hogg's *The Private Memoirs and Confessions of a Justified Sinner*, which is read as a model of

---

[21] Devendra Varma, *The Gothic Flame: Being a History of the Gothic Novel in England, Its Origins, Efflorescence, Disintegration, and Residuary Influences* (London: Morrison and Gibb, 1957), 219.
[22] Chris Baldick and Robert Mighall, 'Gothic Criticism', in *A Companion to the Gothic* (London: Blackwell, 2000), 217.
[23] A notable exception to this would be Sage's excellent *Horror Fiction in the Protestant Tradition*, as well as more recent work which this book is deeply indebted to (see Alison Milbank, *God and the Gothic: Religion, Romance and Reality in the English Literary Tradition* [Oxford: Oxford University Press, 2019]) and Marsden, *The Theological Turn in Contemporary Gothic Fiction*).
[24] Vijay Mishra, *The Gothic Sublime* (New York: SUNY Press, 1994), 17.
[25] For examples of this kind of criticism which makes frequent reference to the supposed 'depth' or 'subversion' of Gothic literature, see Maggie Kilgour, *The Rise of the Gothic Novel* (London: Routledge, 1995), Devendra P. Varma, *The Gothic Flame*, (London: Arthur Baker Ltd, 1957), Anne Williams, *Art of Darkness: A Poetics of Gothic* (Chicago: Chicago University Press, 1995), Montague Summers *The Gothic Quest*, (London: The Fortune Press, 1938) and Rosemary Jackson, *Fantasy, The Literature of Subversion*, (London: Routledge, 1981). For examples of Gothic criticism that conducts its analysis through emphasizing the cultural anxieties of a particular moment, see Stephen Arata, *Fictions of Loss in the Victorian fin-de-siècle, Identity and Empire* (Cambridge: Cambridge University Press, 1996) as well as Kelly Hurley, *The Gothic Body: Sexuality, Materialism and Degeneration at the Fin-de-Siècle* (Cambridge: Cambridge University Press, 1996).

schizophrenia rather than a text deeply invested in a specific religious milieu and within complex theological traditions.[26] However, scholarship more attuned to the religious elements of the Gothic text has become more prominent in recent years, for example, with the work of Diane Long Hoeveler, whose book *The Gothic Ideology* focuses rather exhaustively upon the religious and frequently anti-Catholic details in much of the early Gothic.[27] Yet the focus on religion still comes at the cost of theological ideas, which ties into the broader history of the development of literary criticism. As David Jasper points out, the study of religion and literature has become increasingly popular from the 1950s onwards. He links this to the legacy of structuralism, which moved 'the whole enterprise' away from theology, towards an essentially 'trivial' notion of religion.[28] Religion, as a concrete system of signs and rituals was more critically palatable than the rather more abstract and less immediately tangible field of theology. As a result, what appears in criticism is the study of literature and religion 'without commitment',[29] a disappointing 'theological dilettante-ism'[30] that damages theology through increasingly isolating it from the public realm of literature and culture. As Robert F. Geary argues, in his much neglected and, sadly, little read study *The Supernatural in Gothic Fiction*, theology is a somewhat old-fashioned pursuit and perhaps even embarrassing for modern rationalist criticism:

> These critical presuppositions, in many cases, turn out to be based on the denial of what the supernatural tale asserts – the persistence of the numinous reality in the modern world. Predictably then, many critics have difficulty taking seriously the essence of much supernatural fiction, for doing so would call into question their assumptions not simply about such writing but the nature of modern people and the status of belief in the modern world.[31]

Geary argues that both the Gothic supernatural tale and theology insist upon the insufficiency of vulgar materialism and thus require a reassessment of the assumptions that underpin both literary criticism and theological expression. Throughout his detailed study, Geary notes the difficulties of 'how to employ

---

[26] See David Punter, *The Literature of Terror: A History of Gothic Fiction* (Two Vols) (London: Routledge, 1996). For a further response to this, see Chapter 2.
[27] Diane Hoeveler, *The Gothic Ideology: Religious Hysteria and Anti-Catholicism in British Popular Fiction, 1780-1880* (Cardiff: University of Wales Press, 2014).
[28] Jasper, *The Study of Literature and Religion*, 5.
[29] Ibid., 2.
[30] See David Jaspers, ed., *Postmodernism, Literature and the Future of Theology* (London: Palgrave, 1993), 2.
[31] Robert F. Geary, *The Supernatural in Gothic Fiction Horror, Belief and Literary Change* (Lampeter: The Edwin Mellen Press, 1992), 122.

the supernatural in a credible manner in narratives laying claim to a degree of realism',[32] yet outside of the confines a clear context of belief, this task often leaves formal tensions that novelists struggle to negotiate.[33] The important task from a critical point of view is to negotiate the stubborn persistence of numinous reality while at the same time acknowledging the fact that this cannot be easily or conveniently explained through an unambiguously orthodox Christian paradigm (if only for the reasons that to speak of *one* singular orthodox Christian model for reading the Gothic is theologically reductive in the extreme). It is quite arguable that this persistence of the numinous within the Gothic tale and the need for some form of explanation is behind the critical proliferation of psychoanalytic studies of the Gothic. Yet, as Eagleton points out, one of the markers of modernity is the 'transition from the soul to the psyche, or if one prefers, from theology to psychoanalysis'.[34] Andrew Smith notes the Gothic fascination with the ineffable but ties this to a discourse of 'internalization', traced from Burke to Freud which is contrasted to the Kantian idea of the sublime whereby the dissolution of the subject is triggered by a transcendent experience in nature. The Gothic challenges to Enlightenment rationality are acknowledged as an 'aesthetic feature . . . an ontology and, paradoxically, a kind of epistemology',[35] which is easily read through a psychoanalytic topography.[36] Yet what is missed in this analysis is the fact that Christian theological discourses refuse the notion of a distinction between an interior and an exterior sublime. Theology, broadly conceived, depends upon both the internal experience of the divine and the idea that God can be (and is) revealed through nature and language – both individual revelation and natural theology are key. Furthermore, rather than seek an explanation for this in psychoanalysis (for which the nineteenth-century Gothic text functions as a kind of forerunner) 'theology contains, at the subjective level, a complete, pre-emptive description of the most obscure processes of the mind'.[37] Perhaps unsurprisingly, then, the theological content of the Gothic has

---

[32] Ibid., 31.
[33] See Geary's discussion of *The Monk* (1798) in *The Supernatural in Gothic Fiction Horror*, 60–9.
[34] Terry Eagleton, *On Evil* (New Haven: Yale University Press, 2008), 17.
[35] Andrew Smith, *Gothic Radicalism: Literature, Philosophy and Psychoanalysis in the Nineteenth Century* (London: Palgrave, 2000), 1–2.
[36] An exhaustive list is not possible here, but for other key readings of the Gothic through a psychoanalytic model, see Andrew Smith and William Hughes, eds, *Bram Stoker: History, Psychoanalysis, and The Gothic* (London: Palgrave Macmillan, 1998). See also Michelle A. Massé, 'Psychoanalysis and the Gothic', *A New Companion to the Gothic*, ed. David Punter (London: Blackwell, 2012), Valdine Clemens, *The Return of the Repressed: Gothic Horror from the Castle of Otranto to Alien* (New York: SUNY, 1999) and Williams, *Art of Darkness*.
[37] Sage, *Horror Fiction in the Protestant Tradition*, xvii.

been critically repressed – a theo-drama made over into a psychodrama, yet, theological resources and readings can, it will be shown, provide readings and insights that psychoanalysis alone cannot fully articulate. The quotation from Geary highlights the potential reasons for the absence of theological criticism on the Gothic as well as reinforcing the preference for the concrete actualities of religious symbol, practice and trope over the more diffuse ideas of theology. This distinction is important, as religious tropes, symbol and linguistic expression are all too frequently abstracted from a connection to their wider theological ideas and philosophical concepts, which underpin the religious expression within the texts.

What critical moves there have been rest upon either a historicizing analysis of anti-Catholicism, particularly in the work of critics such as Diana Long Hoeveler[38] mentioned previously, or a nostalgic return to a kind of medieval Romantic spirituality for which there is little evidence.[39] However, to theorize the interactions of the Gothic and religion as solely a political or social discourse is to ignore the causal role theology holds in the formation of cultural discourses as well as ignore the body of literature and philosophy that makes up Christian theology over the past two thousand years. While it is undeniable that Christianity is a religion with a certain broad range of symbols, language and ritual, it is also a set of theological ideas and philosophical concepts which serve to give meaning to the religious aspects of the faith.

Here I follow Graham Ward in defining religion (broadly conceived) as 'inseparable from liturgy, community and the practice of faith' whereas theology is a 'speaking about the God who is believed in'.[40] Furthermore, both of these aspects are intimately bound up in other discourses – of political, social and historical contexts and cultural expression. Without examining the theological ideas which inform and define the religious symbolism, an accurate understanding of the relationship between Christian belief and Gothic writing remains, at best, merely half complete – dependent upon a structuralist understanding of religious pattern, but without the necessary commitment (to use Jasper's phrase) that would give those patterns coherence. Critics like Hoeveler have identified the

---

[38] See Diane Long Hoeveler, *Gothic Riffs: Secularizing the Uncanny in the European Imaginary 1780-1820* (Ohio: Ohio University Press, 2010); also *The Gothic Ideology: Religious Hysteria and Anti-Catholicism in British Popular Fiction, 1780-1880* (Cardiff: University of Wales Press, 2014).

[39] As Chris Baldick and Robert Mighall point out in their essay 'Gothic Criticism', in *A Companion to The Gothic* (2001), this seems to stem largely from Walpole's foreword to *The Castle of Otranto* (1764) and in twentieth-century scholarship a too close adherence to the influential work of Montague Summers, see *The Gothic Quest: A History of the Gothic Novel*.

[40] Ward, *True Religion*, 2–3.

rise of nationalism and anti-Catholicism in contributing to the formation of the early Gothic yet there seems to be all too often a direct correlation equated with causation without examining what is often a more diffuse set of cultural discourses and practices. To examine a theologically formed trope (such as nationalistic anti-Catholicism) without a degree of theological reflection is to ignore Marilyn Butler's point that 'the arts do not exist faithfully to reproduce political realities or real-life political arguments'.[41] While Hoeveler's point about the correlation between the rise of Gothic anti-Catholicism and a political discourse is valid, to ascribe causation to correlation is a reductionist understanding of the ways in which culture and politics interact and one that completely neglects the role that theological reasoning and discourse had in shaping the Protestant bourgeoisie and anti-Catholic politics she so laboriously identifies.

What is often missed by critics is the fact that theology serves simultaneously as both cause and effect in social discourse. While Hoeveler's work recognizes the anti-Catholicism in the production of the early Gothic (a theological effect), it then fails to grasp the theological justification at work in the root causes of this same anti-Catholic sentiment. Perhaps the most famous example would be the reception of Matthew Lewis's *The Monk* (1796). Critics such as Hoeveler rightly connect the almost parodic anti-Catholicism to the political discourses of the time, but the relationship is much more complex. As Victor Sage points out, Protestant theology, while necessarily inclined to a degree of conservatism in order to perform any kind of social cohesion, is also notoriously heterogeneous and hydra-headed.[42] As mentioned earlier in the critical review, the devoutly Anglican Coleridge took issue with Lewis, accusing him of blasphemy, not for his anti-Catholicism but for his use of scripture for seduction. Consequently, Lewis was forced to censor his own text to avoid the serious charge of violation of the King's peace. Here we see the cause-and-effect relationship in full – the theology that Lewis depended upon to exploit popular and political prejudice and anti-Catholicism simultaneously underwrote the law that made his text a politically dangerous one.[43] Theological discourse acts as a grid, holding individuals in a social relationship with one another, yet this should not be understood as a static arrangement. Theology possesses a certain degree of

---

[41] Marilyn Butler, *Romantics, Rebels and Reactionaries: English Literature and Its Background 1760-1830* (Oxford: Oxford University Press, 1981).
[42] See Sage, *Horror Fiction in the Protestant Tradition*.
[43] Andre Parreaux, *The Publication of the Monk: A Literary Event 1796-1798* (Paris: Marcel Didier, 1960).

conceptual elasticity allowing for the unification of disparate social groups – that is, those that share certain theological beliefs – while at the same time ensuring their continued isolation from others. The idea of theology having a real, though shifting, cultural influence is visible throughout the whole of the nineteenth century – for example, Hogg's *Memoirs and Confessions* (1824) draws not just on the homosociality of male desire[44] but on the real theological divisions that existed between the established episcopacy, the dissenting faiths and the radicalism of the Covenanters. To miss these theological markers is to reduce the scope, accuracy and insight of Gothic criticism. Theological rhetoric, tropes and symbolism at work within the Gothic nineteenth-century text allowed for the novels to resonate with various audience members – titillating the sensibilities of anti-Catholic Protestants while at the same time providing theological reinforcement for their own sense of cultural identity and spiritual superiority.

In contradistinction to the work of critics like Hoeveler, Victor Sage's *Horror Fiction in the Protestant Tradition* still represents one of the highpoints in examining the intersections of theology, religion and the Gothic. Sage's book proceeds through rigorous analysis of repeated rhetoric, trope, symbol and style finding in these disparate parts an underlying link to the ideological and discursive currents of English Protestant theology. Yet this is never disassociated from the historical conditions to which theology consistently responds and by which it is shaped. However, at the close of the book, Sage argues that the 'horror fiction is, essentially, fantasy about history'.[45] While the point is well taken, a separation between theology and history is not necessarily so easy to construct, given how deeply bound up in one another the two are. If the horror text is invested in using elements of theological discourse, which is both conditioned by historical circumstances and an ongoing and consistent tradition, then cleanly delineating history and theology is not only difficult but also impossible. Sage's final point rests upon a binary logic that would seek to place theology outside of, or in some way separate to, history, when in fact the two are deeply enmeshed within one another. Easily the most significant follow-up to Sage's work is Alison Milbank's landmark new book on the theological nature of the

---

[44] See Eve Kosofsky Sedgwick, *Between Men: English Literature and Male Homosocial Desire* (New York: Columbia University Press, 1985).
[45] Sage, *Horror Fiction in the Protestant Tradition*, 234.

English Gothic. For Milbank the Gothic is 'a mode of religious historiography'[46] – a case made through a systematic historical study which shows that the English Gothic becomes more, not less, theologically as the nineteenth century develops. Rather than seek to divide theology and history in order to articulate what the Gothic text is 'essentially' about, what is necessary is a theological analysis which is robust enough to deal with ambiguity of the Gothic text, as well as aware of the nuances of historical criticism. While drawing off the pioneering work of Alison Milbank, this study seeks not to construct an historical genealogy, or to make any claim about the denominational commitments of the Gothic text. Rather, the aim here is to use the nineteenth-century Gothic text as an imaginative resource for theological work.

In setting about this aim, this book claims that the nineteenth-century Gothic novel fits with the model outlined by Alison Milbank, of an imaginative form that 'provides an epistemology, a way of knowing, that is inherently religious',[47] albeit in no way orthodox. Milbank argues that imaginative literary forms (mentioning specifically the work of Novalis and Tolkien) can draw the reader into a participatory encounter with the real, to allow a 'stronger role for the "otherness" of reality'.[48] For Milbank, such an encounter aims at creating a kind of 'homesickness for the truth',[49] not simply convincing the reader of a *fact* but rather encouraging a new way of perceiving and participating within the wider world. Such a strategy involves seeing Christian theology as more than a set of truth propositions that are logically assented to but also a set of aesthetic and imaginative qualities that can be expressed through literary form. Crucially, then, the bringing together of the Gothic with theology not only enriches the work of Gothic scholarship but also allows the Gothic to be brought into the ongoing work of imaginative theology, which, despite the growing body of work dedicated to it, makes little to no mention of the Gothic as a site for theological meaning. There has been a far greater focus on poetry and writers who appear perhaps more immediately theologically valuable such as C. S Lewis, J. R. R Tolkien and the work of the Inklings.[50] This frustrating aporia in the field is

---

[46] Alison Milbank, *God and the Gothic: Religion, Romance and Reality in the English Literary Tradition* (Oxford: Oxford University Press, 2019), 305.
[47] Alison Milbank, 'Apologetics and the Imagination', in *Imaginative Apologetics, Theology, Philosophy and the Catholic Tradition*, ed. Andrew Davison (London: SCM Press, 2011), 32.
[48] Ibid., 39.
[49] Ibid., 33.
[50] An exhaustive list is impossible given the way in which the field has expanded in the course of the past three decades and connected with the wider field of literature and theology but for some key works in Imaginative Apologetics, see Davison, *Imaginative Apologetics*; Jaspers, *Study of Literature*

shown in Holly Ordway's point that widening the spectrum of engagement can allow for theological language to find new resonance and meaning with people outside of the faith and even lead to greater sympathy for those suffering.[51] However, Ordway makes no attempt to engage with the Gothic, which in depictions of suffering, horror and fear could prove to be profoundly theologically meaningful. As Milbank claims, Kant's critical philosophy argued for a transcendent spiritual reality but with no possibility of perceptual access to it. This, of course, shares much in common with the neo-reformed orthodoxy of theologians such as Karl Barth who argued that humanity could make no movement towards God outside of his own divine revelation, revealed in Jesus Christ.[52] Under this understanding of the world, 'we are cut off . . . from the noumenal spiritual world, and metaphysics is the science of the limits of our understanding.'[53] In the modern, strictly materialist world, Milbank claims, 'we have lost heaven but also earth, the real and the ideal together'.[54] We live instead in a world of flat phenomenal objects, and thus, an awakening of the imaginative capacity does not just carry with it a religious dimension, but, as Milbank points out, it 'gives us the world itself'.[55] Literature, specifically non-realist modes of fiction, possesses the ability to create a heightened sense of reality – a new world where 'ordinary sites, are rendered eerie and strange'.[56] This might be termed the 'MOOR EEFFOC' effect – drawn from the moment that Dickens sees the mysterious letters on a plate glass door, while walking through a foggy London evening. From the inside of the room, the letters spell out the more prosaic 'coffee room', but that moment of mystery is never fully exorcized, to the point that every time Dickens sees the word 'a shock goes through my blood'.[57] Utilizing theological understanding of literature does not simply add new facts to our understanding but possesses the potential to transform the way in which

and Religion and *Postmodernism, Literature and the future of theology*; David Brown, *Tradition and Imagination: Revelation and Change* (Oxford: Oxford University Press, 1999); *God in Mystery and Words: Experience Through Metaphor and Drama* (Oxford: Oxford University Press, 2011); Malcolm Guite, *Faith, Hope and Poetry: Theology and the Poetic Imagination* (London: Routledge, 2010); Anthony Monti, *A Natural Theology of the Arts* (London: Ashgate, 2003); *Literature and Theology: New Interdisciplinary Spaces*, ed. Heather Walton (London: Ashgate, 2011); Cameron J. Anderson, *The Faithful Artist: A Vision for Evangelicalism and the Arts* (Illinois: InterVarsity Press, 2011).
[51] See Holly Ordway, *Apologetics and the Imagination: An Integrated Approach to Defending the Faith* (Stubenville: Emmaus Road Publishing, 2017).
[52] For a good general overview on Barth, see *The Cambridge Companion to Karl Barth,* ed. John Webster (Cambridge: Cambridge University Press, 2000).
[53] A. Milbank, 'Apologetics and the Imagination', 32.
[54] Ibid.
[55] Ibid., 36.
[56] Ibid., 38.
[57] Detailed in G. K. Chesterton, *Charles Dickens* (Teddington: Echo Library, 2007 [1906]), 21.

analysis and criticism take place, providing a new way of understanding, outside of Kantian metaphysics. As Milbank argues, 'our primary task . . . is surely to awaken people to their own creative capacity, for in so doing we will quite naturally awaken their religious sense.'[58]

Here Milbank shares some common ground with the radical orthodox[59] theologian John Milbank, who in his theological ontology argues that all 'human making participates in a God who is infinite poetic utterance: the second person of the Trinity'.[60] In her landmark essay, Alison Milbank uses the example of Caspar David Friedrich's 1818 painting *Chalk Cliffs at Rugen* as a piece which can be read theologically, as even without crosses or religious iconography, 'it gives us a religious sense of the mystery of the real'.[61] The figures within the painting are, like the viewer of the image, perceiving the view of the infinite sea and taken in by the otherness, the sheer strangeness of the scene and yet, at the same time, they are participating within it. Even without explicit orthodox religious iconography, a painting of a simple natural scene allows for the viewer to be drawn into a familiar scene that is encountered in a strange, new and fundamentally theological way – a point that Ruskin would make back in the nineteenth century in his writing on art but a truth that has not yet been extended to the Gothic by contemporary critics.

As Imfeld claims, the Gothic supernatural tale 'takes up a specific and privileged space in literature . . . in which theological truth claims are doubly immanent and other'.[62] Within the space of the Gothic, ordinary objects are made strange and theological truth claims and metanarratives can be explored by what Imfeld terms the 'non-theological reader'.[63] What this entails is an encounter with a particular theological idea by readers who do not have a pre-existing theological framework and is thus not limited to a particular idea of orthodoxy or even necessarily any kind of religious commitment. This book seeks to extend Imfeld's argument in another direction, by linking it to the work of the theologian David Brown.[64] Brown's work on the history and development

---

[58] A. Milbank, 35.
[59] Radical Orthodoxy is a loose movement in contemporary Christian theology, marked by a Neo-Platonist philosophical commitment and a valorization of theology as the 'queen of the sciences'. Key figures in Radical Orthodoxy are John Milbank, Catherine Pickstock and, to a lesser extent, Graham Ward.
[60] John Milbank, *Being Reconciled: Ontology and Pardon* (London: Routledge, 2003), ix.
[61] A. Milbank, 36.
[62] Imfeld, *Victorian Ghost Story*, 6.
[63] Ibid.
[64] While Brown and others, particularly Alison Milbank, have some fairly major differences in terms of theological method, particularly over the issues of natural theology and revelation outside of

of theology has consistently argued that theological insights can emerge from sources external to church hierarchy and scriptural orthodoxy, which make valuable contributions to the ongoing revelation of God in the world. As Brown writes,

> History invariably throws up new ways of viewing our experience ... what has given Christianity its strength over the centuries is not mere repetition of the past but an ability to respond to new circumstances in new ways.[65]

While Imfeld argues that theology may reveal itself to the non-theological reader, my own position is that this non-theological reading can and must be linked back into the ongoing life of the church.[66] The reader may be 'non-theological', but the insights and challenges brought forth from the text are of vital interest to the ongoing development of Christian theology. The challenge that the Gothic text presents to orthodox Christian belief serves as a spur to make more radical, more open and more generous statements about God, and allow for revelation about the nature of God and his relationship with the world to be manifest in shocking new ways. This strikes me as a vital move for theology to undertake, for while Imfeld is correct to argue for the persistence of a kind of metaphysical language throughout the supernatural Gothic that 'haunts the discipline of literature as a secular task',[67] theology itself is often haunted by its metaphoric, linguistic and imaginative aspects. As David Brown points out, imaginative art is often 'deploying exactly the same tools that make talk of God possible'[68] and therefore it becomes critical to acknowledge the theological potential within the Gothic text but also the ways in which these texts may feed back into the rearticulating and reimaging of theological ideas carried out by the broader community of faith known as the church.[69] Within the environs of the supernatural Gothic text,

---

the Christian faith, their various approaches will be shown through the course of the thesis to be productive antagonisms rather than contradictory.

[65] David Brown, *Discipleship and Imagination: Christian Tradition and Truth* (Oxford: Oxford University Press, 2000), 175. As Brown goes on to argue through the whole book, this is not merely an issue with theological doctrine but something which fundamentally alters the ways in which Christian faith is lived, and members of the community of faith are discipled within faith communities and churches.

[66] I refer here to the church but this should not be taken to mean that I claim the Gothic for a particular denominational strain of Christian belief but rather the ongoing, evolving community of faith that makes up Christian belief in all of its varied forms.

[67] Imfeld, *Victorian Ghost Story*, 6.

[68] David Brown, 'The Arts' Critique of Theology', delivered at the Ian Ramsey Centre – Humane Philosophy Project 2014–2015 Seminar. Available at https://www.youtube.com/watch?v=SgskbXGdHtI, first accessed 26 June 2017.

[69] This challenge is taken up in the conclusion. Here I differ a little from theologians such as Milbank as for the purposes of the argument here, imaginative apologetics is not used simply as a means of

talk of God becomes possible – even if that talk is hostile, or even opposed to the long-running traditions and ideas that make up the broad field of 'theology' or the wider community of religious believers. Paul Fiddes has sought to show how this creative language allows rather than hinders the articulation of dogmatic statements.[70] However, rather than aim for a kind of Gothic systematics, the aim here is to locate the ways in which Gothic texts allow for a more generous and expansive understanding of divine revelation and a wider comprehension about both the nature and means of expressing theological truth. David Brown goes some way towards articulating the theological problem with which the Gothic text may productively engage.

> On the one hand, we have God portrayed as marvellously generous in the way he has disclosed himself in biblical revelation and the Church; on the other, he speaks outside that revelation faintly and only then in a manner that acquires proper legitimacy and intelligibility when set in the context of Christian faith. But if God is truly generous, would we not expect to find him at work everywhere and in such a way that all human beings could not only respond to him, however implicitly, but also develop insights from which even Christians could learn?[71]

The argument from Brown highlights the extent to which Gothic texts serve as a challenge to theological approaches to literature. Within the complex and often-ambivalent relationship to theology that runs throughout the Gothic nineteenth century, the question of the reach of theological revelation becomes more pressing. Brown's question of where God is at work, is one to which the Gothic offers an unorthodox and provocative answer. Even in, and perhaps especially in, the midst of the anti-religious or ambivalently theological Gothic text, there is the very real possibility of finding God at work in unexpected ways. What must be acknowledged is that such a discovery may lead to conclusions that challenge long-standing orthodoxies and belief structures and require a willingness, on the part of theology, to respond hospitably and with humility.

By opening itself to the insights of the Gothic, theology can in turn find powerful new modes of re-expressing old theological truths. As Brown argues, 'a God active outside the control of the Church needs to be acknowledged, and

---

imaginatively engaging and persuading the non-theological reader but also as a way by which the imaginative capacity can be used to engage those within the church.

[70] See Paul Fiddes, *Freedom and Limit: A Dialogue between Literature and Christian Doctrine* (London: Palgrave, 1991).

[71] David Brown, *God and Enchantment of Place: Reclaiming Human Experience* (Oxford: Oxford University Press, 2004), 8.

the implications heeded. That entails a careful listening exercise, the final result of which cannot be predetermined in advance'.[72] Christian thought has long wrestled with issues over theodicy, teleology and the nature of God and religious practice, and the imaginative capacity of Gothic literature offers much by way of potential for contemporary theology that has so far been insufficiently explored.

Outline of the argument: Chapter by chapter

Moving through the Gothic nineteenth century the work that follows offers theological examinations of canonical texts from *Frankenstein* (1818) to *Dracula* (1897), exploring both the historical theological issues which the texts draw upon and respond to and, more importantly, the ways in which the theological register of the texts may be productive for contemporary research. Given the overall aim of facilitating the broadest possible disciplinary dialogue between Gothic studies and creative theology, the choice of texts ranges widely across the nineteenth century and across diverse historical, social, cultural and theological contexts.

The nineteenth century as a whole shows, as Max Weber points out, the rise of both capitalism and a widespread Protestant work ethic.[73] As the manifesto of the V21 Collective points out, the 'aesthetic forms the . . . pioneered and perfected [in the nineteenth century] continue to dominate popular and avant-garde cultural production'.[74] Thus, an examination of the interactions of theology and the nineteenth-century Gothic is essential not only for understanding the development of the historical Gothic novel more fully but also for understanding how theology may still exert an influence on contemporary Gothic forms. All of the texts chosen have been selected for the extent to which they were formative on the development of Gothic writing – both Shelley and Stoker's works were widely adapted and have shaped popular conceptions of the Gothic since their publication.[75]

The book opens with a discussion of Mary Shelley's *Frankenstein*. As a text, *Frankenstein* presents a type of fall narrative yet manages to place the theological

---

[72] Ibid., 2.
[73] See Max Weber, *The Protestant Ethic and the Spirit of Capitalism* (London, Routledge, 2001).
[74] See http://v21collective.org/manifesto-of-the-v21-collective-ten-theses/, first accessed 29 January 18.
[75] This quite arguably holds true even in to the twentieth century with the success and cultural impact of adaptations and appropriations of these two texts.

question of sin and salvation within human material conditions. I argue that Shelley's political liberalism places the theology of the text in concrete terms, rather than the realm of abstract imagination. Furthermore, drawing on the work of theologian David Brown the text will be both placed within the historical and cultural context of the time as well as connected to the ongoing theological tradition within which it participates. The chapter also draws upon the work of Augustine to examine the idea of monstrosity, emphasizing the ways in which the category of evil is often a means by which certain Others are systematically excluded from human community. Given the novel's language, which consistently refers to the evil and monstrous nature of the creature, the concluding section focuses upon the idea of evil, and reads the characters of the novel in Augustinian terms, claiming that of all the characters within the text it is Victor who most closely fits the model of privative evil. Read theologically, then, *Frankenstein* provides both a critique of Romanticism and a practical grounded and material theology that seeks to embrace rather than outcast the Other.

Chapter 2 moves on to consider the influence of Calvin and reformed theology in shaping a specific repeated trend in Gothic literature. Through a close reading of James Hogg's *The Private Memoirs and Confessions of a Justified Sinner* (1824), the ways in which reformed theological ideas inform the techniques used by the text to create fear are examined. Particularly important is the notion of a fundamentally divided world, split between the physical and immaterial. This inculcates a sense of self-doubt and reveals the subject to be adrift in a material world potentially rife with spiritual danger and damnation. Drawing from the work of Alison Milbank, particularly her essay on Covenanter Gothic,[76] the key Gothic symbol of the double is shown to be an idea undergirded by theological ideas derived from the works of Calvin – particularly the highly influential *Institutes of the Christian Religion* (1536). This kind of systematic theology seeks to ultimately secure theological truth, revealed through scripture, but the textuality of language, riven by metaphor, allusion and analogy, consistently resists this kind of enclosure. Here the chapter draws this tension out as a source of much of the Gothic preoccupation with doubling and the unknown as the Gothic co-option of Calvinist theological discourse is designed to prey upon this religious anxiety over the status of language and its role in experiencing the theological. Calvinist epistemology, derived from systematic theological

---

[76] Alison Milbank, 'Calvinist and Covenanter Gothic', in *Scottish Gothic: An Edinburgh Companion*, ed. Carol Margaret Davison and Monaca Germana (Edinburgh: Edinburgh University Press, 2016).

ideas, is, through these Gothic texts, revealed to be both a source of terror and theologically dangerous – far more unstable than systematic writers such as Calvin would be willing to admit. In opposition to this crude Calvinism, the Gothic articulates an ambiguous natural and imaginative religion through its depictions of supernatural encounters in nature. In contrast to the surety and interpretative closure of the systematic, the theological revelation in nature is shown to fit alongside theological doubt, contingency and, crucially, the possibility of destabilizing singular meanings. Despite the consistent ambiguity that runs through the supernatural experienced in nature, Hogg's work refuses to foreclose the theological entirely – even if precision in interpretation cannot be easily maintained.

Keeping the focus upon nature and the theological, Chapter 3 focuses upon the work of the Brontës, specifically *Wuthering Heights* and *Jane Eyre*, both from 1847. As unorthodox theologians, the Brontë texts are deeply invested in the theological contexts of the late 1840s and through a careful close reading of the two texts, the theological resonance of the pieces are explored and the ways in which both authors utilize the Gothic for different ends are explained. Like Hogg, and other Gothic Calvinistic writers, the two texts present powerful theological experiences being closely linked to particular environments. Beginning with Emily Brontë's *Wuthering Heights*, the chapter, rather than attempt to place the text within a particular historical or denominational category, approaches *Wuthering Heights* as a Gothic environment within which theological experience is expressed in haunting and heterodox ways. The chapter also draws upon contemporary criticism, particularly responding to the landmark work of Sandra Gilbert and Susan Gubar,[77] as well as Simon Marsden's work on the religious imagination of Emily Brontë[78] and Marianne Thormählen's study on the link between the Brontës and Anglicanism. *Wuthering Heights* is linked to the work of Schleiermacher, and the idea of theology as profoundly rooted in personal experience, but at the same time, theology allows for ways out of patterns of abuse and pain inflicted by living in a fallen, material world. In the case of *Jane Eyre*, theology provides a model of liberation that leads towards a more complete and fulfilling model of subjectivity than the strictures and boundaries of a life marked by cultural and class contexts. Rather than see the world as something from which one must withdraw in order to maintain some standard of moral

---

[77] Sandra M. Gilbert and Susan Gubar, *The Madwoman in the Attic: The Woman Writer and the Nineteenth-Century Literary Imagination* (London: Yale University Press, 1984).
[78] Simon Marsden, *Emily Brontë and the Religious Imagination* (London: Bloomsbury Academic 2014).

purity, *Jane Eyre* presents theology as a means of entering fully into the world, rather than escaping from the world. Here, then, the reading provided expands upon the idea of the novel as a model of feminine subjectivity, arguing for a Gothicized political theology. Gothic elements are used throughout the text to underscore both the need for liberation into authentic subjectivity and the potential risks of a theological view of existence that can draw the individual away from the full experiences of life. For the Brontës, then, theology is both a matter of material existence in all of its fullness, and an awareness that materiality can exist alongside the supernatural.

Chapter 4 turns to the ghost story as the nineteenth century was a time in which this form found a huge popular readership. Offering close readings from a range of short stories, the chapter makes an argument for reading them in religious and theological terms. The Victorian age is a historical moment that is hugely religious, heavily involved in theological debate and discussion yet at the same moment the truth claims of religious belief become increasingly contingent as new knowledge forms emerge which challenge traditional religious hegemony. As religious discourse becomes one form among many others, this leads to a growth of new concerns, as religion becomes a site of intense debate and study. This finds cultural expression in the form of the ghost story as the supernatural short story becomes a space in which theological anxiety, commitment and scepticism can be explored. The range of ghost stories analysed in the chapter underscore this, yet chime with the previous and subsequent chapters by highlighting the extent to which the Gothic allows for a kind of faith without commitment. Readers are drawn into a theological world, which cannot ultimately make absolute claims to final truth but still has the potential to function as an imaginative form.

The fifth and final chapter of the book moves on to the British fin-de-siècle Gothic text, focusing on *The Picture of Dorian Gray* (1890), *The Strange Case of Dr. Jekyll and Mr. Hyde* (1886) and *Dracula* (1897). Beginning with an exploration of the social and historical contexts, particularly focusing upon materialism and degeneration, the era is articulated as being fraught with the issue of how to maintain a coherent theological understanding of existence in an age of scientific sophistication and increasing secularism. The three texts are read as expressing differing facets of theology and articulating some of the key limitations of scientific materialism. However, despite the explosion in criticism around this issue, as well as evolution and material explanations for existence, the Gothic of the period explores not just cultural fears of atavism but also theological anxieties of what may lie beyond the material. Drawing on the work of Rowan Williams,[79] the chapter argues that this discourse of degeneration is unable to articulate its own limitations, and thus the Gothic persists as a means of exploring beyond the solely materialist. *Jekyll and Hyde* is shown to be an exploration of Pauline theology in the era of scientific explanations of human subjectivity and behaviour. Expanding on work that treats the novel as an examination of anxieties around atavism, the chapter argues that the text responds on a profound level to a fear of divided subjectivity, not simply the divide between human and beast. This connects Chapter Five 5 to Chapter 2, as the theological aspects of the self divided against itself are directly linked back to Calvinist theologies which inform the construction of subjectivity. From there, Oscar Wilde's *Dorian Gray* is read as an exploration of the danger implicit in decoupling aesthetics from theology, as a solely aesthetic view of ethics leads to a profound deprivation of being, which can be subverted through a sacramental theology that reunites both aesthetics and ethics. Wilde's text is read as providing a case study in the application of a particularly extreme interpretation of the aesthetic theories of Walter Pater,[80] and the dangers this carries. The chapter thus engages with the wider critical and historical context of the time, particularly the debates between John Ruskin and Walter Pater, which were highly influential on Wilde's own thought. The chapter turns to the work of Augustine on privative evil as a means of showing the ways in which imaginative apologetics can produce readings that expand the critical debate upon the Gothic while remaining sensitive to the pre-existing critical and historical context. Moving from an Augustinian reading of Wilde to the work of Stoker shows the ways in which theological iconography and sacraments can be used as both a means of combatting evil and a tool of justification for colonialist empire building. Stoker, as an Irish Protestant, combines what might be seen as traditionally more Catholic theological practice (the use of icons and sacraments in particular) with a more stereotypical 'protestant' focus on a kind of evangelical missiology – the quest against Dracula functions as both an evangelical mission and a kind of crusade against evil. The text is read alongside the work of René Girard on sacrifice as providing a model for both how sacramental and sacrificial theology may be used against evil and the ways in which figures of evil, particularly the vampire, are able to produce their own parodic sacramental theologies. Sacrifice is not simply presented as a safe or easily secured theological rite but rather an

---

[79] Rowan Williams, *Faith in the Public Square* (London: Bloomsbury, 2015).
[80] Walter Pater, *The Renaissance: Studies in Art and Poetry, The 1893 Text*, ed. Donald L. Hill (London: University of California Press, 1980).

often bloody and materially costly endeavour that carries with it the potential to reorder material relationships between individuals and communities. This focus on the material aspect of theological practice links the chapter back to the opening chapter on *Frankenstein* and further reinforces the ways in which theology is not simply concerned with abstract matters of belief or faith but the ways in which faith is lived. Theology, then, in the era of the fin-de-siècle, both proliferates and diversifies but at the same time becomes more vulnerable and contingent.

The conclusion offers some arguments for the broader implications of the readings explored. The challenge of the Gothic to theology is in the emphasis given to the possibility of theological failure. Rather than a system of thought invulnerable to corruption, to historical and social conditions or to mistaken belief, theology throughout the Gothic is presented as deeply fragile, often unable to cope with divine revelation or supernatural encounters which manifest in ways outside of the boundaries of orthodoxy. As Davison writes, 'like the sublime cathedrals that first bore its name, the Gothic's supreme levelling effect reminds us of how we are most human.'[81] Yet this should not be seen as a chance to reiterate the old comparison of Summers, who contrasted the Gothic novel to the cathedral. Rather, like the cathedrals of the past, the Gothic ultimately reflects back upon human subjectivity, in all of its theological and material instability, contingency and fragility – the two are mutually constitutive. To reinstate the idea of the Gothic novel as textual church is an act of theological arrogance that the texts provide no evidence for, and which would forcibly detach the texts from the social and historical contexts in which they were produced. Rather, the supernatural Gothic emerges from a multiplicity of discourses and material influences that have shifted and changed in response to historical changes. In this, it shares something with the nature of theology. Despite the theologian's efforts at a kind of theoretical closure, revelation is never completely certain but rather consistently contested and mediated through the supernatural encounters in the texts. The imaginative critique of theology offered by Gothic literature does not invalidate the insights of the theological tradition but rather offers a profound and serious challenge to orthodox theological approaches to issues like evil, the supernatural and revelation. Seen as a literary site of theological critique, the Gothic requires a return to theology, to the ongoing work of rethinking theological truth and the constant challenge to take seriously the myriad ways in which divine revelation functions.

---

[81] Davison, 225.

1

Monstrosity and the problem of evil

A theologico-literary understanding of personhood in *Frankenstein* and *Paradise Lost*

Mary Shelley's *Frankenstein* (1818) has become deeply embedded in the textual canon of the Gothic,[1] yet for a text that deals so closely with the 'theological consequences of creation'[2] criticism on the theological elements of the text is distinctly lacking. Criticism generally falls into two separate spheres: the assessment of the creature in a social or political context or the assessment of the creature as an embodiment of concerns around gender or the body.[3] This section will build on the work covered in the introduction and argue for the necessity of a theological understanding of Shelley's text. Through a theologically inflected reading of the novel, the link between ontological status, morality and aesthetics can be decentred and the vital role of community and mutual recognition in the formation of subjectivity re-emphasized. Shelley's representation of Victor Frankenstein and his creature serves to present a supremely practical theology of personhood and being, and shows that, for all of the Romantic-era interest in the transcendent and poetic potential of creativity, that creativity alone can have disastrous consequences. In short, while the Romantics may have co-opted Milton, they fatally misunderstood the vision of creativity he espoused.[4] The figure of the monster is thus only superficially monstrous, as Shelley presents

---

[1] The book has been a recurrent part of Gothic scholarship for at least fifty years. See *Mary Shelley*, ed. Harold Bloom (London: Modern Critical Voices, 1985), which collects critical essays and scholarship from 1951 onwards.
[2] Mark Knight, *An Introduction to Religion and Literature* (London: Continuum Books, 2009), 9.
[3] Exemplary of the first type would be Chris Baldick, *In Frankenstein's Shadow; Myth, Monstrosity and Nineteenth Century Writing* (Oxford: Clarendon Paperbacks, 1990). An exemplar of the second would be Judith Halberstam, *Skin Shows: Gothic Horror and the Technology of Monsters* (London: Duke University Press, 1995).
[4] See J. A. Wittenreich, *The Romantics on Milton* (Ohio: Case Western University Press, 1970), esp. p. 11.

Frankenstein's creature as, like us all, seeking a connection to that which brought us into being; or, to put this another way, seeking a theology. It is this aspect that must be understood to grasp the significance of the Gothic's theological underpinnings and further the critical understanding of the link between theological belief, tradition and other, more 'numinous' Gothic writings.[5]

The opening of *Frankenstein* (1818) quotes from *Paradise Lost*, using as the novel's epigraph: 'Did I request thee, Maker, To mold Me man? Did I solicit thee From darkness to promote me?'[6] Quite deliberately, this epigraph and the monster's own speech and thought are linked, as the monster repeatedly echoes Miltonic and biblical language: 'I ought to be thy Adam, but I am rather the fallen angel whom thy drivest from joy for no misdeed.'[7] Typically, criticism has given rather less attention to Milton's text as a theological influence, with some critics even going so far as to claim, quite erroneously, that in *Frankenstein* 'the universe is emptied of God and of theistic assumptions of "good" and "evil"'.[8] This argument seems, at best, untenable, as the sheer depth of theological language that recurs throughout the novel is impossible to ignore. The theo-linguistic register of the novel culminates with 'the rationalist [Victor] who . . . ends up execrating his Creature as a fiend and a devil'.[9] When this is coupled with the influence and connection to Milton, such a critical claim for a lack of theology is rendered naïve and untenable, as *Frankenstein* repeatedly shows itself to be a profoundly theologically influenced text. Shelley goes so far as to link Frankenstein's monster to a theological tradition that extends as far back as the book of Job, namely the theodicy question of the purpose and justice of a creator.[10] As philosopher and theologian David Brown points out throughout his work *Tradition and Imagination* (1999), theological orthodoxy has always been creatively re-imagined outside of the confines of doctrine in response to the

---

[5] I borrow the term 'numinous Gothic' from Devendra Varma's pioneering study *The Gothic Flame: Being a History of the Gothic Novel in England* (1957) as this book consistently argues for an understanding of the Gothic nineteenth-century novel as texts which possess a theological aspect. See also Milbank's argument mentioned in the introduction in the essay 'Apologetics and the Imagination'.
[6] John Milton, *Paradise Lost,* ed. Gordon Teskey (London: Norton Critical Editions, 2005), 250.
[7] Mary Shelley, *Frankenstein* (London: Penguin Classics, 2012), 98.
[8] Joyce Carol Oates, 'Frankenstein's Fallen Angel', *Critical Inquiry*, no. 10 (March 1984): 550.
[9] Nora Crook, 'Mary Shelley, Author of Frankenstein', in *A Companion to the Gothic*, ed. David Punter (London: Blackwell, 2000), 61.
[10] For a more detailed exploration of the notion of theodicy see *Problems in Theology: Evil – A Reader*, ed. Jeff Astley, David Brown and Ann Loades (London: Continuum, 2003) as well as Joseph F. Kelly, *The Problem of Evil in the Western Tradition: From the Book of Job to Modern Genetics* (Minnesota: The Liturgical Press, 2001).

changes in circumstance brought about through the progress of history.¹¹ This re-imagining takes place in a variety of ways across shifting historical contexts – less a rejection of theological concerns than an ongoing and constant retelling of these concerns brought about through new stimuli.¹²

Shelley's novel functions as a creative re-imagining of a well-established theological position that finds imaginative expression within Gothic writing. Since the equation of the Good with notions of self-identity and sameness in early Western philosophy, 'the experience of evil has often been linked with notions of exteriority'.¹³ Frankenstein's response to his creature certainly seems to fit this model. After working himself to nervous and physical exhaustion, Frankenstein succeeds, and yet immediately the 'beauty of the dream vanished' and he himself is unable to 'endure the aspect of the being I had created'.¹⁴ Rather than attempt to reduce the other to the level of metaphor or elide all difference, theology offers new way of thinking through the ethical implications of the Other in its understanding of personhood. Furthermore, through an awareness of the historical development of both the Gothic and theological traditions, there must also be an acceptance of the possibility of imaginative revelation as historical contexts shift and theological truths are articulated in fresh ways. This twin movement of both traditional canonicity and imaginative reinterpretation can be understood as expressing the 'capacity of the Christian faith for renewal, reform and even revolution'.¹⁵ If, as Kevin J Vanhoozer has argued, 'the Bible is God's instrument for doing revelatory and redemptive things with words in the context of the church'¹⁶ then the numinous literature of the Gothic can be seen as doing theologically revelatory things in the context of the wider cultural world.

However, received theological revelation is never static. It is always mediated through various textual forms and thus always subject to a degree of interpretation.¹⁷ One of the issues at stake within *Frankenstein* is the mediation

---

¹¹ See Fiddes, *Freedom and Limit*, for his discussion of the false binarism between the 'open-ness' of imaginative literature and the 'closure' of doctrinal statements.
¹² A similar point is raised here by Milton A. Mays who refers to the novel as a 'black theodicy' – see Milton A. Mays, '*Frankenstein*, Mary Shelley's Black Theodicy', in *The Southern Humanities Review* (1964): 146–53.
¹³ Richard Kearney, *Strangers, Gods and Monsters* (London: Routledge, 2003), 65.
¹⁴ Shelley, *Frankenstein*, 50.
¹⁵ Knight and Mason, *Nineteenth Century Religion and Literature*, 5.
¹⁶ Kevin J. Vanhoozer, *Remythologizing Theology: Divine Action, Passion, and Authorship* (Cambridge: Cambridge University Press, 2010), xiv.
¹⁷ For a recurrent theological issue but one perhaps most famously expressed in the Barth/Brunner debates of the early twentieth century, see Emil Brunner, *Natural Theology, Comprising Nature and Grace by Professor Dr. Emil Brunner and the Reply No! by Dr Karl Barth* (London: Wipf & Stock, 2003).

of competing texts and the worrying status that the act of creation (whether that be literary or otherwise) takes on because of this. The novel is a complex palimpsest of texts exhibiting a multiplicity of characters and distinctive voices. That said, critics such as Newman argue that

> We are more apt to be struck by the similarities in the way the Monster and Frankenstein express themselves, since they both use the same kind of heightened language, and since both speak with an eloquence more expressive of a shared Romantic ethos. . . . The novel fails to provide significant differences in tone, diction and sentence structure that alone can serve, in a written text, to represent individual human voices.[18]

Yet, what this misses is the ways in which Shelley uses specifically theological language to clearly delineate the relationship between the creature and Victor (seen most sharply in their first conversations on the mountainside in chapter two of Volume two and discussed in greater detail here).[19] Even if the question of who may be using that language is complicated by the framing narrative structure, the separation of story from character shapes the combination of different forms (letters, diaries, journals and even personal testimony) into 'a text, divested of its originating voice'.[20] Here this disparate collection of texts becomes the means by which the essentially symbolic story can be transmitted. Like scripture, the text works to destabilize the idea of any kind of singular narrative authority, shifting the reader's conception of authority from a singular source to a collection of texts that must necessarily be interpreted. Given the emergence of the novel form in the eighteenth century and the accompanying debates about 'realism', *Frankenstein* is tied not only to the issue of the epistemology of novel writing[21] but also to a deeply held theological concern, namely the tension between theological certainty and theological expression, which out of necessity must always be riven by metaphor and analogy. Literature, specifically non-realist forms such as the Gothic, 'reaches out towards mystery, towards a reality that is our final concern but which eludes empirical investigation and bursts rational concepts'.[22] This holds true even if, as with *Frankenstein*, the ostensible format, in this case the epistolary or testimony narrative, is one that

---

[18] Beth Newman, 'Narratives of Seduction and the Seductions of Narrative: The Frame Structure of Frankenstein', *English Literary History [ELH]*, 53 (1986): 146.
[19] Shelley, *Frankenstein*, 98.
[20] Newman, 'Narratives of Seduction', 147.
[21] Dealt with in detail by Ian Watt, *The Rise of the Novel* (London: The Hogarth Press, 1987).
[22] Fiddes, *Freedom and Limit*, 11.

lends itself to empirical understanding. Victor's testimony 'reaches out' beyond the verisimilitude of testimony narratives through the novel's content. *Frankenstein* – as a text heavily influenced by theology – participates within a tradition of 'searching for something of ultimate concern', framing this search by 'taking as [its] theme the telling of a story'.[23] The framing device in the form of a series of conversations between Walton and Frankenstein ensures that the character of Frankenstein can only make sense of his life in the act of narration – his existence can only be understood in retrospect. As Walton articulates it, 'strange and harrowing must be his story, frightful the storm which embraced the gallant vessel on its course and wrecked it – thus!'[24] It is through the telling that the events contained within the text may become coherent to Victor and some kind of meaning drawn from it. Victor himself seems to recognize this as he refers throughout the novel to a sense of predestination at work. Even towards the end of his life, he frames his struggle in retrospect as one that is ordained by spiritual forces: 'you may give up your purpose, but mine is assigned to me by heaven.'[25] Through framing his own narrative through the older, wider narrative of the preordination of the world, it 'gives him a pattern by which he can find *himself* in what would otherwise be a meaningless end to his journey'.[26] Thus, the displacement of the narrative voice of the text is not simply a result of the multiplicity of forms that it covers (such as diary entries, letters and journals) or a problem of hermeneutics but ties the novel into a tradition of theological quests whereby it is through a larger narrative, through a grander 'story' that sense can be made of one's existence.[27] To phrase things more theologically, the textual creation of the novel is one of multiplicity rather than any univocity of being, all of which are incorporated into and pointing towards a larger theological frame. This, too, ties *Frankenstein* to *Paradise Lost*, as Milton's poem makes space for a creation of multiplicity – 'a multivocality at the heart of creation'.[28] However, this embodies a certain tension regarding ideas around creation that *Frankenstein* enables us to grasp more clearly. Human participation in creation can affirm

---

[23] Ibid., 8.
[24] Shelley, *Frankenstein*, 22.
[25] Ibid., 223
[26] Fiddes, *Freedom and Limit*, 8
[27] Here *Frankenstein* is connected to not only John Milton's *Paradise Lost* (1667) but also *The Pilgrim's Progress* by John Bunyan (1678). Furthermore, this idea of finding some purpose within a larger narrative idea links *Frankenstein* to the early epistolary novels, wherein the ethical problem of their 'fictionality' was solved through the potential virtue of the story in informing a larger ethical narrative. See Samuel Richardson's book (and its extremely telling subtitle) *Pamela: or Virtue Rewarded* (1740).
[28] Knight, *An Introduction to Literature and Religion*, 13.

difference, but the line between individual freedom as part of some harmonious vision of creation and free participation that strays into Miltonic Pandemonium seems perilously fine. In both *Paradise Lost* and *Frankenstein*, human participation in the act of creation is seen as potentially highly dangerous.[29] As a result, there is a common critical position to see God, in *Paradise Lost* at least, as a tyrant – a creator who maintains his control by allowing there to be only one way or one set of possibilities for the whole of existence to function within. C. S. Lewis decries Milton's presentation of God as 'unsatisfactory... giving us a cold, merciless or tyrannical Deity',[30] and for William Empson the 'reason that the poem is so good is that it makes God so bad'.[31] The common complaint seems to be that in Milton's poem, all of creation is placed under the tyranny of the divine, and any action is mediated and controlled through God. Frequently it is the speech at the beginning of Book Three that draws most critical attention[32] as God sets out not only the plan for humankind but his foreknowledge of their fall and eventual redemption alongside the necessity of Christ's sacrifice on the cross for the satisfaction of divine justice and atonement for sin.[33] While the criticism of God as a rather removed absolute ruler has proven remarkably consistent within a certain school of Miltonic criticism, it ignores a theological issue that states that it is only in Christ that creation can continue to exist in the first place.[34] Despite the issues that the Puritan Milton had with the concept of Trinitarian theology[35] his work is motivated 'less by a rejection of the doctrine per se and more by a desire to focus attention on the role of mediation in creation'.[36] On a textual level, Milton resolves this apparent theological tension

---

[29] A concern which seems deeply ingrained in the popular cultural legacy of the text, some of which is still felt today. One only need note the fears and concerns around so-called 'Frankenstein foods' for example.

[30] C. S. Lewis, '*A Preface to Paradise Lost*' (Oxford: Oxford University Press, 1942), 92, reprinted in Milton, *Paradise Lost*.

[31] William Empson, *Milton's God* (London: Chatto & Windus, 1961), reprinted in Teskey (London: Norton Critical Editions, 2005), 439.

[32] See Stanley Fish, 'The Milk of the Pure Word', in *Surprised by Sin: The Reader in Paradise Lost* (Cambridge: Harvard University Press, 1998). Also see Northrop Frye, 'The Garden Within', in *The Return of Eden: Five Essays on Milton's Epics* (Toronto: University of Toronto Press, 1965).

[33] Milton, *Paradise Lost,* 59–62.

[34] For the biblical justification for this belief see Colossian 1 15–19, particular verse 16, 'for in him, all things on heaven and earth were created' – all subsequent quotations and references are taken from *The Bible, with Apocrypha, NRSV Anglicized Edition* (Oxford: Oxford University Press, 1995). For the theological exegesis on this point of doctrine and its implications, see Marilyn McCord Adams, *Christ and Horrors: The Coherence of Christology* (Cambridge: Cambridge University Press, 2008).

[35] See Milton's descriptions of God in *On Christian Doctrine* wherein Milton struggles to detach himself from the monistic viewpoint as well as his licence for publication in 1650 of a version of a non-Trinitarian creed, the Racovian Catechism.

[36] Knight, *Introduction to Literature and Religion*, 15.

between his Puritan leanings and more orthodox Trinitarian doctrine by ensuring the continuation between the new life of Eden and the pre-existence of God (and thus by implication Christ too). This echoes the opening of the book of Genesis, which 'focuses on how God forms this world out of pre-existing materials, thereby opening up space for human beings to continue to participate in its development'.[37] Shelley herself seems to share a similar creative philosophy, writing in the preface to the 1831 edition of the novel, that 'the materials, must in the first place, be afforded: it [literary invention] can give form to dark shapeless substances but cannot bring into being the substance itself'.[38] The creative act in Milton's work is one that is ongoing and furthermore, one in which all participants are said to be in a 'charming symphony . . . [m]elodious in their harmony'.[39] In Milton's vision of creation, difference flourishes within the ongoing harmonious work of God's overall creative schema as different instruments involved in the performance of a single symphony. Adam and Eve are participants within this ongoing process – to quote from Book Four: 'God hath set Labour and rest as day and night to man . . . man hath his daily work of body or mind/Appointed which declares his dignity'.[40] As Regina Schwartz articulates it, far from a totalizing homogeneity of vision, *Paradise Lost* does not depict the 'cosmic creation as a privileged beginning, a single event that occurred once-upon-a-time and for all time'.[41] Rather, creation in *Paradise Lost* is, like textual creation itself, a multi-vocal and ongoing exchange – as Adam discusses later in Book Four, 'millions of spiritual creatures walk the earth . . . sole or responsive to each other's notes, Singing their great Creator'.[42] On the other hand, Shelley's novel seems to have a much more pessimistic understanding of the role of the human in creation. Victor Frankenstein, in claiming that 'life and death appeared to me ideal bounds, which I should first break through, and pour a torrent of light into our dark world',[43] is arguing for his own revelatory act of *creation ex nihilo* with the expressed aim of bringing about a reality over which he has completely unmediated control. Yet, what remains acknowledged by

---

[37] Ibid.
[38] See Mary Shelley, *Frankenstein, 1818 Text*, ed. Marilyn Butler (Oxford: Oxford University Press, 1998) 195.
[39] Milton, *Paradise Lost* IX, 736–7, II. 379–80
[40] Milton, *Paradise Lost* IV, 613–18, 94
[41] Regina Schwartz, *Remembering and Repeating: Biblical Creation in Paradise Lost* (Cambridge: Cambridge University Press, 1988), 1.
[42] Milton, *Paradise Lost*, 677–83, 96.
[43] Shelley, *Frankenstein*, 47.

Victor is the truth that *creation ex nihilo* is precisely what he is unable to do – science will only allow him to assemble out of pre-existing material.

Once again, in Shelley's own understanding of the creative process she shares much in common with the theological Milton than Victor: 'invention, it must be humbly admitted, does not consist in creating out of void, but out of chaos . . . in the power of moulding and fashioning ideas suggested to it.'[44] Whereas within *Paradise Lost* the mediation of God allows for the flourishing of creation, Frankenstein seeks instead to explain and restrict his own creation. In the character of Victor, we see this combination of exploration of the physical world, representative of the new rise of science and discovery, coupled with a semi-religious and imaginative fervour or 'rapture'. Whereas his cousin Elizabeth continues that Miltonic tradition of the exegesis and description of the world (in her upbringing she spends her time 'contemplating the magnificent appearance of things')[45] Victor is established as a character that seeks mastery over it. Victor, rather than merely be a part of the wider creative work of the divine, seeks to take on the powers of divine itself. The ability to imbue life is not simple a scientific quest but a means to bring back and restore those who have been lost (particularly his own mother). Victor seeks the imaginative and 'Christ like capacity of redemption and reconciliation that mimes God's own creative power'.[46] It is no longer in Christ that creation holds together but in the mind of the singular genius who can, like the Christ he has replaced, resurrect the dead and create life. Within the Romantic Imagination, man is the centre of and dominant force within a larger universe. Placing man at the core of the vision of the universe grants not just exploratory or descriptive powers but also, and perhaps most importantly, creative powers. Victor's discovery of metaphysics – the 'secrets of heaven and earth',[47] as the novel puts it – leads him to the creation of life. The 'new man' of Romanticism does not just describe and explore creation (as Milton's retelling of the creation story did) but actively participates in the process of bringing new elements of creation into being. The theologically gnostic language of 'a torrent of light'[48] adds credence to the notion that the Romantic reorientation of the universe as centred around the subject had dispensed with the traditional theological view of creation as something within which humanity

---

[44] Shelley, *Frankenstein, 1818 Text*, 195.
[45] Ibid., 28.
[46] Terry Eagleton, *Culture and the Death of God* (London: Yale University Press, 2014), 101.
[47] Shelley, *Frankenstein*, 29.
[48] Ibid., 47.

was a participant (that grand Miltonic harmony), and instead had placed man as the creative force at the centre of it, in place of the divine.[49] Victor Frankenstein has no patience for the necessary participation in the continuing harmonious work of God's creation but seeks a new, and entirely separate, realm of creativity. Coupled with the characteristically gnostic subordination of ethics to cognition, the consequence is that the position of man at the centre of the universe, rather than God, seems assured. Victor figures as a type of the Romantic ideology more generally as in various ways Romantic poets, writers and philosophers sought to go beyond the material into the realm of imaginative transcendence.[50]

Victor refers to himself as the creator and source of a new species, saying that 'no father could claim the gratitude of his child so completely as I should deserve theirs'.[51] What this neglects is that he himself admits that he is not creating from nothing but rather visiting the charnel houses to piece together his 'dark materials', disturbing the 'secrets of the human frame' with his own 'profane fingers', and assembling his monster in a 'workshop of filthy creation'.[52] His own participation in creation is heavily mediated and reflects very poorly on Victor's inability to grasp the social context of revelatory knowledge. His successful acquisition of the ability to create life ignores the reality that life is dependent upon the co-existence of different forms. Scientific revelation within the novel leads only to solitude and undeniable catastrophe. For this, we need only see Victor's inability to concede his responsibilities towards his creation, his constant litany of negative terms and vituperation towards the unfortunate creature throughout the novel and his complete failure to grasp how his invention might bring others killed in the course of the novel back to life. All of these examples reinforce the view that knowledge outside the social milieu is, at best, dangerous. Victor embodies the very essence of imaginative engagement but without the stabilizing influence of tradition his imaginative excesses inflict terrible consequences as his own failure to acknowledge his involvement and participation in the ongoing

---

[49] For further detail on this, see Taylor, *A Secular Age*. For a more detailed focus on the secular age in the context of Western Europe within the 1800s see Owen Chadwick's *The Secularization of the European Mind in the Nineteenth Century* (Cambridge: Cambridge University Press, 1975). A recent counterargument to this thesis, which presents the recent capitalist history of the West in religious terms, see Eugene McCarraher, *The Enchantments of Mammon: How Capitalism Became the Religion of Modernity* (Cambridge: Harvard University Press, 2019).

[50] This is dealt with in great detail by M. H. Abrams, *Natural Supernaturalism: Tradition and Revolution In Romantic Literature* (London: Norton, 1971). For example, see Abrams's discussion of Wordsworth's poetic programme pp. 21–32 as well as the theodicy of landscape that Abrams details on pp. 97–117.

[51] Shelley, *Frankenstein*, 47.

[52] Ibid., 48.

act of creation leads to his abnegation of responsibility and the eventual death of those close to him.

Whereas Victor is the embodiment of the so-called Romantic 'great man', who thrives on a kind of solitary revelation, Frankenstein's creature is the direct opposite. Abandoned by his creator the creature is motivated by a desire for not just a sense of community or companionship but also a need to understand himself as a created being-in-the-world. 'The words induced me to turn towards myself'.[53] Later, the monster is led into that most basic of ontological questions: 'I had never yet seen a being resembling me, or who claimed intercourse with me. What was I?'[54] It is this desire that leads him to forge his own textual canon – first finding Frankenstein's own journal notes, then moving onto Volney's *Ruins of Empires* (1791), then Goethe's *Sorrows of Young Werther* (1774), Plutarch's *Lives* (second century) and, most importantly, Milton's *Paradise Lost* (1667). The choice of texts is striking, as Frankenstein's creature uses these texts to ground his being in the historical, social and cultural contexts of the time. The text's function is extremely formative upon the creature's notion of his own subjectivity. From Volney, his being is placed within a historical context, as he learns of 'the manners, governments and different religions of the earth . . . the strange system of human society was explained to me'.[55] Moving on from the historic and the general the creature's engagement with Goethe and *The Sorrows of Young Werther* allows for a more personal articulation of subjectivity:

> The gentle and domestic manners it described, combined with lofty sentiments and feelings, which had for their object something out of self, accorded well with my experiences . . . and the wants alive in my own bosom.[56]

Moving forward from the engagement with the subjective comes the engagement with the theological. Being grounded in a historical tradition with a subjectivity moulded by the literary tradition the creature is guided towards a more explicitly theological tradition. Milton's *Paradise Lost* allows the creature to frame his position in theological terms, as both created and abandoned by his creator. It is from these initial encounters with traditional texts that the creature's recognition of himself and the vital duties that Frankenstein has abandoned emerges. The

---

[53] Ibid., 119.
[54] Ibid., 120.
[55] Ibid., 119–20.
[56] Ibid., 128.

engagement with tradition gives insight to his own ontological state but little comfort, as he compares his own condition with that of Milton's Adam:

> Like Adam, I was apparently united by no link to any other being in existence; but his state was far different from mine in every other respect. He had come forth from the hands of God a perfect creature, happy and prosperous, guarded by the especial care of his Creator . . . but I was wretched, helpless and alone . . . the bitter gall of envy rose within me.[57]

This sense of exile from God is reinforced when Victor and the creature come face to face for the first time. Resisting his creator's attempts at his destruction the creature puts his case to him, arguing for the vital and central needs of companionship and for community. Drawing from Job 23 the language here reverses the power dynamics established by the more disingenuous Frankenstein. Job, seemingly forsaken by his creator and suffering for reasons that seem not only vague but also deeply unfair, wishes for an audience with God to put forward his case and seek some kind of justice. As Job says:

> I would lay my case before him, and fill my mouth with arguments. I would learn what he would answer me, and understand what he would say to me. Would he contend with me in the greatness of his power? No; but he would give heed to me. There an upright person could reason with him, and I should be acquitted forever by my judge.[58]

The language of Job presupposes both the duty of care of the creator towards the created and, simultaneously, the possibility of a kind of rational communication between the two. These two elements are interdependent, as without the possibility of rational conversation between the two (the 'upright reasoning' mentioned by Job) Job cannot be acquitted in the sight of his judge. Frankenstein's creature shares this desire, asking,

> let your compassion be moved, Listen to my tale when you have heard that, abandon or commiserate me, as you shall judge that I deserve. But hear me . . . listen to me, Frankenstein![59]

The monster's own subjectivity is revealed to be deeply similar to Job's from scripture. Here, the creature combines appeals to justice, wisely noting that 'even the guilty are allowed, by human laws, bloody as they are to speak in their

---

[57] Ibid., 129.
[58] Job 23: 4–7.
[59] Shelley, *Frankenstein*, 99.

own defence',[60] with an awareness of the theological nature of the relationship between himself and Victor: 'if you can and if you will, destroy the work of your hands.'[61] Here, the creature takes on the role of the rationalist, becoming the 'supreme rhetorician of his own situation'.[62] He is aware of his own nature and his position in relation to divine power. On the other hand, Victor, ostensibly the novel's hero, becomes an extremist. Victor's language takes on theologically apocalyptic tones as he lambasts his creation as a devil and a vile insect.[63] Victor goes further still as he seeks to use divine power to undo his own creative act: 'Cursed be the day, abhorred devil, in which you first saw light! Cursed (although I curse myself) be the hands that formed you!'[64] Victor, in essence, disavows his own subjectivity as the creature he has brought into the world shows the effort of attaining his own. Unknowingly or not, Victor's outburst articulates a vital theological point – as a fallen individual in creation, the hands that formed the creature are not the perfect hands of the divine presence that Milton details but are cursed by the stain of original sin. As a created being-in-the-world, Victor is literally incapable of creating in any other way, despite his imaginative reach – an imaginative capacity which is, in a sense, an aspect of his fallen nature. As a human subject, Victor is himself bound up within the network of human relationships that always carry with it the potential for failure, hurt and sin. Because of this theologically inflected vitriol, the conversation between Frankenstein's creature and Victor is not a rational exchange between the person and the divine that the creature (and Job) has desired. Rather, the reader sees the rational, created man come into contact with the terrible genius of the Romantic Imagination. The aw(e)ful Other in the novel is not the creature but rather Victor himself. 'You my creator, detest and spurn me . . . You purpose to kill me! How dare you sport thus with life?'[65] Victor takes on here the role of the divine speaking out of the whirlwind at the end of the book of Job but too committed to his revelatory act of creation, he lacks the grounding in tradition to make sense of what he has done and the duty that creation carries with it.

With this understanding of the relationship between the creature and Victor in place, further attention can be given to the theology of creation that *Frankenstein*

---

[60] Ibid.
[61] Ibid.
[62] Peter Brooks, '"Godlike Science/Unhallowed Arts": Language, Nature, and Monstrosity', in *The Endurance of 'Frankenstein': Essays on Mary Shelley's Novel*, ed. George Levine and U. C. Knoepflmacher (Los Angeles: University of California Press, 1979), 205–20.
[63] Shelley, *Frankenstein*, 97.
[64] Ibid., 99.
[65] Ibid., 97.

puts forward. Once more Milton forms not only the poetic and discursive influence on Shelley but also provides an essential theological stimulus. On his arrival into Paradise in Book Four of *Paradise Lost* Satan espies Adam and Eve for the first time: 'into our room of bliss, thus high advanced creatures of other mold, earth borne . . . yet to Heav'nly spirits bright'.[66] The God-created Adam and Eve are both earth borne or fully material, and yet theologically aware, bright to the 'Heav'nly Spirits'. Milton's Devil goes on to note how 'lively shines in them divine resemblance, and such grace the hand that formed them on their shape hath poured'.[67] The physical appearance of Adam and Eve is entirely bound up in the grace (a deliberately non- material choice of word) used by the hand which created them – to put this another way, their physical appearance is a reflection of their spiritual condition. By contrast, Frankenstein deliberately problematizes this relationship as the link between physical appearance and spiritual nature is shown in a more complex light:

> It was on a dreary night of November that I beheld the accomplishment of my toils . . . I saw the dull yellow eyes open; it breathed hard, and a convulsive motion agitated its limbs. . . . Oh! No mortal could support the horror of that countenance . . . I had gazed upon him while unfinished; he was ugly then; but when those muscles and joints were rendered capable of motion it became a thing such as even Dante could not have conceived.[68]

The passage repeatedly links aesthetics with the theological. The inability of the mortal to support the horror of the creature's appearance and the reference to the great religious poet Dante manage to construct a theologically inflected aesthetics – the creature transforms from a scientific object of curiosity and becomes a 'demonical corpse'.[69] The hybridized combination of the 'Earth bound' and the transcendent that, in Milton, is used to show the divine influence on Adam and Eve is here transmuted. The combination of the material (the corpse) and the non-material (the demonic) serves to render Frankenstein's creation as not mere metaphor or allegorical fear but as horrific and theologically abject. Whereas the creation of Adam and Eve in *Paradise Lost* forms a smaller part within the melodious harmony of the ongoing act of divine creation and, vitally, allows for the participatory flourishing of the individual within the Edenic setting, Victor's

---

[66] Milton, *Paradise Lost*, Book IV 359–60, 88.
[67] Ibid.
[68] Shelley, *Frankenstein,* 50–1.
[69] Ibid., 51.

own creative act reveals his lack of awareness about the theological implications and duties that accompany bringing life into being. The quoted passage shows the dangers of his Romantic world view – the great man of the Romantic ideology is catastrophically prone to dangerous arrogance in terms of ego and is completely unable to translate effort into aesthetic appearance. Here, Victor is linked back to Goethe's *Faust*, for 'it is obvious that Frankenstein is in some sense a Faustian over-reacher'.[70] Victor's creative aspirations are great, but unlike Prometheus, who brought fire from the gods, he creates something he regards as abhorrent. More theologically, unlike the created works of God in *Paradise Lost*, Victor's creature shows none of the 'divine resemblance' or 'grace the hand that formed them on their shape hath poured' as Milton writes. Simply put, creation for Victor Frankenstein is a singular event – a great revelatory act of insight – yet as Milton understands, the act of creation depends upon a necessary and deep-seated continued involvement with that which has been brought into being. For as Seed points out, 'creation is articulated partly in terms of birth and consequences in terms of parental responsibility'.[71] Within *Paradise Lost*, God as Divine Father does not simply create Paradise for Adam and Eve and then leave them. Rather, the Garden, their involvement with it and the relationship between the human subject and the divine are assiduously maintained. God goes so far as to send angels to warn his creation that their enemy is at hand in Book Five[72] – the notable reason given for this continued intervention in the created world being, as Milton writes, 'to fulfil all justice'.[73] The creative act without the continued involvement of the creator is, therefore, deeply unjust. The idea of the Romantic man as a lone figure of genius is, according to Milton, held up as being guilty of a moral failure to fulfil the role of creator that Victor is so keen to seize. This move from physical involvement within the world to abstracted consideration is not unique but rather inextricably bound up in Romantic era thought around the nature of creation itself which rejected the notions of interdependence and mutuality for the figure of the lone creative genius. As Young's *Conjectures on Original Composition* (1759) argues, 'An Original may be said to be of a *vegetable* nature; it rises spontaneously from the vital root of genius; it *grows*, it is not *made*'.[74] Rather than emerging from the material conditions of

---

[70] David Seed, '*Frankenstein*: Parable or Spectacle?' *Criticism*, 24:2 (Fall, 1982): 327–40, 330.
[71] Ibid., 331.
[72] Milton, *Paradise Lost*, 106.
[73] Ibid., 112–3.
[74] Edward Young, 'Conjectures on Original Composition', in *Critical Theory Since Plato*, ed. Hazard Adams and Leroy Searle (London: Wadsworth Publishing, 2004), 347–57.

a particular historical moment, art, in the time of Romantic individualism, is seen as a product of the individual imagination that can make it grow – rather than an interaction between the creative individual, their world and the work. As a result, the creator is reduced down to a singular, decontextualized 'genius' figure. This 'new idea of a superior reality, and even of superior power',[75] finds expression across Romantic-era writing that consistently refuses the demand of interpersonal relationship and reaches towards the infinite.

This refusal or failing on Victor's part is well noted by the creature in their first face-to-face encounter: 'do your duty towards me . . . I am thy creature, and I will be even mild and docile to my natural lord and king, *if thou wilt also perform thy part, the which thou owest me*'[76] (emphasis mine.) At a later stage, the creature adds to this, 'but on you only had I any claim for pity and redress'.[77] What is owed to Frankenstein's creature is first, the involvement of the creator with creation, and second, a degree of ontological recognition from a source external, and prior, to the self. Frankenstein's creature has, by this point in the narrative, begun to engage with the textual tradition of the Enlightenment (as previously discussed) but comes to his creator seeking the recognition of his personhood from an external source.[78] His desire for Victor to create for him a companion is not simply to fulfil a desire for companionship, but a subtle awareness that companionship carries with it the acknowledgement of personhood. Through identification, through sympathy and through the intimacy of relationship that acknowledges a basic familiarity and shared personhood, the Other can be brought from the status of the monstrous to join with human society. As the creature himself articulates it, 'everywhere I see bliss, from which I alone am irrevocably excluded . . . am I not alone, miserably alone? You, my creator, abhor me; what hope can I gather from your fellow-creatures who owe me nothing?'[79]

The status of the Other as Other is constructed, and therefore dependent upon, first, the abandonment of the created by his creator and, second, a refusal to acknowledge the figure of the Other as possessing a degree of personhood. The comparison once more comes from Milton as Shelley deliberately draws a

---

[75] Raymond Williams, *Culture and Society 1780-1950* (London: Penguin Books, 1961), 55.
[76] Shelley, *Frankenstein*, 98.
[77] Ibid., 150.
[78] The theological position articulated here shares a relevant theoretical line with the neo-Hegelianism of Judith Butler. See specifically Chapter two of *Precarious Life: The Powers of Mourning and Violence* (London: Verso Books, 2004). While Butler (and, of course, Hegel in the *Phenomenology of Spirit*) share an interest in the vital nature of relationality, both elide the transcendental signifier that is the divine, which both Milton and *Frankenstein* put forward as essential here.
[79] Shelley, *Frankenstein*, 98.

contrast between the monster's own awakening to self-awareness and the earliest memories and subsequent recognition of Eve in Book Four of *Paradise Lost*. Eve awakens and comes to consciousness 'under a shade of flowers . . . not distance far from thence a murmuring sound of waters issued from a cave' and like Frankenstein's creature she is 'much wond'ring where/And what I was'.[80] From there she comes to recognize herself and experience the joy of self-recognition: 'A shape within the wat'ry gleam appeared . . . pleased I soon returned'.[81] By contrast, while Frankenstein's creature also comes to and gains consciousness by a brook, the creature comes to no such understanding of himself. 'I was a poor, helpless, miserable wretch; I knew and could distinguish, nothing; but feeling pain invade me on all sides, I sat down and wept.'[82] Frankenstein's creature too has a moment of self-regarding, catching sight of his reflection, but in contrast to Eve who is drawn towards the pleasing shape, 'I was terrified when I viewed myself . . . when I became fully convinced that I was in reality the monster that I am, I was filled with the bitterest sensations of despondency and mortification.'[83] However, to simply describe the creature as monstrous based solely on appearance is far too reductive and fails to appreciate the significance of the contexts that both Eve and the creature are placed within. Eve is drawn away from her own reflection and told by the divine voice to 'follow me and I will bring thee where no shadow stays thy coming and thy soft embraces'.[84] Her creator places her within a relationship with Adam and here Milton makes clear that the relationship they share is not simply a degree of biological necessity or even romance but something bound up with their theological status:

> Whom fli'st thou? Whom thou fli'st, of him thou art, His flesh, his bone. To give thee being I lent
> Out of my side to thee, nearest my heart, Substantial life to have thee by my side Henceforth an individual solace dear
> Part of my soul I seek thee and thee claim My other half.[85]

The relationship between Eve and Adam is presented as a constituent element of not just a material understanding of personhood but rather as distinctly non-material. Adam and Eve share a physical connection, a recognition of their

---

[80] Milton, *Paradise Lost*, 90.
[81] Ibid.
[82] Shelley, *Frankenstein*, 102.
[83] Ibid., 113.
[84] Milton, *Paradise Lost*, 91.
[85] Ibid.

sameness but this recognition goes beyond the material into the spiritual. The physical connection and similarity they share is merely the visible sign of the non-material connection. They are brought together through the active involvement of their creator and through relationship, which in itself reflects the ongoing act of divine creation; they find in each other the other part of their souls, and, as a result, an answer to the question that Frankenstein's creature is unable to resolve: 'what was I?' This theological truth goes some way to explaining the desire of Frankenstein creature for a mate of his own. The creature's request for a mate and entreaties towards Victor Frankenstein do not simply show a need for the satisfaction of a human desire. Rather, the creature's request is framed as a need to 'become linked to the chain of existence and events from which I am now excluded'.[86] Frankenstein's creature seeks a visible reflection of the link between the God and his creation that is ongoing and participatory, and that allows for the affirmation of the individual's personhood within it. Shelley here draws on the liberal philosophy of Rousseau, particularly *The Social Contract* (1762), wherein Rousseau argues for a social compact as the basis of secure and just societal organization. In the case of the creature, the relationship he asks Frankenstein to provide is something Frankenstein is incapable of granting as Frankenstein refuses to recognize that his creation requires his ongoing involvement and that the relationship that the creature desires reflects this ongoing process.

Frankenstein's creature is made monstrous, not through his material creation (a facet of being shared by all, regardless of our aesthetic qualities) or through being stitched together from the filthy fragments of the earth but rather through the complete failure of his creator to understand either the significance of what he has made or the act of creation more generally. Materiality is something shared by all, but it is the inclusion of the individual within relationship that seems to be the determining feature in the acknowledgement of personhood and the awareness of the 'various relationships which bind one human being to another in mutual bonds'.[87] The closest that Frankenstein's creature gets to this state is through the observations of the De Lacy family – the creature even goes so far as to hope that they may 'become acquitted with my admiration of their virtues, they would compassionate me and overlook my personal deformity'.[88] Here then the creature not only seeks an involvement within an seemingly idyllic

---

[86] Shelley, *Frankenstein*, 148.
[87] Ibid., 120.
[88] Ibid., 130.

community but articulates a desire to be drawn into a social contract, echoing Rousseau in *The Social Contract*.

> Each of us puts his person and all his power in common under the supreme direction of the general will, and, in our corporate capacity, we receive each member as an indivisible part of the whole.[89]

The desire for a relationship and the implied acknowledgement of some shared essence which relationship carries with it are touchingly conveyed: could they 'turn from their door one, however monstrous, who solicited their compassion and friendship?'[90] Yet the broader question here is whether to consider this as an entirely secular move – a desire to enter into the *polis* in some form. Rather, this desire to enter into sociality, to form a social contract still rests upon, and requires, a certain degree of theological logic. As Simon Critchley points out, 'if the problem that Rousseau is trying to solve . . . is the problem of politics, then the solution to that problem requires religion.'[91] As Critchley argues even in Rousseau's model of politics not based on natural law but free association, equality and popular sovereignty, there still must be an element of *theologia civilis* or civil theology. Even in the most immanent of communities there must be a kind of belief through which the community can be maintained. In the case of the De Lacy family it seems to be their shared bond, predicated upon their shared familial connection and empathetic recognition of their shared state. As the narrative progresses the link between this understanding of personhood as dependent upon the acknowledgement of another becomes more clear – 'the more I saw of them the greater became my desire to claim their protection and their kindness . . . my heart yearned to be known and loved by these amiable creatures.'[92]

Crucially there is also a sense of this reciprocity being deserved – as a created being the creature seems aware of the intrinsic value he possesses – 'I required kindness and sympathy; but I did not believe myself unworthy of it.'[93] On the brink of forming a new association (to use Rousseau's term) the creature makes

---

[89] Jean Jacques Rousseau, *The Social Contract, Or, Principles of Political Right,* trans. G. D. H. Cole (public domain, available here: https://www.ucc.ie/archive/hdsp/Rousseau_contrat-social.pdf, first accessed 7 August 2017), 11.
[90] Ibid.
[91] Simon Critchley, *Faith of the Faithless, Experiments in Political Theology* (London: Verso Books, 2014), 23.
[92] Shelley, *Frankenstein*, 131.
[93] Ibid., 132.

himself known to the blind old man of the family, who seems to offer a degree of reassurance in fairly Rousseanian terms:

> To be friendless is indeed to be unfortunate; but the hearts of men, when unprejudiced by any obvious self-interest, are full of brotherly love and charity. Rely, therefore, on your hopes; and if these friends are good and amiable, do not despair.[94]

However, the moral aesthetics that repulsed the theologically naïve Victor proves to be sadly irresistible to the De Lacy family and the social compact between them is never formed. Simply put, the creature is unrecognizable – when the De Lacy's come back to the cabin, the first question is one from the old man, 'Great God ... who are you?'[95] The creature flees this potential reciprocal relationship in a fit of violence, physically driven from the brink of humanity back out towards its limits and the position of the monster. Simply put, it would be a mistake to assume the relationship with the De Lacy family would offer all the creature assumes. Far from being a straightforward Rousseauian idyll, the life of the De Lacy family is built upon the alienated labour of the creature, who clears their paths of snow and fetches their fuel.[96] He remains invisible; a 'good spirit' who delivers the benefits of his labour to his superiors and as long as he does so, the idea of the social contract that could potentially be formed remains coherent.[97] It is not the creature that causes the violence of the De Lacy family but rather it is his desire to make himself known – to make himself visible for recognition – that brings the virulent response. Strikingly, however, the creature never lays blame at the feet of the De Lacys exclusively, only going so far as to admit that he 'could with pleasure have destroyed the cottage'.[98] Notably, however, he does not do so until the De Lacy family is safely out of harm's way. Immediately following his violent expulsion from their midst, the creature turns his attention to the source of his unrecognized humanity – his creator. 'Cursed, cursed creator!

---

[94] Ibid., 133.
[95] Ibid., 135.
[96] I use alienation here in the Marxist sense of the term. In *The Economic and Philosophical Manuscripts of 1844* Marx writes that the 'object which labour produces – labour's product – confronts it as *something alien*, as a *power independent* of the producer'. In the case of the creature, it is his labour power which provides for the De Lacy family, but at no point does he benefit from the work he has done – he is estranged from it, only gaining the benefit of the fire (fuelled by his own work) before the De Lacy family physically attacks him. See Karl Marx, *Economic and Philosophical Manuscripts of 1844*. https://www.marxists.org/archive/marx/works/1844/manuscripts/labour.htm, first accessed 30 August 2017.
[97] For more on this, see Daniel Cottom, '*Frankenstein* and the Monster of Representation', *SubStance*, 28 (1980): 60–71.
[98] Shelley, *Frankenstein*, 136.

Why did I live?'⁹⁹ Forcibly expelled from the boundaries of the human world of identification and relationship, the creature's humanity is neglected – 'I was like a wild beast that had broken the toils, destroying the objects that obstructed me and ranging through the woods with a stag like swift-ness'.¹⁰⁰ Denied the acknowledgement of his personhood by his fellow men and entirely ignored by the force that brought him into being, Frankenstein's creature truly appears as monstrous for the first time.

From this point, examination can turn to what kind of moral discernment or judgement can be made about the figure of the creature within the text and where the figure of the monstrous may be said to truly reside. The purpose of this section will be to attempt to come to an ethical judgement about the text and explore what the previously discussed theological re-readings of *Frankenstein* may offer by way of recasting the figure of the creature in a more philosophically and theologically nuanced way.

Frankenstein himself clearly believes his creature to be evil, but, as discussed earlier, the link between aesthetics and morality serves only to indict Victor's failings as a creator and positions the book as highly critically of key tenets of Romantic thinking, particularly ideas on selfhood, creation and the theological. The revulsion and aesthetic disgust that Frankenstein feels towards the creature begin first with his creation, where the aesthetic repulsion ensures that his dreams and pleasant rest 'become a hell'¹⁰¹ and where a 'frightful fiend/Doth close behind him tread'.¹⁰² Even before Frankenstein's creature has committed any act that might reasonably be described as evil, Frankenstein himself attempts to link the creature to the language of hell and damnation. It is not enough to consider evil as a category of behaviour, as Victor positions his creature as such before the creature has any ability to do anything, good or not. Rather, as Eagleton claims, 'evil is a condition of being' as well as 'a category of behaviour'.¹⁰³ With the notion of evil as a condition of being (a certain kind of constructed being at that) the evil actions would certainly seem to follow from that – there would be no other kind of action that those who are evil could perform. However, this lends itself to a remarkably circular logic, 'if some people really are born evil . . . they are no more responsible for this condition that being born with cystic fibrosis. The

---

⁹⁹ Ibid.
¹⁰⁰ Ibid.
¹⁰¹ Ibid., 52.
¹⁰² Ibid.
¹⁰³ Eagleton, *On Evil*, 152.

condition which is supposed to damn them succeeds only in redeeming them.'[104] To hold Frankenstein's creature as morally responsible, and for the moral judgement of evil to hold any weight, it requires evil to be something freely chosen and if Frankenstein has created the monster to be evil then said monster is rendered incapable of being anything else. If we are to label the monster as 'evil' this depends upon an understanding of evil as something that is fundamentally *willed* into action, a series of actions carried out for their own sake, frequently labelled as 'radical evil'.[105] Ewan Fernie calls this understanding of evil 'a form of existence founded upon destruction'[106] where actions are the result of evil beings rather than any kind of external factors. The attraction of such a position is clear but ultimately reductive – too often radical evil is used as an ideological means of ensuring that those who have committed acts that are met with disapproval cannot be excused or explained away by appeal to circumstance, mistakenly conflating what is understandable with what is commendable and explanation with absolution.[107] The idea that evil actions are performed by evil persons because they are evil persons is an unsatisfying conclusion and gets no closer to the ontological reality of Frankenstein's creature despite the great effort that Shelley goes to provide the creature with a detailed subjectivity. Without a theological understanding of both creation and personhood, interpretation of the novel and the moral culpability (or otherwise) of the creature is morally reductive and fails to reflect the true complexity of the issue at stake.

From this, it follows that for Frankenstein's immediate condemnation of the creature as evil to be tenable and taken seriously, a closer examination of the link between evil and subjectivity is necessary. Frankenstein's extreme and theologically inflected language constantly tries to link the creature to not just a moral position but to the ontological state of evil. What renders this untenable is the novel's lengthy subjectivizing of the creature, with the middle third of the novel dedicated to prioritizing the creature's narrative voice. This voice serves as insight into the nature of the creature's being and shows a rather more complex image than Victor's own rather reductive and totalizing theological language. 'Evil', as a term, suggests a transcendence, something that goes beyond the solely

---

[104] Eagleton, *On Evil*, 5.
[105] The term is drawn specifically from Kant and his work *Religion within the Bounds of Reason Alone* (1793). For a more modern summary of the philosophical underpinnings of Radical Evil, see *Radical Evil*, ed. Joan Copjec (London: Verso Books, 1996).
[106] Ewan Fernie, *The Demonic: Literature and Experience* (London: Routledge, 2013), 10.
[107] See Eagleton's example of the police response to the Bulger murders at the beginning of *On Evil*, 'as soon as I saw them, I knew they were evil'. See Eagleton, *On Evil*, 1–2.

materialist moral categories of good and bad. To phrase things in more theological language, evil forms the inverse negative of the goodness of the divine. However, Frankenstein's creation shows himself to be far from transcendent or all that interested in negation; rather his aims and actions are often close to prosaic. The creature's concerns are with satiating hunger and thirst (pp. 101, 103–6) with shelter and rest (pp. 101, 104 and 106), and ultimately with companionship (pp. 119–20). The concerns of the creature are rather human as opposed to the demonical or truly evil labels that Frankenstein assigns. Even when the creature experiences negative emotions, they are contextualized in such a way as to make the creature more empathetic:

> I continued for the remainder of the day in my hovel in a state of utter and stupid despair. My protectors had departed, and had broken the only link that held me to the world. For the first time the feelings of revenge and hatred filling my bosom, and I did not strive to control them; but allowing myself to be borne away by the stream, I bent my mind towards injury and death. When I thought of my friends, of the mild voice of De Lacy. The gentle eyes of Agatha . . . these thoughts vanished . . . but again when I reflected that they had spurned and deserted me, anger returned, a rage of anger.[108]

Here, alongside a confessional tone that once again links Frankenstein's creature to the lamentations of Job, we see a broad gamut of human emotion and the perilous emotional trauma tied up in the expulsion of the subject from any kind of community. The anger and thoughts that bend towards injury and death become understandable if not justifiable. To call the creature 'evil' seems at best an ethical overreaction, in fact close to irresponsible, and highlights the fundamental flaw in the radical evil conception of the term. While arson and murder can by no means ever be granted as acceptable actions, it would seem that the creature's actions and behaviours are too closely interrelated with the behaviours and motives of those around him to be classified as 'evil'. While these actions are wrong, it seems extreme to label them as 'evil' for these actions do not come from the creature themself but from multiple causes, including the great network of relationships and peoples that the creature has been introduced to by the very act of being created. Frankenstein's creature cannot be called radically evil with any sincerity – Shelley's portrayal all too clearly shows the creature as less ontologically monstrous and rather socially constructed as such. Radical

---

[108] Shelley, *Frankenstein*, 112.

evil's emphasis on the ontological reality of evil is insufficient to comprehending the interconnectedness of Shelley's novel. Frankenstein's creature is *made* to appear monstrous, and the narrative neatly highlights both the interrelated nature of the self with the other and the dangerous trauma and violence that emerge when the personhood of the Other is ignored. Like all of humanity, the actions of the creature within the novel are violent, destructive but cannot be immediately reduced to a singular ultimately destructive and private will. What Shelley documents, then, is an example of original sin, which 'allows theologians to acknowledge that evil is endemic to human activity and indissolubly associated with the most basic aspects of our experience'.[109] However, to focus on the notion of 'original sin' does not require any kind of moral relativism as the doctrine 'links evil to human activity without making the crass and simplistic suggestion that the world's faults are directly attributable to the sins of one particular person'.[110] In other words Frankenstein's creature is evil in as much as we all are morally responsible and morally compromised through the very notion of acting in the world and thus should not be called evil at all. If this is the case, Victor's appropriation of theological language becomes more significant as it reveals the extent to which he is invested within theological logics while disavowing his own complicity in the creature's actions. Fundamentally, the creature is not evil in any coherent sense of the term – but rather capable of wrongdoing and capable of inflicting harm, just as other fallen creatures are. In effect, this is merely a theological extension of the same argument made by Rousseau: if the social contract ensures that humanity 'all bind themselves to observe the same conditions and should therefore all enjoy the same rights',[111] then all are at risk of inflicting harm upon one another. Shelley takes seriously the idea of a kind of social contract without lapsing into a naïve utopianism, for as the novel shows, to be in the world is to be fundamentally vulnerable to the other, bound up and connected to them in ways which go beyond the political or social. The case of Justine and William seems fitting here, as simply through virtue of being-in-the-world the two are both killed. Their own actions are arguably not the cause of their deaths, but their involvement with others (even if that involvement was involuntary) is far more to blame. Elizabeth's question, of how 'shall I ever again believe in human goodness',[112] does not simply reflect

---

[109] Knight, *Religion and Literature*, 97.
[110] Ibid.
[111] Rousseau, *Social Contract*, 23.
[112] Shelley, *Frankenstein*, 80.

a moral judgement upon the individual actions of Justine but raises far more complex questions of the fragile nature of the connections between people and how easily the connections that are undeniably good can also result in great damage.[113] Furthermore, the novel emphasizes the vital role of community in the recognition of the ontological status of the individual, and the high costs when aesthetics is equated with morality or ontology. Understood as a theological text then, *Frankenstein* becomes more than simply 'part of the Gothic', but presents an imaginative theology, declaring the value, worth and personhood of Frankenstein's creature beyond the reductive readings of Gothic studies that would see this theologically abjected, compelling human figure as nothing more than mere metaphor or political allegory.

However, the novel does not merely put forward the figure of a monster as a constructed product of human relationships but further extends its theology by providing a stern critique of Romanticism more generally. If, despite the theological extremity of Frankenstein's language, his creature resists the label of 'evil' the same cannot be said of Victor Frankenstein himself. As previously discussed, 'evil' as a term is not simply a moral judgement but must be treated as a metaphysical concept. The turn to theology allows for a move beyond the totalizing and reductive moral ontology that has been criticized earlier. As John Milbank notes, 'Traditionally, in Greek, Christian and Jewish thought evil has been denied any positive foothold in being', being instead 'the privation of being itself'.[114] Evil, in theological terms, is 'violent hostility to being',[115] and from this point, it becomes easier to see Victor as not merely irresponsible, but as embodying the evil of the Romantic ideology that Shelley so trenchantly criticizes. This privation theory, key to Christian theology since at least the time of St Augustine, argues that evil is not a positive presence but rather an ontological *lack*. As God is creative and always good, it follows that all of God's creation must be good too, in some way. Theologically speaking, this renders evil a problem – if evil is a thing in the world then (as all created things are in some way reflective of the goodness of God) evil must in some sense *be* good. The other option is that evil is in some way outside of the control of God. The Augustinian solution

---

[113] It is for similar reasons that the philosopher Simon Critchley claims that one of the fundamental ontological states is that of being in debt, due mainly to the fact of our 'thrown-ness' into the world. See *Faith of the Faithless*, particularly 155–203.
[114] For a detailed exposition of the coherence of privation theory, see Charles T. Mathewes, *Evil and the Augustinian Tradition* (Cambridge: Cambridge University Press, 2008) as well as Milbank, *Being Reconciled*.
[115] Fernie, *The Demonic*, 10.

of privation theory solves this problem by placing evil outside of the realm of being – something which instead of embodying positive presence, embodies rather negation and often hostility towards that which exists. At stake here is a deep-seated and radical critique to early Romantic ideology. The emphasis on imagination and the primacy of the individual genius is prone to not just great imaginative creativity but also dangerous annihilationist overreach. Through a privative view on evil, the Romantic ideal of a new metaphysical reality is revealed as not simply dangerous but, more importantly, potentially hostile to the materiality of the world it inhabits. Overly enamoured with its own imaginative capacity, the Romantic Imagination that Victor embodies 'dissolves the everyday world into so much meretricious show . . . as such it is as much a divisive capacity as a unifying one'.[116] This is rather primly understating the case here, as Shelley's presentation shows Victor's imagination to be not only divisive but also actively hostile to the created world, contributing in the end towards his own bodily dissolution.

With this understanding in place, it becomes more possible to see Victor as the figure within the novel that comes closest to embodying evil. Whereas the creature is presented as a subject concerned with basic, mundane needs, Victor is uninterested in and detached from the physicality and materiality of existence. From the very beginnings of his narrative his interests stretch beyond the limitations of the physical world to the idea of something that can only be conceived of as beyond. Frankenstein speaks of Elizabeth and her interest in the 'magnificent appearance of things',[117] but the realities of the created world are to Frankenstein a means of concealing a 'secret which I desired to divine'.[118] Beyond the created world, beyond the physical world, Frankenstein seeks another kind of reality and access to a metaphysical realm of power.

> So much has been done, exclaimed the soul of Frankenstein, – more, far more will I achieve . . . I will pioneer a new way, explore unknown powers and unfold to the world the deepest mysteries of creation.[119]

In theological terms, Frankenstein's failure is not simply in his inability to understand the actuality of creation but in the fatal and hubristic pride, that, like that of Milton's Satan, seeks the knowledge and ability of the divine. Pure

---

[116] Eagleton, *Culture and the Death of God*, 104–5.
[117] Shelley, *Frankenstein*, 28.
[118] Ibid.
[119] Ibid., 41.

autonomy, as Eagleton notes, 'is a dream of evil',[120] as it removes the human subject from the host of relations and network of interdependence through which humanity is constructed. Whereas his creature is drawn into the mutual co-dependence that constitutes a basis of personhood, Frankenstein, as his own narrative unfolds, becomes increasingly solitary – 'I was now alone. In the university, whither I was going . . . I must be my own protector'.[121] Cut off from the network of familial relationships and obsessively searching for access to a realm of knowledge beyond the knowledge of man, Frankenstein begins to embody the ideal Romantic man, 'too voraciously ambitious for his own well-being, perpetually driven beyond his own limits by the lure of the infinite'.[122] Victor's withdrawal from the bonds of the social contract is not only a political issue – a violation of the compact that sustains the Frankenstein family – but also the physical and social echo of his desperate theological experiments in making himself the father and creator of a new species. His journey from Switzerland to Ingolstadt marks the beginning of his own *felix culpa* or 'fortunate fall' away from the world of human relations and 'up' into the deeply unstable realm of abstract thought and creative powers. The imaginative realm of Romanticism that has attracted such interest from scholars of religion and literature is revealed to be profoundly theologically unstable, more concerned with striving towards abstract metaphysical and poetic re-imaginings than the distasteful physical world that it resoundingly spurns.[123] A theology removed from any kind of notion of the divine becomes emotionally unsatisfying, and as such, there should be little surprise in the prevalence of new, transcendent possibilities being explored in imaginative writing. Such a thirst for the infinite can, if left isolated and removed from the plane of the human, carry with it a 'puritanical distaste for the fleshly'.[124] Within the novel, this certainly holds true as Victor's own experiments turn from the physical with a striking disengagement from materiality. He himself speaks of being motivated by 'almost supernatural enthusiasm'[125] but once again, his misunderstanding of the nature and importance of the physical

---

[120] Eagleton, *On Evil*, 12.
[121] Shelley, *Frankenstein*, 37.
[122] Eagleton, *On Evil*, 31.
[123] To see the resurgent interest in Romanticism in scholarship on religion and literature, see Gavin Hopps and Jane Stabler, eds, *Romanticism and Religion from William Cowper to Wallace Stevens* (London: Ashgate, 2006); also Bernard Reardon, *Religion in The Age of Romanticism* (Cambridge: Cambridge University Press, 1985) plus J. Robert Barth, *Romanticism and Transcendence: Wordsworth, Coleridge and the Religious Imagination* (Missouri: University of Missouri Press, 2003).
[124] Eagleton, *On Evil*, 31.
[125] Shelley, *Frankenstein*, 44.

is clear. Spending his time in graveyards and churchyards there is no connection to the dead as those who were once people, friends and family members, rather 'a churchyard was to me merely the receptacle of bodies deprived of life'.[126] As before, Frankenstein seeks to look beyond the veil of the physical, ignoring the true metaphysical significance of the human frame. His work examining how the 'fine form of man was degraded and wasted . . . how the worm inherited the wonders of eye and brain'[127] shows an understanding of creation as singularly and solely physical. There can be no greater significance to the human if, like the secrets of nature, they are concealed behind their physical appearance. Yet Victor, despite his eagerness to seize the restorative and resurrection powers of Christ, reveals himself as a theological sceptic, rejecting the possibility of any kind of physical or bodily resurrection in his treatment of the bodies which he uses to create his creature. Eagleton, in his book *On Evil*, summarizes the depth of Frankenstein's arrogance in greater detail:

> We think from inside a particular perspective on the world. This is not an obstacle to grasping the truth. On the contrary, it is the only way we can grasp it. The only truths we can attain to are those appropriate to finite beings like ourselves. And these are the truths of neither angels nor anteaters. Overreachers, however, refuse to accept these enabling constraints. For them, only truths which are free of all perspective can be authentic. The only valid viewpoint is the God's eye viewpoint.[128]

Yet, as Frankenstein is finite, his actions are catastrophic. His construction of the creature is described as a pursuit of nature but it is rather a warping of it. Whereas the creative act of Milton's *Paradise Lost* is a great ongoing hymn involving the relational participation of all concerned, Frankenstein 'dabbles with the unhallowed damps of the grave' and tortures the 'living animal to animate the lifeless clay',[129] enacting his own grisly parody of Genesis One. As he comes closer to the act of creation and to attaining the knowledge for which he is disastrously underprepared, the conflict between the appropriate knowledge of the human and the seemingly supernatural encouragement towards hubris is rendered starkly:

> In a solitary chamber, or rather cell, at the top of the house, and separated from the other apartments by a gallery and staircase I kept my workshop of

---

[126] Ibid., 45.
[127] Ibid.
[128] Eagleton, *On Evil*, 32.
[129] Shelley, *Frankenstein*, 47.

> filthy creation . . . The dissecting room and slaughter house furnished many of my materials; and often did my human nature turn with loathing from my occupation, whilst, still urged on by an eagerness which perpetually increased, I brought my work near conclusion.[130]

Here we see a dangerous and appealing paradox; Frankenstein reaches beyond the limits of human knowledge yet at the same time this reach into the abstract and transcendent realm of knowledge is hugely generative. It is this ambition that Ewan Fernie observes: 'it involves a potential for creativity, over and against what merely is, which is something other than evil – and indeed, if we are to pay heed to contemporary philosophy and culture, may be a central component of the Good'.[131]

Yet the great tragedy of Frankenstein is his seeming inability to recognize the potential good of his creation – his belief in the secret knowledge *behind* the physical ensures this, and so his response to the physical actuality of creation is violent disgust and a theological revulsion. That which is actually present in the world is merely an impediment to the working of his abstracted will. In the night of his successful animation of the creature comes Frankenstein's famous dream, wherein the reader sees Frankenstein's aversion to physical contact. 'I thought I saw Elisabeth . . . delighted and surprised, I embraced her, but as I imprinted the first kiss on her lips, they became livid with the hue of death . . . and I saw the grave-worms crawling in the folds of flannel'.[132] This process of revulsion begins with Frankenstein's first view of the creature's completed physical form and accelerates Frankenstein's own isolation. Even his cousin's attempts to draw him back to the world of human relationship, of interdependence and intimacy, fail; 'Remember the friends around you . . . have we lost the power of rendering you happy?'[133] If he could be drawn back into human relationship it is arguable the narrative as it stands would never unfold. Yet Victor is too self-contained, self-reliant and too disengaged from the physical and material to be reached in such a way.

It is this detachment that leads to his solitary hikes and the vicious theologically inflected rage with which he attacks his creature. The linguistic attack being an expression of Victor's own inability to confront and comprehend the physical actuality of his created work while at the same time serving as a

---

[130] Ibid., 48.
[131] Fernie, *The Demonic*, 10.
[132] Shelley, *Frankenstein*, 51.
[133] Ibid., 90.

loaded reminder of Victor's own physical limitations he is so desperate to transcend and go beyond. The creature is labelled as 'demonic' but is in reality simply too physically human for the transcendentally inclined Victor to accept. Frankenstein's attempt to go beyond himself and create *ex nihilo* has only succeeded in creating a profoundly physical rather than abstract being. Rather than 'pour a torrent of light into the world'[134] Frankenstein instead creates a man – physical and flawed – something that the ascetic Victor cannot accept. The ending of the novel also serves to show Victor's essential self-imposed isolation. Pursuing his creation across Europe, he is only kept alive through the work of his creature yet he seems incapable of appreciating his own dependence on others – involving as it would an unsustainable commitment to materiality.

Through the course of the novel it is Victor that comes the closest to the negation of being that in the Augustine tradition is known as evil, as he admits he 'trod heaven in my thoughts'[135] and as such he is not without pathos. His inability to stand the physical interconnectedness of all things is what motivates his desires and yet at the end of his life he comes to recognize not only the moral but also theological error he has made. 'Like the archangel who aspired to omnipotence, I am chained in an eternal hell'.[136] The claim is somewhat histrionic as Victor finds himself not in hell, but in the unbearable physicality of the material world, and yet with a typical egoistical flourish compares himself to the fallen Lucifer. Dependent upon the generosity of Walton and the sailors and trapped within the impassable physical ice of the Arctic his death is perhaps inevitable.

To conclude, Shelley's *Frankenstein* articulates that which the Romantic ideology fails to – that theology is simultaneously a matter of transcendence and immanence, of the sublime and the deeply material. Thus, the novel is a deep-seated and much-needed corrective to a Romantic ideology that is morally reductive, removed and aloof from a material world that it finds somewhat distasteful and theologically naïve. Victor Frankenstein's own creature literally embodies this paradox, brought forth from the very basest of all materials; he articulates the all too human and hence familiar desire to connect with the divine that brought him into the world. While Romanticism seeks the transcendent in the sublimity of the imagination, *Frankenstein* shows that such searching may be both creative but is also deeply dangerous and theologically

---

[134] Ibid., 40.
[135] Ibid., 218.
[136] Ibid.

naïve. Despite the oft-stated Romantic interest in and debt owed to Milton,[137] the Romantic Imagination 'plays a role equivalent to that of the Redeemer in Milton's providential plot',[138] neatly excluding the need for a genuine theological engagement. On the contrary, it is in *Frankenstein* and the trash of the circulating libraries that is the canonical Gothic that a more sincere theological engagement can be found. However, when this theology itself can be warped to evil ends the theological and the Gothic can only become more deeply intertwined. It is this increasingly close relationship that will be the subject of the next chapter.

---

[137] One only need see Wordsworth's 1802 poem 'MILTON! thou shouldst be living at this hour' or Keats's own 'On seeing a lock of Milton's Hair'.
[138] Abrams, *Natural Supernaturalism*, 119.

2

'Sinners in the hands of an angry God'

Gothic revelation and monstrous theology in the Gothic's Calvinist legacy

This chapter will consider a certain theological tradition within nineteenth-century Gothic writing, namely the discursive legacy of reformed theology.[1] Shown in the recurrent Gothic fascination with ideas such as election, predestination and fate, this wide-ranging and diverse set of theological ideas will be considered under the broad label of the 'Calvinist Gothic'.[2] This follows the work of Alison Milbank, particularly her essay on Calvinist and Covenanter Gothic but seeks to widen the scope of analysis beyond the Scottish connection with Calvinistic Presbyterianism.[3] This Calvinist Gothic forms a distinct theme, repeated throughout the different iterations of Gothic writing. Within this subset of the Gothic there is a complex problematizing between what things are and what they appear to be, with a concomitant suspicion of appearances as opposed to essences. Whereas certain critics assert this problematizing as a characteristic of Gothic writing this tension between appearances and actualities links inextricably to the epistemological frameworks of systematic

---

[1] By 'reformed theology', this term is used to focus on the theological ideas and discourses produced in the work of European theologians such as John Calvin in their break with the dominant orthodoxies of the Roman Catholic Church during the Reformation. For more on this, see Jaroslav Pelikan, *The Christian Tradition: A History of the Development of Doctrine Volume Four, Reformation and Dogma 1300-1700* (Chicago, IL: University of Chicago Press, 1985).
[2] While the theological tropes, ideas and discourses the Gothic concerns itself with are drawn from the reformed theology of John Calvin, Calvinism is a broad and often conflicting set of ideas (particularly since the controversy between Calvinism and Arminianism). Despite the conflicts over specific points of dogma, the broader discourse of Calvinistic theology that finds expression in the Gothic canon draws upon the reformed ideas of Calvin (even if only to disagree with those same ideas), particularly in relation to predestination, revelation and soteriology. Therefore, even if on specific points there may be a theological disagreement, these discussions take place within a unified discursive whole that allows the Calvinist legacy to function as a broad, though ultimately coherent term.
[3] See Milbank, 'Calvinist and Covenanter Gothic', 89–101.

theology, specifically to Calvinist scepticism over the appearance of things (shifting, insubstantial and changing) versus the divinely revealed 'true' nature of the world. Through a close analysis of James Hogg's *The Private Memoirs and Confessions of a Justified Sinner* (1824) this link between theology, revelation and the Gothic will be positioned as central. Furthermore, this chapter aims to examine the Calvinist legacy in Gothic writings, explore how it articulates the tensions between revelation and knowledge, and argue for the Calvinist Gothic as performing both a valuable critique of and necessary contribution to the reformed theological tradition. What is at stake here is a crucial intervention within the debate between systematics and natural theology, as well as essential insight into the importance of Gothic texts as both contributing to and expressing theological truth. Rather than argue that the Calvinist Gothic is solely condemnatory or even critical of this kind of theology, this chapter will show that while there may be no escape from the narrative pattern of duality, it provides what Milbank refers to as 'a productive episteme through which to think'[4] through the multiplicity of identity in connection to theological belief and expression.

Both theology and the Gothic are discourses of writing and thus of language. Both discourses attempt to articulate what perhaps cannot be completely expressed through language alone, yet the very mode of their articulation determines much about them. There is, within the Gothic canon, a highly productive set of tensions between the desire to systematically explain and delineate the supernatural and transcendent and at the same time, an unmistakeable ambiguity wherein explanation and rationalist pragmatism can all too often fail or collapse into sheer undecidability.[5] As a result, these Gothic texts, which respond to Calvinist theology, pose a substantial challenge to the epistemic and discursive frameworks of systematics as the texts are susceptible to a reading that produces a radical and potentially ambiguous natural theology. Revealed knowledge or revelation of the divine and the supernatural cannot be attained solely through scripture or the word. Rather, in its depictions of revelation – whether that revelation be within nature, or through experience, the Gothic foregrounds and emphasizes the very instability of systematic theology

---

[4] Ibid., 89.
[5] Despite the predilection for the explained supernatural, most evidently in the early Gothic work of Ann Radcliffe, the supernatural and divine is often left open and unresolved in texts that are influenced by the tradition of reformed or Protestant theology. Hogg's *Memoirs and Confessions of a Justified Sinner* (1824), Henry James's *The Turn of the Screw* (1898), and the work of Stevenson and the Brontës would all serve as excellent examples of this.

and thus of strict or fundamentalist religious faith.⁶ Throughout the texts in question, it is not certainty that should be sought. Rather, resolution must come after the process and experience of ambiguity. Therefore, despite the best efforts of systematic theological systems, revelation can never be entirely secured; and the certainty of knowledge, indeed of all absolutes, whether that be identity of the self or other, divinity or the demonic, is brought into question through these narratives. It is in such *questioning*, rather than in systematic certainty, that the theological can be found. Rather than easy didacticism, or moralistic judgement, the Calvinist Gothic text is both closely linked to systematic theology as well as the theological traditions of negative theology or apophatic theology that seeks to speak of the divine, not in terms of concrete or positive statements but through negation and through what is fundamentally unknowable.⁷ Thus, even in the experience or encounter with the supernatural, as Brown writes, 'something is revealed or explained, [yet] a continuing element of mystery remains.'⁸ While commenting on the strictures and legal epistemic frameworks of systematic theology, Gothic Calvinism advances a more imaginatively engaged theology that in its questioning allows revelation to emerge through experience and through the process of narrative rather than through faith alone. Placing theology as central allows for the theological claims made within the text to be taken seriously as *theology*, rather than as a representation or sublimation of another critical concern.⁹

This chapter consists of three sections. Analysis will initially focus upon the different ways knowledge and revelation are presented in these texts, highlighting how Calvinist revelation is produced, necessitating some close attention to Calvinist theology. Furthermore, consideration will be given to the way in which religious models of revelation come into conflict with rationalist, empirical

---

⁶ As David Brown points out, the search for definition versus the acceptance of mystery has been a long- standing concern of theology, and the search for definition has been in ascendency from around the Middle Ages. See David Brown, *God in Mystery and Words: Experience through Metaphor and Drama* (Oxford: Oxford University Press, 2008), especially Chapter One.
⁷ The tradition of negative theology emerges in the early Church Fathers, such as Tertullian and St Cyril of Alexandria, but some of the most influential early works are from Pseudo-Dionysius the Areopagite. Other influential writers include Meister Eckhart and Saint John of the Cross. Aquinas drew heavily from the tradition of negative theology in his formulation of the analogical way in the *Summa Theologica*. For more on the development of negative or apophatic theology see, *The Wiley Blackwell Companion to Mystical Theology*, ed. Julia A. Lamm (London: Wiley-Blackwell, 2013).
⁸ Brown, *God in Mystery and Words*, 5.
⁹ Perhaps the most notable example of this is in David Punter's dismissal of Hogg's *Memoirs and Confessions* as nothing more than 'detailed and terrifying account of schizophrenia'. Such a short-sighted critical statement shows a startling lack of interest in the impact of theology and a profound a-historicism as to the theologico-cultural realities of the texts production. See Punter, *The Literature of Terror: The Gothic Tradition*, particularly Chapter Five.

means of knowledge – usually in the guise of encountering or experiencing supernatural manifestations within the text. From there, analysis will move to consider in-depth and specific examples of this tension in the revelation of the supernatural in nature. It is in the encounter with the supernatural in nature, outside of the systematic and linguistic expressions of faith that the Calvinist Gothic prefers, that reveals the instability inherent in the systematic approach to theology, as language consistently fails to suitably contain or secure the natural world. The final section of the chapter will argue for a Gothic natural theology, drawing on the role of story, narrative and ambiguity in constructing a more expansive, and generous understanding of experiences of the supernatural and the theological more generally. The vital contribution of the Calvinist Gothic is in articulating not simply a systematic theology of revelation but in seeking to express an imaginative and natural theology of revelation through the mysteries of the supernatural encounter expressed in the text. Crucially, Calvinist Gothic texts should not be considered as antithetical to, or critically dismissive of, religious experience. Through analysis of the texts, what can be revealed is that there is, as Paul Fiddes writes, 'not only a parallel, but actually a *union* between [theological] revelation and [literary] imagination'.[10]

In order to analyse Calvinist conceptions of revelation and knowledge within the texts it is first necessary to engage with the modes of knowledge production within Calvinism more generally. Two factors are of particular importance to the issue at hand: first, the status of the Word, namely the certainty of scripture; and second, the understanding of the world as essentially concealing a spiritual reality behind worldly appearances. Calvin's own work is instructive on both of these points. After establishing the nature of the innate knowledge of God in man, and man's subsequent ultimate depravity through sin, Calvin's work leaves no way for the subject to have any means of access to the divine.[11] It is these 'tenets of the great Reformers'[12] that leads to the next important theological move Calvin makes in the *Institutes*, namely the epistemic security of scripture as the means for revelation or knowledge of God. Calvin claims in Book One of the *Institutes* that 'scripture . . . deigns not to submit to proofs and arguments, but owes the full conviction with which we ought to receive it to the testimony

---

[10] Fiddes, *Freedom and Limit*, 26.
[11] For the knowledge of God, see John Calvin, *Institutes of the Christian Religion*, trans. Henry Beveridge (Grand Rapids, MI: WM. B. Eerdman Publishing, 1998), 38–9. For man's ultimate depravity, see Chapters One to Three of Book Two of the *Institutes* (210–64).
[12] James Hogg, *The Private Memoirs and Confessions of a Justified Sinner* (London: Wordsworth Classics, 2003), 4.

of the Spirit'.¹³ Revelation of the truth of God comes through the unchanging and unchangeable *logos* of scripture in conjunction with the work of the Holy Spirit and in no other way.¹⁴ It is for this reason that Calvin goes so far as to claim in Chapter Seven, Book One of the *Institutes* that it is 'impiety' to draw upon the interpretative judgement of the church in matters of hermeneutics.¹⁵ In this formulation of theology, interpretation is secondary to application, and the church, the heterogeneous practising community of faith, is entirely incidental to theology.¹⁶ Milbank points out that the issue with Calvin's model of redemption is that it is 'wholly extrinsic',¹⁷ reliant not on works, or even the natural world but on nothing other than the imputed righteousness of an otherwise wholly mysterious God.

As a result, the Calvinist Gothic is often riddled with an interpretative anxiety over the truth status of revealed knowledge, despite the long-standing theological idea that 'reading sacred texts involves a conversation'.¹⁸ The Calvinist Gothic functions as a site of tension, embodying the conflict between the epistemic certainty of systematics and the ambiguities of the metaphoric. Yet as David Brown points out, 'words ... are not just a medium for conveying something else but sometimes themselves are an essential constituent in [religious] experience'.¹⁹

Despite this, the systematic theology of the Calvinist tradition states that the duty of those who receive the Word is not to understand or to interpret but rather to *obey*. Scripture is taken as the final revelation of God and is held as ultimately true in all things. As a result, revelation is inherently deterministic, as exhibited in the murderous convictions of Gil-Martin. Yet it is precisely the deterministic nature of the theology that powers the horror and tragedy of these Gothic narratives. Despite the Calvinist insistence on the inviolate and permanent status of revealed knowledge through scripture, the potential theological richness of metaphor, ambiguity and textuality is latent within the Gothic despite the influence of Calvinism that seeks to exert a limitation to

---

[13] Calvin, *Institutes*, 72.
[14] Ibid., 64–7.
[15] Calvin, *Institutes*, 68–74.
[16] For a more in-depth exploration of this issue See Stanley Hauerwas, *Unleashing the Scripture: Freeing the Bible from Captivity to America* (Tennessee: Abingdon Press, 1993) as well as Stephen D. Moore, *Literary Criticism and the Gospels: The Theoretical Challenge* (New Haven, CT: Yale University Press, 1989).
[17] Milbank, 'Covenanter Gothic', 94.
[18] Knight, *An Introduction to Religion and Literature*, 71; also see David Brown's extensive exploration of this, particularly throughout *God in Mystery and Words*, as well as *Discipleship and Imagination: Christian Tradition and Truth* (Oxford: Oxford University Press, 2000).
[19] Brown, *God in Mystery*, 17.

multiplicity of meaning. However, as post-Saussurian structuralist theory and narrative theology maintain, '[e]xperience occurs within language. All that we have has been given in words'.[20] For the Calvinist, the function of language is to reveal the truth of the divine, yet this revelation is not clearly and finally separable from the ambiguity and multiplicity of language itself. The Gothic co-option of Calvinist theological discourse is designed to prey upon this religious anxiety over the status of language, its role in experiencing the theological and the necessity for interpretation.

With the status of scripture as the final theological and epistemological authority, received by man rather than interpreted, the Calvinist Gothic suspicion of interpretation applies not just to imaginative literature such as the Gothic (which frequently draws upon this very suspicion) but extends towards a suspicion of the world as it is. There is a strong focus throughout the Calvinist tradition of understanding the sensual world as deceptive, whereby even apparently benign worldly appearances conceal a spiritual conflict. Such a theological trait is evident in much of the Calvinist Gothic,[21] but is perhaps most clear in the structural subtlety of Hogg's famous novel. Comprising an editor's introduction, an apparently found manuscript and an editorial after-word, the novel details the life and suicide of a young religious fanatic in Scotland. Set in the aftermath of a particularly violent time in Scottish political and religious history (the 'Killing times' of Presbyterian history) the novel is informed by the complex and shifting political, social and religious discourses resonant in Scottish culture. Following the life and religious extremism of Robert Wringhim allows Hogg to examine not just the state of a nation but its theological sins. In its examination of the minutiae of a single religious fanatic, Hogg shows the broader theological dangers inherent in such beliefs and the very real experiential element of supernatural encounters in forming and refining subjectivity. The editor's narrative shows the material reality of Robert's life – his religious prejudice, his vanity and physical weaknesses are all shown in detail (particularly in the rather embarrassing physical confrontation with George Colwan). However, during the sinner's part of the narrative, these same events are instead revealed as moments of divine significance. Whereas the editor's narrative presents George Colwan as a somewhat typical example of aristocratic masculinity in his fondness for

---

[20] Gerard Loughlin, *Telling God's Story: Bible, Church and Narrative Theology* (Cambridge: Cambridge University Press, 1996), 20.
[21] For more on this, see R. L. Stevenson's *The Strange Case of Dr. Jekyll and Mr Hyde*, discussed in Chapter 4.

sports, games, drinking and 'all that constitutes gentility',²² the memoirs section of the narrative sees to the spiritual 'truth' of his character. Wringhim regards his brother with 'utter abhorrence', and desires him to be 'carried quick to hell'.²³ Thus, not only does Colwan become a legitimate target for destruction, but his destruction also serves as a necessary precondition for the salvation and security of the elect.

This attitude, which sees spiritual reality concealed behind material appearances, is applied to events as well as to the representation of subjectivity. The fight at the tennis match is recast from George's 'slight strike' into Robert nobly suffering 'in the name of righteousness'.²⁴ While such narrative reinterpretation and reworking is key to the novel's narrative ambiguity as well as the development of character, it serves to expose the epistemic and theological discourses which shape the coherence of Calvinist subjectivity. No matter the individual perception and awareness of reality, the real world merely conceals a deeper spiritual truth. While the nonbeliever may ignore an event or dismiss it as insignificant, for the Calvinist, every moment, no matter how banal, can be deeply loaded with cosmic, albeit non-material, signification, and most crucially, events are interpreted to one's own advantage as long as the subject's certainty of election does not waiver.

Historically these discourses were spread through the extremely effective means of distribution that Calvinistic theology created with its focus on evangelism, preaching and exegesis. One of the most famous examples is Jonathan Edwards's sermon 'Sinners in the Hands of Angry God' (1741), which gives special emphasis to the religious non-material element of existence elided in the material present. Edwards argues in his sermon that, thanks to the ultimate depravity of man, the condemnation of the wicked is assured. Furthermore, Edwards argues that 'it is no Security to wicked Men for one moment, that there are no visible means of death at Hand'.²⁵ Whatever the material circumstances of subjectivity may be, the reformed theological position is that it is irrelevant, and the wrath of God as determined through scripture is the reality. This reality is fundamentally non-corporeal and inaccessible. This point crops up repeatedly throughout Hogg, used by Gil-Martin and Wringhim as justification for their

---

[22] Hogg, *Memoirs*, 15.
[23] Ibid.
[24] Ibid., 18, 103.
[25] Jonathan Edwards, *Sinners in the Hands of Angry God: A Sermon Preached at Enfield, July 8, 1741*. Electronic Texts in American Studies. Paper 54, 8.

various crimes. For example, when discussing the 'worthy, pious divine Mr. Blanchard',[26] the life of one man is contrasted with the non-material nature of Wringhim's theology, which demands a refusal of the ethics of the world for the theological absolutism of hyper-Calvinism:

> Was it not my duty to cut him off, and save the elect? 'He who would be a champion in the cause of Christ and His Church, my brave young friend', added he, 'must begin early, and no man can calculate to what an illustrious eminence small beginnings may lead. If the man Blanchard is worthy, he is only changing his situation for a better one; and, if unworthy, it is better that one fall than that a thousand may perish. Let us be up and doing in our vocations'.[27]

The logical extension of the Calvinist refusal of the material world for the realities of the spiritual and immaterial ensures that planning the murder of a man has no ethical ramifications because of the spiritual realities at play.[28] Thus, abnegation of the accepted moral standards of the moment is by no means a failure but rather an overcoming of a flawed moral idea for the implementation of the perfect system of theological truth. Importantly then, such an action does not call into question the status of the elect but rather reflects the novel's preoccupation with the idea of antinomianism. Freed from the constraints of both the morals of the world and the standards of accepted religious behaviour through the surety of election, subjective behaviour is uncoupled from any moral consequences.

The Gothic element of the novel (and of the Calvinist Gothic as a whole) is generated by this very tension and incongruity between the realist and the materialist appearances of things, and the fear and anxiety of the spiritual conflict that exists behind or beyond the material. Hogg's titular Calvinist exhibits his own signs of subjective dissonance throughout the novel, exemplified in the following famous passage:

> I generally conceived myself to be two people. When I lay in bed, I deemed there were two of us in it, when I sat up I always beheld another person and always in the same position from where I sat or stood, which was about three paces off towards my left side . . . over the singular delusion that I was two persons my reasoning faculties had no power.[29]

---

[26] Hogg, *Memoirs*, 90.
[27] Ibid., 92.
[28] The idea of the man compelled by God to commit murder is a common Gothic theme, with some real historical examples discussed further in the chapter. This further links Gothic writing with the reformed theological tradition.
[29] Hogg, *Memoirs*, 106.

While the modern-minded critical response to this may turn to a psychoanalytic reading (some key texts on psychoanalysis and the Gothic are footnoted here),[30] this fractured subjectivity is a direct consequence of the theological discourses that shape the novel as a whole. Milbank draws this theology out, as follows:

> If in Calvin's system salvation is purely by the imputed righteousness of Christ and not by the individual's good actions or by his faith, how can someone know he is of the Elect? Such dubiety opens a space of self-conscious inner examination whereby the subject potentially splits, divides and doubles itself.[31]

Thus, to focus on psychoanalysis to the detriment of theology is simultaneously to ignore the historical and cultural conditions of the texts production as well as the role theology plays in structuring the Gothic conception of the subject.[32] It is a theme often repeated throughout Hogg's novel as the titular sinner increasingly becomes unable to function or maintain a coherent grasp upon his own subjectivity. The split between the real world and the spiritually violent and conflicted realm that is normally immaterial becomes increasingly hard to maintain. This suspicion is one that Hogg's novel expertly captures, as many of the characters exhibit the belief that material identity is something ultimately deceptive. Gil-Martin is frequently referred to as being able to change his appearance, and even Robert, after spending only the briefest time within his company, is thoroughly 'transformed'.[33] As Bessy Gillies so accurately notes at the courthouse, when she is questioned on the nature of the stolen goods, the items presented may be very *like* the ones taken but '*like* is an ill mark'.[34] The Calvinist theological discourses, which in many ways shape the novel, seek to neutralize the fundamental instability of material identity through the imposition of the immaterial, unchanging and revealed Word. However, this absolutism is further complicated by the various textual and structural strategies the work employs in order to dramatize the quest for the truth. The editor's narrative reveals the editor to be extremely hostile to Calvinism in favour of 'nature, utility and common

---

[30] For example, see Andrew Smith, *Gothic Radicalism: Literature, Philosophy and Psychoanalysis in the Nineteenth Century* (London: Palgrave Macmillan, 2000), also Joel Faflak, *Romantic Psychoanalysis: The Burden of the Mystery* (New York: State University of New York Press, 2009) as well as Michelle A. Massé, 'Psychoanalysis and the Gothic', in *A Companion to the Gothic*, ed. David Punter (London: Blackwell, 2001).

[31] Milbank, 'Covenanter Gothic', 93.

[32] For the historical context of Calvinist controversy in the Church of Scotland and the ways in which Hogg was almost certainly aware of them, see Louis Simpson, *James Hogg, A Critical Study* (London: Oliver & Boyd, 1962), 170–99. For an overview of the theological debates around the Reformation in Scotland, with a particular focus on atonement, Christology, election and the doctrine of the Church see Donald Macleod, 'Reformed Theology in Scotland', *Theology in Scotland*, 17.2 (2010): 5–31.

[33] Hogg, *Memoirs*, 83.

[34] Ibid., 49.

sense', as opposed to seventeen-hour discussions on points of doctrine.[35] Yet despite this, the search for any kind of narrative certainty reveals the editor of the manuscript, and by extension Enlightenment values more generally, to be utterly powerless to inform the reader of the ultimate truth of things: 'With regard to the work itself, I dare not venture a judgement for I do not understand it.'[36] In addition, the fight that breaks out after the altercation at the Black Bull is investigated to the fullest extent of the law, and yet, once more, true knowledge cannot be revealed: 'Finally it turned out that a few gentlemen, two-thirds of whom were strenuous Whigs themselves, had joined in mauling the whole Whig population of Edinburgh.'[37] The strategies of asserting and securing 'truth' – whether this be the truth of identity, the legal truth or even narrative truth – are consistently undermined throughout the course of the novel.[38] Just as Calvinist discourse seeks to ascertain who belongs to 'the society of the just made perfect'[39] and by the end of the narrative fails to secure an answer, so too does the novel fail to resolve the ambiguities of the supernatural into solely material causes. As Milbank puts it, 'the reader is thus left in a position of hesitation, unable to discount or to believe . . . parodying Calvinist doubt'.[40] This doubt is only exacerbated through the course of the novel for, as the text progresses, the demarcation between the material and the spiritual becomes more porous, and both the systematic revelation of Calvinism and the rationalist theories of the editor begin to break down. Accused of horrendous crimes and increasingly unable to maintain a coherent grip upon the actualities of his own life, Robert becomes a fugitive, moved from place to place and increasingly beset by the strange and supernatural. The supernatural manifestations reach a head upon his reaching the village of Ancrum, where he is

> momentarily surrounded by a number of hideous fiends, who gnashed on me with their teeth, and clenched their crimson paws in my face . . . my dreaded and devoted friend, who pushed me on and, with his gilded rapier waving and brandishing around me, defended me against all their united attack.[41]

---

[35] Ibid., 10.
[36] Ibid., 176.
[37] Ibid., 23.
[38] As Jan-Melissa Schraam explores in *Testimony and Advocacy in Victorian Law, Literature and Theology* (Cambridge: Cambridge University Press, 2000), the undermining of the truth of testimony and narrative was a long-standing preoccupation and anxiety throughout nineteenth-century literature, an anxiety which in many ways still haunts contemporary Gothic writing – see Marsden's *Holy Ghosts* for more examples.
[39] Hogg, *Memoirs*, 79.
[40] Milbank, 'Covenanter Gothic', 94.
[41] Hogg, *Memoirs*, 161.

Such an episode is easily enough read as a hallucination, or a psychosomatic manifestation of guilt for his various hideous crimes, but this misses the situation's theological language and semiotics. The language describing 'hideous fiends with crimson paws' echoes the apocalyptic and annihilationist language of Edwards's sermon:

> The Wrath of God burns against them, their Damnation don't slumber, the Pit is prepared, the Fire is made ready, the Furnace is now hot, ready to receive them, the Flames do now rage and glow. The glittering Sword is whet, and held over them, and the Pit hath opened her Mouth under them. The Devil stands ready to fall upon them and seize them as his own, at what Moment God shall permit him. They belong to him; he has their Souls in his Possession, and under his Dominion.[42]

As argued in the opening section, the Calvinist predisposition towards the perception of the world as concealing a conflict-riven spiritual reality is one that has a profoundly damaging impact upon subjectivity. Guilt often emerges in strange and unaccountable ways as a direct result of the theological positions that Calvinistic religion espouses. Neither is the effect upon subjectivity limited to the subjectivity contained within narrative. The story of Major Thomas Weir serves as an instructive example. After a life 'characterised externally by all the graces of devotion', the Major confesses to crimes and sins so removed from the material realities of his life that 'the provost, Sir Andrew Ramsay refused for some time to take him into custody'.[43] Weir's response to the possibility of repentance was to cry 'Torment me no more – I am tormented enough already'.[44] Weir was eventually sentenced to death by strangulation and burning, 9 April 1670. His final words, instead of the to-be-expected call for divine mercy, were, 'Let me alone – I will not, I have lived as a beast and must die as a beast'.[45]

In a similar real-world example, Charles Brockden Brown's *Wieland* draws influence from another religiously inspired criminal case. In late July 1796, James Yates, 'bidden by a "spirit" to destroy all his idols', murdered his two sons and baby daughter, and beat his wife to death with a stake from the garden fence.[46] When caught by the authorities, as with Weir, he refused any opportunity to repent, instead exclaiming that 'my father, thou knowest that it was in obedience

---

[42] Edwards, *Sinners*, 7.
[43] Robert Chambers, *Traditions of Edinburgh: A New Edition* (Edinburgh: W&R Chambers, 1847), 33.
[44] Ibid.
[45] Ibid., 34.
[46] Peter Kafer, *Charles Brockden Brown's Revolution and the Birth of American Gothic* (Pennsylvania: University of Pennsylvania Press, 2004), 113.

to thy commands and for thy glory, that I have done this deed'.[47] As with Weir, the religiously inspired belief in an immaterial spiritual reality manifests itself in the justification of horrific crime. As with Weir, Yates too refuses the possibility of repentance and forgiveness as both his belief in the necessity of obedience to the spiritual world, and the ability to ignore the ethics and moral standards of the present and material world manifestly prove. Importantly, these Calvinist subjects believe that they are more pious in accepting their damnation rather than seeking any kind of repentance. By accepting the deterministic nature of Calvinist faith, obedience to the glory of God and his will is framed as an ultimate virtue, and, in keeping with typically Gothic concerns, predestination proves to be inescapable even to the point of death. What this suggests is that the Gothic double is a profoundly Calvinist concern – or, in other words, it is through the figure of the double that the Gothic gives form to the Calvinist notion of the divided self. As Chapter Four outlines, the Calvinist idea of the divided self is hugely influential on Stevenson's *Jekyll and Hyde*, which, as Milbank points out, is 'rarely connected to its Calvinist origins'.[48] Milbank correctly identifies the interest in duality as a 'protest against a murderous dualism'[49] – a dualism, that as the stories of Weir and Yates proves, is able to exert genuinely dangerous consequences.

Again, while it is perhaps enough to approach these narratives as apocryphal or simply the testimony of a disturbed mind, the parallels between the story of Weir, the story of Yates and the subjectivity of Hogg's sinner cannot be easily ignored. Like Weir, Robert cannot endure the material realities of the world, too burdened by the spiritual conflict and sins that exist beyond the material realm. Like Weir, Robert ends 'dying like a beast'. Hogg's sinner believes that the 'hour of repentance is past and now my fate is inevitable',[50] and, 'ordered to the byre, or cowhouse'[51] he dies in a manner far removed from his class status and far away from the ideal of a sinner made righteous before God. The Calvinist discourse that shapes his subjectivity, that in many ways, constitutes his identity as *human*, reduces him to the level of a beast. Despite the best efforts of Calvinist discourses to elevate humanity, the instability of Calvinist systematic revelation achieves exactly the opposite. In other words, revelation can never be entirely secured,

---

[47] Ibid.
[48] Milbank, 'Covenanter Gothic', 98.
[49] Ibid., 101.
[50] Hogg, *Memoirs*, 165.
[51] Ibid., 164.

and the forced division that Calvinist theological discourse enacts between the word and the world provides much of the narrative power of the Calvinist Gothic.

At the same time, subjectivity is placed under an enormous tension, as the material world is presented as essentially false and concealing a deeper, non-material spiritual reality. Thus, despite the disavowal of interpretation, the world must constantly *be interpreted* in order to reveal the spiritual that it conceals. What is important to note is that it is not the issue of interpretation per se that causes the issue – rather, tension emerges from the idea that interpretation must in some way be concealed in order for the systemic totality of Calvinist discourse to be maintained. Such tensions reveal themselves to be profoundly stressful, as the individual subject begins to fracture under the pressures of a world and self that is deeply unstable, with a revealed Word or *logos* that is believed to be unchangeable. Confronted by the supernatural that runs counter to the fixed idea of what it *should be*, Calvinist subjectivity struggles to maintain any coherence.

However, despite these theological tensions and often-challenging ambiguity found in this conflict between the deceptive physical world and the revealed truth of scripture, the Gothic Calvinist text is not entirely antithetical to the religious possibilities of nature – wherein characters experience a revelation of the divine through a natural setting. Here's Hogg's novel proves useful in illustrating the point – despite the Calvinist extremism of its protagonist, the text offers the potential for a Gothic natural religion. By 'natural religion', what is referred to is not the systematic revelation of the divine through scripture that Calvin espoused but rather the argument that theological revelation and experience can be derived from sources other than scripture (e.g. nature). Alison Milbank points out that this kind of theological idea is common to the more Radcliffean tradition of Gothic writing, 'drawn to scenes of Romantic beauty experienced properly by characters of moral worth'.[52] As Emil Brunner argues, in what is widely regarded as the classic text on the issue, 'the creation of the world is at the

---

[52] Alison Milbank, 'Gothic Theology', in *Romantic Gothic: An Edinburgh Companion*, ed. Angela Wright and Dale Townshend (Edinburgh: Edinburgh University Press, 2016), 372. The connection, theologically speaking, is to the theistic thought of writers such as Shaftsbury who was hugely critical of religion derived from scriptural revelation alone, as Calvin had argued for:

> Tis indeed no small Absurdity, to assert a Work or Treatise, written in human Language, to be above human Criticism, or Censure. For if the Art of Writing be from the grammatical Rules of human Invention and Determination; if even these Rules are form'd on casual Practice and various Use: there can be no scripture but what must of necessity be subject to the reader's narrow scrutiny and strict judgment.

See Anthony Ashley Cooper Shaftsbury, *Characteristicks of Men, Manners, Opinions, Times*, Volume 3 (Indiana: Liberty Fund Press 2001), 140.

same time a revelation, a self-communication of God'.[53] Brunner's rather narrow natural theology drew a furious polemical response from his long-time friend Karl Barth who argued passionately against natural theology in all of its forms. Tellingly, Barth was long seen as winning the debate, determining the direction of much twentieth-century theology towards systematic theology at the expense of natural theology and imaginative apologetics.[54] The Gothic presents moments wherein characters experience a revelation of the divine in nature, and from these presentations it is possible to move towards a broader understanding of the model of revelation that the Gothic Calvinist text advances. Certain passages from the texts in question bear closer examination – in pursuit of his brother and 'desperate for an opportunity of executing divine justice on a guilty sinner',[55] Robert pauses, experiencing a rare moment of doubt. 'I tried to ascertain, to my own satisfaction, whether or not I really had been commissioned of God to perpetrate these crimes in his behalf'.[56] Following this moment of doubt is a clear moment of theological revelation as,

> Involved in a veil of white misty vapour, and, looking up to heaven, I [Robert] was just about to ask direction, when I heard as it were a still small voice close by me which uttered some words of derision and chiding.[57]

The still small voice is a direct reference to a moment of revelation within scripture. The prophet Elijah is told to stand upon the mountain and is assailed by wind, earthquake and fire, but 'the Lord is not in the wind' or any of these physical manifestations. Finally, there is sound like 'sheer silence' and 'then came a voice to him that said, "What are you doing here, Elijah?"'[58] Crucially, Wringhim's theological revelation comes from a moment not of dogmatic certainty but rather of doubt, directly echoing a scriptural story of a devout prophetic figure beset by spiritual insecurities. This 'still small voice' is followed by another theological revelation as Robert meets a figure 'robed in white' who possesses supernatural insight into his spiritual condition:[59] 'Preposterous wretch! How dare you lift your eyes to Heaven with such purposes in your

---

[53] Brunner, *Natural Theology*, 25.
[54] For a good overview on the debate and the ways in which the thought of Brunner has undergone re- evaluation in recent years, see Alister McGrath, *Emil Brunner: A Reappraisal* (London: Wiley-Blackwell, 2013).
[55] Hogg, *Memoirs*, 108.
[56] Ibid.
[57] Ibid.
[58] See I Kings 19: 11–13.
[59] Hogg, *Memoirs*, 109.

heart? Escape homewards, and save your soul, or farewell forever!'[60] Unlike the theological revelation of his sure election to salvation, however, these undeniably supernatural experiences are not forcibly imposed upon him but are rather mediated through (in this case) what appears to be a human figure. He goes on to justify his behaviour with a theologically loaded rhetorical question: 'How is this interested and mysterious foreigner a proper judge of the actions of a free Christian?'[61] Carrying on with his journey, he encounters Gil-Martin who, upon hearing what the mysterious woman has said, interprets the words in such a way as to allow the attempted murder to continue. From this episode, a few formative points on the nature of natural theology as a source of revelation of the divine begin to emerge. First, and perhaps most importantly, Hogg's natural revelation is necessarily *interpretable*. As opposed to the view on revelation drawn from the Calvinist discourse, here the experience can, and indeed *must* be interpreted – even if the ultimate interpretation is a disingenuous attempt to justify murder. Secondarily, and crucially, natural revelation comes at the moment of subjective spiritual doubt. This moment from Hogg suggests that in the still small voice and the revelation within nature, there is space (however quickly extinguished) for the notion of predestination to be questioned. This moment of indecision ('I be thought the rashness of my undertaking')[62] proposes a theological revelation of the divine which is, at core, non-deterministic and allows for the possibility of different action. This can be profitably contrasted with an earlier episode in the novel, wherein Robert confesses that 'my faith began to give way a little and I doubted most presumptuously of the least tangible of all Christian tenets, namely *the infallibility of the elect*'.[63] The infallible knowledge of election is a doctrine that is placed beyond the possibility of questioning, and to even be concerned about one's own theological status is a 'disingenuous sin'. Yet, in contrast, the emergence of doubt, the possibility of failure and, most strikingly, the fear of an absent salvation mark the moments of theological revelation within nature. The close of the sinner's narrative is rich with language which echoes the prophetic laments of the Old Testament – 'Lord thou knowest all that I have done for Thy cause on earth! Why then art Thou laying Thy hand so sore upon me? Why has thou set me as a butt of Thy malice?'[64] Once again, the rigidity of systematic

---

[60] Ibid.
[61] Ibid.
[62] Ibid., 108.
[63] Ibid., 101.
[64] Ibid., 164–5. For the scriptural correlates, see Habakkuk 1, and the entire book of Job.

Calvinist belief is unable to allow for ambiguity, doubt and the possibility of failure. In epistemological terms, where the systematic revelation imposes a theology of certainty, the destabilizing of the Calvinist legacy within the Gothic text opens the possibility for a theology of doubt. The theological experience of the divine in nature resists the systematic imposition of unchanging and unchangeable words imputed by an external hierarchical figure. Natural revelation is incommensurable and the experience within nature continually eludes the semiotic certainties that dominate Calvinist theological thought.[65] It seems then that Gothic depictions of theological revelation in nature draw out the tension between explanation and mystery, 'between the conviction that something has been communicated by the divine (revelation) and the feeling that none the less, God is infinitely beyond all our imaginings'.[66]

This tension between the systematic and the natural theologies present within the Gothic Calvinist legacy is not necessarily anti-theological. Notably, the tradition of doubt, of questioning and ambiguity that drives the justified sinner to the grave is drawn from the same *sola scriptura* that Calvinist revelation is built upon. Rather than seeing the moments of revelation in nature as a direct challenge to the Calvinist tradition, the Gothic draws from the same sources and traditions that the Calvinist discourse uses, and at the same time, both subverts and opens this tradition to new readings. This final section will thus seek to draw together the shortfalls of theological revelation that the Gothic exposes while at the same time offering a revised model of revelation that significantly contributes to this ongoing theological tradition. The Calvinist understanding of revelation as coming solely through the Word, a-historical and final in its meaning, 'revealed a strategy all too concerned with human control of the divine'.[67]

Revelation for the Calvinist legacy is one dominated by the desire to control, and such control is exerted through a vision of language that is entirely fixed on a definitional level. Calvin's comment on the opening of John's gospel serves as an excellent case in point here. Just as men's speech is called the expression of their thoughts, so it is not inappropriate to say that God expresses himself

---

[65] The awareness of this is behind much of the American transcendentalists and their move away from this kind of theological Calvinism towards new models of community and politics. For more on this, see Lawrence Buell, ed., *The American Transcendentalists: Essential Writings* (New York: Modern Library, 2006).
[66] Brown, *God in Mystery and Words*, 22.
[67] Brown, *God in Mystery and Words*, 33. In reference to this point it is important to note that it is his father that welcomes Robert into 'the society of the just made perfect' (Hogg, *Memoirs*, 79) rather than anything else which assures Robert of his own election.

to us by his speech or Word . . . the other meanings of the word are not so appropriate. The Greek certainly means 'definition' or 'reason' or 'calculation'; but I do not wish to enter into philosophical discussion beyond the limits of my faith.[68] Calvin's fundamentally a-historical and rather literalist view on language prevents the full metaphoric richness of the work from emerging, and thus leaves his commentary lacking theological depth.[69] However, the alternative, namely to see divine revelation only in nature also comes with significant issues, which have been well explored in the intellectual history of the Christian faith, having formed perhaps the most notable theological debate of the twentieth century in the reformed tradition.[70] What the Gothic text allows for is not simply a continuation of the divide between systematic or natural revelation and theology but rather the creation of an imaginative revelation which opens space for the reconsideration of theology as not monstrous system but rather as something experiential. Thus, the Gothic novel is intimately bound up in the process of belief. To quote Graham Ward,

> Novelists do not create ex nihilo. These worlds are exercises of imaginative transformation. That is, taking what is perceived and configuring a new presentation of what is meaningful. And, if they are to be successful exercises of imaginative transformation, they have to be believable – they have to persuade, even seduce, the receptive reader. The art of good novel writing is to arouse belief by awakening the imagination of whoever reads it.[71]

Rather than perceive imagination as antithetical to systematic statements and practices about theology, the Calvinist Gothic tradition positions them as complementary. Hogg here argues for a literary experience that can 'open onto the theological'.[72] The proliferation of theological language, concerns and allusions throughout the texts under consideration leaves these writers in the service of 'expressing a reality, which in some way transcends what can be

---

[68] John Calvin, *Commentary on John*, ed. A. McGrath and J. I. Packer (Wheaton, IL: Crossway, 1994), 13.
[69] For a brief, but extremely illuminating, exposition of Calvin's literalism and a small taste of the vitality and metaphoric depth of John 1, see Brown, *God in Mystery and Words*, particularly 22–43.
[70] See Brunner, *Natural Theology* . . . For background and context to this debate, see Trevor Hart, 'A Capacity for Ambiguity? The Barth/Brunner Debate Revisited', in *Tyndale Bulletin* 44.2 (1993): 289–305. Also see Stephen Andrews, 'The Ambiguity of Capacity, A Rejoinder to Trevor Hart', *Tyndale Bulletin* 45.1 (1994): 169–79.
[71] Graham Ward, 'Belief and Imagination', in *Theology and Literature After Postmodernism*, ed. Zoë Lehmann, Alison Milbank and Peter J. Imfeld (London: Bloomsbury T&T Clark, 2015), 74–95, 82.
[72] Ibid.

empirically verified, by sense and rationality'.[73] Both the Gothic text and the theological tradition from which it draws are attempts to use language in the reaching out towards mystery. However, where the theological discourses of Calvin seek epistemic certainty, the medium of this reaching, language itself, betrays the theological endeavour. Systematic theology seeks to use language to provide a secure foundation of theological knowledge and directly map the eternal Word of the revealed God onto the lives of the faithful. However, as David Brown notes, 'no detailed precision in such mapping is anymore possible'.[74] Thus the Gothic exploits the textuality of the language of systematic theology, which despite the systematic attempt at foreclosure, consistently points outward towards multiplicity of meaning. It is this desire for epistemic and religious certainty and the frustration of this desire that allows the texts discussed to generate much of their narrative power. To express it another way, the event can be 'true' in the sense of conveying a significant meaning even if it is not something which actually took place. The editor in Hogg's manuscript might open the final section of the text asking, 'what can this work be . . . I cannot tell',[75] yet even in this final section the theological and supernatural cannot entirely be explained away. Hogg once again expertly destabilizes any kind of epistemic certainty, first through the letter to *Blackwood*'s and finally the discovery of the body. In short, the imaginative revelation proposed by the Gothic Calvinist legacy is one that exists on 'the edge of the incredulous, seeking out new terrain where what is visible and reasonable and familiar meets what is invisible, miraculous and *Unheimlich*'.[76] Thus, the Gothic text functions as a powerful and necessary corrective to the oversimplification of Calvinist theological discourse while at the same time refusing to foreclose the theological entirely. An exceedingly strict Calvinist theology is shown to be potentially dangerous, prone to either ignore the material realities of the world or violently force the world to conform to an immaterial spiritual reality. At the same moment, the Gothic text resists the closure of systematics for the ambiguities of theological revelation in nature. Theological faith is depicted as strange, unstable and potentially far from benign but nevertheless one that is experientially and imaginatively real. The Gothic Calvinist legacy proposes a model of revelation that is inescapably bound up within 'the tense possibility of welcoming what is strange and highly

---

[73] Fiddes, *Freedom and Limit*, 35–6.
[74] Brown, *God in Mystery and Words*, 44.
[75] Hogg, *Memoirs*, 167.
[76] Ward, *Belief and Imagination*, 90.

dangerous: an act of faith'.[77] However, the theological discourses which manifest themselves throughout the Gothic nineteenth-century novel are not necessarily solely concerned with the abstractions of theological discourse and dogma. Theological belief and practice are concerned with the immaterial as has been discussed, but theology is also a powerful and effective tool for social regulation. Theology, in addition to being a discourse of political emancipation, can also be used as a means of enforcing expected social norms and hegemonies. It is this social aspect of theology which the next chapter will consider.

---

[77] Ibid.

3

Gothic writing and political theology

Wuthering Heights and *Jane Eyre* as theological texts

The connection between the Brontës' writing and religion is well established – hardly surprising given the Brontë siblings' familial biography and the close involvement and awareness of the theological issues of the day that their work reflects.¹ For the Brontës, influenced by theologians and writers such as Coleridge and his *Aids to Reflection* (1825), as well as the evangelical focus on personal piety and practical discipleship, Christian belief was understood as not simply a set of creeds but a mode of life, influencing all aspects of living.² However, as with all of the fictions under consideration throughout this book, the relationship to theology is not simply didactic, moralistic or evangelistic but far more ambivalent and frequently antagonistic towards certain forms of Christian orthodoxy and various manifestations of institutional forms of religion.³ As Miriam Elizabeth Burstein notes, 'contemporaries found the religious tendencies of their works ranging from glum to heterodox.'⁴ One of the early reviews of *Jane Eyre*, for example, condemned it as 'pre-eminently an anti-Christian composition'.⁵ Yet such lack of orthodoxy should by no means exclude these novels from being considered as theologically motivated works for '"religion" is a capacious category that includes more than expressions of doctrinal

---

¹ For an in-depth exploration of this, see Marianne Thormählen, *The Brontës and Religion* (Cambridge: Cambridge University Press, 2004).
² Thormählen, *Brontës and Religion*, 144.
³ Not for nothing does Tom Winnifrith categorize the influence of religion on the Brontës as 'both obvious and obscure'. See Tom Winnifrith, *The Brontës and Their Background: Romance and Reality* (London: Palgrave Macmillan, 1988), 28.
⁴ Miriam Elizabeth Burstein, 'The Religion(s) of the Brontës', in *A Companion to the Brontës*, ed. Diane Long Hoeveler and Deborah Denenholz Morse (London: Wiley-Blackwell, 2016), 433.
⁵ Elizabeth Rigby, 'Vanity Fair – And Jane Eyre', *Quarterly Review*. 84 (December 1848): 153–85 http://www.quarterly-review.org/classic-qr-the-original-1848-review-of-jane-eyre/ first, accessed 24 April 2017.

orthodoxy'.[6] Furthermore, as Gilbert and Gubar point out, what attracted the charge of anti-Christian writing was not the apparent coarseness and sexuality of the texts but rather the 'refusal to accept the forms, customs and standards of society'.[7] What emerges from this conflation of social norms with Christianity is not a conflict between Christian belief and anti-Christian sentiment but rather religious expression that is far enough outside of the orthodox standards of the day to be considered oppositional to a certain conception of the theological status quo. Too frequently, as Simon Marsden argues, the 'complexities and ambiguities of religious discourse have not always been acknowledged',[8] with criticism frequently depending upon a fixed notion of Christian belief that the Brontës either resist and oppose or move beyond entirely. Therefore, rather than reproduce the simplistic binary of sceptical versus faithful, this chapter seeks to follow the work of Micael M. Clarke – that of seeking 'a hermeneutics that considers religion in relationship to secular epistemologies'.[9] This is in line with the overall aim of the book generally, which seeks to consider the ambivalently secular Gothic in hospitable dialogue with the hermeneutics of imaginative apologetics.

Therefore, this chapter will not seek to place the Brontës within a particular theological or dogmatic position (as Thormahalen explains, such an exercise, while perhaps valuable, would be deeply contested for a variety of reasons)[10] but rather will examine how, through the use of Gothic technique, language and theme, theological ideas may be examined and critiqued. Particularly pertinent to this chapter will be the two Gothic novels, *Wuthering Heights* (1847) and *Jane Eyre* (1847), in which Emily and Charlotte present two differing comments on theology. Thus, rather than attempt to label the Brontës as Christian or not, this chapter will seek to examine the ways in which the Gothic novel functions as both a type of theological criticism and theological model, allowing for both Emily and Charlotte to explore, however ambivalently, a variety of theological concerns. *Jane Eyre* will be read as providing a kind of social theology concerned with a personal theological response to a specific social and political configuration of society. In *Wuthering Heights*, Emily Brontë offers a radical vision of openness

---

[6] Burstein, 'Religion of the Brontes', 434.
[7] Sandra M. Gilbert and Susan Gubar, *The Madwoman in the Attic: The Woman Writer and the Nineteenth Century Literary Imagination*, 2nd edn (London: Yale University Press, 2000), 338.
[8] Marsden, *Emily Brontë and the Religious Imagination*, 19–22.
[9] Micael M. Clarke, 'Emily Brontë's "No Coward Soul" and the Need for a Religious Literary Criticism', *Victorians" Institute Journal* 37 (2009): 195–224.
[10] Thormählen, *Brontës and Religion*, 13–24.

and hospitality towards the Other at the very limits of language as well as an ambiguous theological vision that embraces both religious and imaginative experience. *Wuthering Heights*, within the generic setting of the Gothic country house, outlines a highly original and compelling imaginative theology that emphasizes the contingency and fragility of the separation between the spiritual and the material, as well as the ways in which religion and theology not only reinforce one another but can often emerge as in tension with one another. In the case of *Jane Eyre*, which uses the same kind of generic setting, theology is anchored in the material relationships between people, articulating, in a sense, a type of political theology that encompasses both social and theological ideas on the nature of relationships between individuals.

Wuthering Heights, religious tensions, theology and grace

Wuthering Heights as a novel has often attracted attention from critics, who saw in it a complex work of art beset by various structural and thematic inconsistencies and problems. Q. D. Leavis in her influential 'A Fresh Approach to Wuthering Heights'[11] divides the text into two parts: a sociological narrative, which is broadly realist in tone, and a narrative of far more violent section revolving around the relationships of Catherine, Heathcliff and Edgar. This section argues that, theologically speaking, the divide that Leavis notes is instructive, highlighting as it does not only a divide within the text's structure but rather more significantly a fundamental divide within theological belief and religious practice. In her piece, Leavis writes that

> If we were to take the sociological novel as the real novel and relegate the Heathcliff-Cathy-Edgar relationship, and the corresponding Cathy-Linton-Hareton, as exciting but ex-centric dramatic episodes, we should be misconceiving the novel and slighting it, for it is surely these relationships, and their working out that give meaning to the rest.[12]

Leavis's point is well taken, but the argument is not extended far enough in the direction of theology. Rather than see it as simply a reflection of structural issues within the text, the divides within the narrative serve to illustrate the ways in which religious tradition, expectation and culturally ingrained norms

---

[11] See F. R. Leavis and Q. D. Leavis, *Lectures in America* (London: Chatto and Windus, 1969), 85–138.
[12] Ibid., 101.

can conflict with theology and doxology.[13] Throughout the novel, there is a clear tension explored between the accepted practices of culturally normalized 'religiosity' and theological experience and encounters with the numinous which exist outside of what is accepted and normalized. While in orthodox religious and theological practice these two ideas would be ideally held as mutually reinforcing, *Wuthering Heights* explores the tensions that arise when the two constituent parts of faith – religion and theology – begin to come into conflict with one another, rather than mutually reinforce one another. However, despite this tension between religious practice and theological experience, there is not necessarily a contradiction or an opposition to Christian belief and practice per se through the novel.

The critical opinion of Emily Brontë as being opposed to either an institutional religious expression or, at best, a heterodox believer is well established. For example, Stevie Davis's reading of Brontë's poem 'No Coward's Soul is Mine' argues that the poem has 'a quality of out of doors: no church could hold it. The roof would blow off.'[14] As Marsden points out, Brontë's most famous fictional church Gimmerton Kirk 'seems less likely to be blown off than to fall down'.[15] Yet, as J. Hillis Miller points out, in a widely influential but much-misunderstood reading, Brontë may have moved away from a specific understanding of Christianity, wrestling with the absence of a divine presence, but she also sought to try to find some way of rebuilding the connection between humanity and God – 'for only a recovery of God will make possible a renewal of society'.[16] As Clarke expresses it, the religious spirit that 'overflows doctrinal boundaries' should not be conflated with 'hostility to religion itself'.[17] Therefore, the question of what type of religious and theological critique the text articulates becomes clearer. First, the text functions as a theological critique of certain organized religious institutions and the behaviours and cultural expectations within which these institutions are bound up. Undeniably, the text is deeply antagonistic towards some notions of organized religion – the character of Joseph being a particularly vicious satire of Calvinist Christian religion, prone to mangling Scripture for

---

[13] Here I follow Graham Wards argument about the distinction between theology and religion outlined in *True Religion*. See particularly 2–4.
[14] Steve Davis, *Emily Brontë: Heretic* (London: The Women's Press, 1994), 144.
[15] Marsden, *Emily Brontë*, 57.
[16] J. Hillis Miller, *The Disappearance of God: Five Nineteenth Century Writers* (London: Oxford University Press, 1963), 209. This is a fight that later natural theologians would take up, as the nineteenth-century popular discourse increasingly turned to issues of materialism. For more on this, see Chapter 4.
[17] Clarke, 'Religious Literary Criticism', 212.

his own particular ends. He is, as Nelly eloquently explains, 'the wearisomest, self-righteous Pharisee that ever ransacked a Bible to rake the promises to himself, and fling the curses on his neighbours'.[18] Importantly, however, what seemingly attracts most criticism is not Joseph's devoutness but rather his use and interpretation of Scripture and the ways in which his particular literalist hermeneutics informs his behaviour. On the same night that Heathcliff leaves the Heights, after overhearing Catherine's rejection of him as a potential future spouse, Joseph comes to berate Catherine:

> This visitation worn't for nowt, und Aw wod hev ye tuh look aht, Miss, – yah muh be t'next. Thank Hivin for all! All warks together for gooid tuh them as is chozzen, and piked aht froo' th' rubbidge! Yah knaw whet t'Scripture ses[19]

Here, like the Calvinists discussed in Chapter 2, Joseph uses scripture to assure himself of his own salvation while condemning those who are outside of, or behave in a way that is resistant to, his own religious tradition. Throughout the novel he proves to be 'actively and aggressively malignant',[20] a religious hypocrite who delights in assuring himself of his own righteousness.[21] An extreme version of this kind of hermeneutic manipulation and the violence which emerges from it is in the famous dream of Lockwood and the sermon of Jabes Branderham. After listening to Branderham's interminable sermon, Lockwood rises to his feet and tries to depart before being stopped by a response from the preacher:

> *Thou art the man!* Cried Jabes, after a solemn pause, leaning over his cushion. 'Seventy times seven didst thou gapingly contort thy visage – seventy times seven did I take counsel with my soul – Lo, this is human weakness; this also may be absolved! The First of the Seventy First is come. Brethren, execute upon him the judgement written!'[22]

From this distorted reading of Mt. 18:22 erupts violence – again, institutional religious practice is seen as both prone to perverting the sacred texts they adhere to and, more fundamentally, inspiring dangerous levels of physical violence. Not only does this echo the critique of Calvinism offered by writers like Hogg but also shows the extent to which Gothic writing serves as a site that destabilizes

---

[18] Emily Brontë, *Wuthering Heights* (London: Penguin Classics, 2012), 44.
[19] Ibid., 92.
[20] Thormählen, *Brontës and Religion*, 82.
[21] The links and similarities between Joseph and the justified sinner of Hogg's earlier novel suggest a degree of cultural awareness of Calvinist thought and practice that was continuous and widespread throughout the period.
[22] E. Brontë, *Wuthering Heights*, 25.

normative theological practice. With tongue-in-cheek subversion, the message of the sermon and its example of the unforgiveable sin is to refuse to listen to a seemingly never-ending sermon – neatly highlighting the careful hermeneutic literalism of the preacher. Branderham's sermon is an exercise in biblical legalism, taken to a grossly exaggerated degree. His sermon exposes the extent to which this type of religious hermeneutics seeks outward conformity of behaviour and social propriety, enforced through strict disciplinary mechanisms. At the same time, the text highlights the level to which these controls and limitations of behaviour, which are constantly presented throughout the text, are ultimately intolerable. The suggestion is clear: 'legalistic and literalist readings of the Bible have reverted to a distorting insistence upon vengeance under the guise of forgiveness'[23] – a point highlighted in Chapter 2 on Calvinism. Even Lockwood, at best a rather lukewarm orthodox believer, is not immune to practising such violence when confronted with that that exists outside of his experiences. After reading Catherine's diary he dozes off. Awakened from his dream, he encounters the spirit of Catherine for the first time; his response is brutal:

> Terror made me cruel; and finding it useless to attempt shaking the creature off, I pulled its wrist on to the broken pane, and rubbed it to and fro till the blood ran down and soaked the bed clothes: still it wailed, 'Let me in'![24]

The scene neatly juxtaposes the Gothic with the theological – it is a classic example of the Gothic idea of the past forcibly reappearing into the present. As Sedgwick writes, 'Catherine's ghost represents the unquiet past that has not found continuity with the present.'[25] Yet this same moment of the violent re-emergence of the past comes alongside a record of the ways in which Catherine engaged with religious texts. The journal that Lockwood reads is written by Catherine in the margins of various sacred texts – her thoughts and narrative positions her as a kind of textual ghost – haunting the orthodox theological writing. As Marsden notes, 'her diary literally plays with the borders of authoritative texts, enacting the convergence of sacred and secular discourses.'[26] Not only is this an important theological point but further links the text to the Gothic, with its own long record on blurring and falsifying textual boundaries.[27] After reading

---

[23] Marsden, *Emily Bronte*, 81
[24] E. Brontë, *Wuthering Heights*, 27.
[25] Eve Kosofsky Sedgwick, *The Coherence of Gothic Convention* (London: Methuen Press, 1986), 99.
[26] Marsden, *Emily Bronte*, 79.
[27] Hogg's *Memoirs and Confessions* discussed in the previous chapter is an excellent example of this, with the Editors Introduction and the letters in *Blackwood's Magazine* but perhaps the most famous

it, Lockwood experiences this blurring of secular and sacred discourses as Catherine makes her 'Gothic return' from the past. Understood theologically, the moment is extremely significant in exploring the tension between religious tradition and theological experience. Religious tradition, focused on binding together a community of believers in faith, emphasizes a historical continuity and consistency of belief and behaviour. This is often practised and maintained through various strategies such as the supposedly educational texts and pamphlets that Catherine uses as the basis of her diary as well as the interminable sermons and proselytizing of figures like Joseph. However, theology, specifically doxology and eschatology, acknowledges the distinct possibility that God can, and indeed does, disrupt the historical continuities of faith communities. Revelation can manifest itself unexpectedly and radically affect the idea of a seamless continuation and progression between the past, the present and the future. The Gothic, then, allows for not only the return of the past into the contemporary present but also a dangerous destabilizing of the boundaries between the religious and the secular. Such a destabilizing frequently provokes a violent reaction from religious institutions and more fundamentalist believers who seek to preserve the clear boundaries of the spiritual. The violence of religious institutions is not necessarily triggered through their religious nature or through faith per se but through their religiosity – a culturally appropriate set of behaviours that either has little to do with Scripture or more to do with the various culturally sanctioned expressions of religious faith.[28] A literalist, vengeful hermeneutics inevitably results in a limitation of behaviour and sets in place often violent disciplinary mechanisms by which conformity is policed. Sedgwick picks up on this in relation to Catherine, writing that 'her ambition is always to break through, and if that involves pushing aside a wall of books, she would no doubt find the symbol a satisfying one'.[29] The best example of the ways in which this kind of religion seeks to limit behaviour comes immediately after Heathcliff's return – Catherine, now married to Edgar, welcomes home Heathcliff and brings him into the parlour. Edgar's response highlights the ways in which this kind of religion is more a question of acceptable behaviour than actual Christian living, as Nelly details the incident:

example is in one of the most successful early Gothic novels, Horace Walpole's *The Castle of Otranto* (1764) with its 'found narrative' conceit.

[28] It's quite arguable that this idea is something easily observed in the discourses of Calvinism that were discussed in Chapter 2 – as there is a clear divide between the work of Calvin and the expression these writings found in the religious communities that fit the label of 'Calvinist'.

[29] Sedgwick, *Coherence*, 100.

'You bid him step up' he said, addressing me, 'and, Catherine, try to be glad without being absurd! The whole household need not witness the sight of your welcoming a runaway servant as a brother'.[30]

Of course, once again, the biblical text is misinterpreted. The reference to a runaway servant being welcomed as a brother is the Prodigal Son, from Lk. 15:11-32 (as well as discussed in Paul's letter Philemon). The irony of the situation is that if truly committed to following biblical models of behaviour as literally as possible, Catherine would do exactly what Edgar disallows – propriety would be cast aside and she would welcome him *as a brother*, which is, in a certain sense, precisely what Heathcliff is to her. Here then, spiritual impulse collides with religiosity in order to limit and restrict the range of behaviours that are deemed acceptable, subsuming and reducing faith to a set range of class appropriate behaviour. The novel presents these restrictions as both physically and emotionally coercive and constraining, illustrated in a brief exchange between Catherine and her father. Exasperated by his daughter he asks, 'Why canst thou not always be a good lass Cathy?' to which she responds, 'why cannot you always be a good man, Father?'[31] In this short exchange, the complexities and ambiguities of the divide between religious acceptability and theological experience come into sharp relief. Catherine's father judges the issue of goodness as a matter of propriety, respectability and the performance of certain social functions and behaviours. By contrast, Catherine refuses this value judgement, asking the far more theologically interesting question of her father of why, despite his apparent performances of goodness, he is incapable of being a truly good man. Quite arguably, she has a far more thorough grasp of issues such as Original Sin – men cannot always be good simply because 'good' does not depend upon issues such as the public performance of proper behaviours but rather reflects a more fundamental truth about human ontology. Religiosity is a limit – a barrier that prevents the individual from being truly good no matter how devotedly religious behaviour is maintained and demonstrated as it fails to deal with the fundamentally fallen nature of humanity.

This idea of praising the performance of particular religious practice over a more substantive engagement with the realities of human life is something that occurs throughout the text. The grouchy old Calvinist Joseph goes so far as to insist upon the futility of the family's grief when their father dies, asking 'what

---

[30] E. Brontë, *Wuthering Heights*, 102.
[31] Ibid., 46.

we could be thinking of to roar in that way over a Saint in Heaven?'[32] Yet it would be a mistake to dismiss the novel as simply an anti-Christian or heretical piece of work – a mistake predicated upon a narrow understanding of Christian tradition and theology that reduces theology down to a specific and rather narrow binary of either orthodox or heretical. While the text excoriates the religiosity of a specific set of Christian beliefs, belief structures that exist outside the contemporary understanding of orthodoxy have generally been dismissed as heretical by theological or ecclesial authority at some point in history. However, as has been consistently demonstrated, the Christian tradition has, throughout its history, been able to express a capacity for imaginative renewal, brought about by changes in historical circumstance and, hence, to bring forth new forms for expressing theological concerns. While critiquing the religious civilities and practices that limit individual freedoms and disguise violent behaviour behind the veneer of piety, the novel also extends its own theological ideas. Such a theological vision is constructed through the use of specifically Gothic techniques and strategies wherein theological language and Gothic ideas coexist and inform one another. The Gothic haunts the theology within the text, as shown in the scene with Catherine's ghost, and this is directly connected to the ways in which the sacred is presented and understood.

The novel's own positive contribution of/to a theological tradition (however ambivalent or antagonistic that tradition may be) has been noted among some of the key readings of the novel, although often not fully developed. Gilbert and Gubar link Emily Brontë, along with Mary Shelley, to various restagings of the work of Milton.[33] As discussed in Chapter 1, Milton's influence on the Gothic novel is not simply poetic or aesthetic but also theological, connecting the Gothic tradition to theology in under-acknowledged ways. From the outset, *Wuthering Heights* is replete with references to both heaven and hell, perhaps most famously in the much-quoted speech from young Catherine:

> If I were in heaven, Nelly, I would be extremely miserable . . . I was only going to say that heaven did not seem to be my home; and I broke my heart with weeping to come back to earth; and the angels were so angry that they flung me out, into the middle of the heath on the top of Wuthering Heights; where I woke, sobbing for joy.[34]

---

[32] Ibid.
[33] See Gilbert and Gubar, *The Madwoman in the Attic*, 2nd edn, particularly Chapters six, seven and eight.
[34] E. Brontë, *Wuthering Heights*, 86.

What is striking about the passage is the extent to which the novel disavows normative theological standards. Heaven rather than being a place where every tear is wiped away is instead a place of misery, for it would involve union with God, rather than her desired union with Heathcliff. There is an element of sacrilege here, picked up by contemporary reviewers, as it seems Brontë moves away from a traditional or more orthodox conception of heaven. One anxious contemporary reviewer found the work threatening to the morality of the readership:

> If we did not know that this book has been read by thousands of young ladies in the country, we should esteem it our first duty to caution them against it the book is original; it is powerful. But still, it is coarse . . . . Setting aside the profanity, which if a writer introduces into a book, he offends against both politeness and good morals, there is such a general roughness and savageness in the soliloquies and dialogue.[35]

Yet, rather than see this as a violation of orthodoxy or a threat to the general morals of readers,[36] it is possible to read this section of the novel in another light. Read imaginatively, the speech from Catherine can be seen as proposing a critique of theological understandings of heaven that challenges its spatial and hierarchical aspects,[37] through a shocking, and fundamentally relational, understanding of heavenly paradise. Rather than see heaven as a spatial configuration, wherein the soul is reunited with God in a place that is both geographically distinct and removed, paradise for Catherine is found in her union with another.

For Catherine, the traditional idea of a paradise after death is anathema, and like Milton's Devil and, indeed, Frankenstein's creature, the fall from the heights of paradise is a *fortunate* fall, back to the environment of Wuthering Heights. She literally sees herself as a cast-out from paradise, a fallen angel, exorcized from heaven and forced back into the material world. Yet, at the same time, the world that Catherine 'falls' into (or rather, is thrown back into) is one irreducibly fallen itself – as Hillis Miller puts it, the characters of the novel 'are, for the most part, without pity or forgiveness for one another, and their conscious defiance of the law by which God reserves vengeance to himself echoes throughout

---

[35] G. W. Peck, from an unsigned review of *Wuthering Heights*, America Review, June 1848, vii, 572–85 in *The Brontë's: The Critical Heritage*, ed. Miriam Allot (London: Routledge, 1974), 235–48, 236.
[36] The concern here being somewhat similar to anxieties expressed by Coleridge in his review of *The Monk*.
[37] For more on the ways in which Victorian theology saw heaven in spatial terms, see Albert Myburgh, 'Spaces of Death in Emily Brontë's *Wuthering Heights*', *Journal of Literary Studies* 30.1 (March 2014): 20–33.

the novel'.[38] Forgiveness, redemption and, most importantly, grace are seen throughout the text as both desperately needed but also 'conspicuously absent'.[39] Here, Brontë expresses a long-held theological idea: that the obsessions of Branderham and Joseph with individual transgressions of morality are reductive and caricature the Christian understanding of sin. Theologically speaking, Brontë acknowledges that, as Ricoeur argues, '[sin] is not the transgression of an abstract rule – of a value – but the violation of a personal bond'.[40] Sin is, to use a much-repeated theological analogy, a kind of stain – a distortion of the *imago Dei* and a corruption of the world from how it should be. Like the Gothic past that constantly seeks to reassert itself in the present, so too does sin constantly emerge into the world of the novel. Just as the religious seeks consistently to secure itself from the intrusion of the heterodox, unorthodox and secular so too does the society seek to disguise the essentially universal nature of sin. From the outset of the novel, the world of *Wuthering Heights* is presented as already fallen, tainted by a kind of inexpungable blot – rather than a state 'caused by a loss of an earlier state of civilised restraint'.[41] 'Why is *Wuthering Heights* so Miltonically hellish'[42] ask Gilbert and Gubar – the answer to this is because it could be no other way. There is no singular villain of the text but, within the Gothic environs of the novel, all are implicated and all are culpable in various degrees for the bitterness and destructiveness that runs through the text. There is no singular monster but rather a collection of people who are placed within a specific Gothic environment that brings forth the very worst within human nature by refusing the societal niceties of respectable religious behaviour. Violence and Sin, then, are not shielded by the pious orthodoxies of religiosity but brought to the fore, and all are shown to be, in some way, bound up within the behaviours. Heathcliff at the beginning of the novel is not introduced into a kind of metaphoric Eden that he fatally destabilizes – rather, he merely conforms to the already existing structures of relationship and sin that are in place throughout the text. Thormählen describes the text as a 'nineteenth-century Revengers Tragedy',[43] but, that said, there is no identifiable cause – the novel 'refuses to trace its cycles of vengeance and violence to a secure point of origin'.[44] Heathcliff, for example,

---

[38] Miller, *Disappearance*, 188.
[39] Marsden, *Emily Bronte*, 87.
[40] Paul Ricoeur, *The Symbolism of Evil*, trans. Emerson Buchanan (Boston: Beacon Press, 1969), 2.
[41] Miller, *Disappearance*, 168.
[42] Gilbert and Gubar, *Madwoman*, 263.
[43] Thormählen, *Brontes and Religion*, 119.
[44] Marsden, *Emily Bronte*, 102.

enters the narrative at the beginning, but on his arrival, he comes loaded with the mystery of what has happened to him already and his origins. Mr Earnshaw simply announces that he has been found on the street but provides no details as to what may have brought this about. There is a pre-story, a point further back from where the narrative begins that determines much about him but to which we, as readers, have no access. Heathcliff, then, is not simply the model of a Byronic hero that critics have pointed to,[45] or some sort of supernatural force of evil, but is rather the product of some tragedy in his past, which is further exacerbated with his introduction into the hostile environment of the Earnshaw family. Rather than consider the text as a kind of Revenger's Tragedy then, it is far more precise to consider the text as a Gothic castle. Within its limits all of the characters prove themselves to be imbricated in the idea of sin as an indelible stain upon their nature. Nelly admits as much that 'we plagued and went on with him shamefully, for I wasn't reasonable enough to feel my injustice',[46] and the injustices of the past become motivation for further injustices as the novel progresses. Heathcliff, of course, inherits some of the tragedies of the Earnshaws, as he is given the name of a child who died in childbirth, a Gothic bequest, that ensures from the very beginning Heathcliff functions as a presence that haunts the Earnshaw family. Hindley, in response, 'comes to regard his father as an oppressor rather than a friend, and Heathcliff as a usurper of his parent's affections ... he grew bitter brooding over these injuries'.[47] The novel dramatizes the prophetic warning of Num 14:18 as the sins of the fathers are visited upon the children, yet at the same time there is a sense in which the 'sins of the fathers' are diffuse and have no clear point of origin. There is a distinctly Gothic sense of inescapable predestination at work here, as the familial dynamics between the Earnshaw's become increasingly unstable. Trying to locate a single or discreet cause would be futile as 'each generation is marked by the failures of its predecessors; their individual stories are conditioned by their inheritance'.[48] While Marsden's point here is instructive, inheritance is a somewhat unhelpful term, as with its implications of economics and familial relationships, it essentially reduces the scale of the problem to one that is socially mediated and passed down, rather than a reflection of the fundamentally fallen character of

---

[45] This is a common critical argument and key examples can be found in Gilbert and Gubar (2000) as well as Diane Long Hoeveler, *Gothic Feminism: The Professionalisation of Gender from Charlotte Smith to the Brontes* (Liverpool: Liverpool University Press, 1996), 185–241.
[46] E. Brontë, *Wuthering Heights*, 40.
[47] Ibid., 40–1.
[48] Marsden, *Emily Brontë*, 103.

the human subject more widely. Thus, one of the central conflicts throughout the novel, exemplified by the speech from Catherine quoted earlier, can be seen more clearly – namely, the struggle between the religious, Calvinistic view of human behaviour and history and the exercise of individual agency founded on love that forms the basis of an apparently more authentic religious expression. Marsden argues that Brontë criticizes the extreme and stifling Calvinistic moralism not merely through caricature but through 'depicting a social environment shaped by its paradigms'.[49] This environment is one that refuses the possibility of disguising violence behind the veneer of civility, instead bringing it front and centre to the entire world of the novel. As Eagleton expresses it, *Wuthering Heights* trades in 'spite and stiff-neckedness, but always "objectively" as the power of its tenaciously detailed realism to survive unruffled even the gustiest of emotional crises would suggest'.[50] Interpersonal relations are then inevitably shaped and dictated by the 'objective' nature of the fallen world of the novel. It is a deeply Gothic environment – a point Lockwood brings up in his first visit to the Heights, describing its great fire and cavernous interior, alongside swarms of 'squealing puppies, and other dogs',[51] which haunt the recesses of the building. He details the environment, realizing that it is a reflection, or double, of the spiritual nature of its inhabitants.

Another example of this is the moment where the two children are spotted by Joseph in the act of destroying the various religious tracts they are forced to study. Joseph warns them that '"owd Nick" would fetch us as sure as we were living; and so comforted we each sought a separate nook to await his advent'.[52] Catherine and Heathcliff thus invert the threat of damnation issued by Joseph, awaiting the Devil not out of fear of damnation but an expectation of spiritual liberation. The two are, in many ways, 'of the Devil's party' and seem to acknowledge a distinctly Miltonic Satan, seeing the possibility of being carried off to a hell as a kind of Gothic soteriology – far better than the performance of piety within which neither of them seems to find much truth. Yet this possible redemption is deferred – the two may find solace and a spiritual kinship in the company of one another, and in the wild splendour of the moors, yet this does not serve as a solution to their problem. Leaving the Heights to 'have a ramble at liberty',[53] the

---

[49] Ibid., 108.
[50] Terry Eagleton, *Myths of Power: A Marxist Study of the Brontës* (London: Palgrave Macmillan, 2005), 99.
[51] E. Brontë, *Wuthering Heights*, 5.
[52] Ibid., 23.
[53] Ibid., 51.

two find their way to the Grange, contrasting the life of the Lintons with their own condition. Unlike Heathcliff and Catherine, the Linton children do not spend their time 'reading sermons, and being catechised by their manservant, and set to learn a column of Scripture names'.[54] Rather, the Lintons exist in a pleasant world of frivolous enjoyment, with the children fighting over who gets to hold a puppy. This combination of class position, material comforts and rather childish indulgence receives nothing but disdain from the two observing the scene. As Heathcliff puts it, functioning as a type of ghostly observer, haunting the family at the window, 'we laughed outright at the petted things . . . we did despise them'.[55] While Heathcliff offers Catherine a friendship that 'opens fresh possibilities of freedom within the internal system of the Heights',[56] the encounter at the Linton house offers her a secure class position, a more 'appropriate' spouse and an apparent liberation from the catechizing, spiritually restrictive world of Joseph and Hindley Earnshaw. The true struggle of Catherine, then, throughout the novel, is the struggle against the realization that the world she inhabits is structured in the same way as the Heights – marked by an absence of grace, requiring the same performative religious and social appropriateness. If anything, the discursive codes and disciplinary procedures that the Lintons embody are less explicit than the disciplinary mechanisms enacted at the Heights but just as restrictive. Unlike Catherine, Heathcliff seems to recognize that the life at the Grange is no different from that in the Heights. He furiously tells Nelly that he would not exchange his life for that of the Lintons, for that life of comfort would deny him the possibility of revenge.[57] In the choice between being 'good' (in the sense of social approval) and bad, Heathcliff refuses it, preferring instead to exist outside of those structures which make such a choice necessary. While Heathcliff is a social inferior but a spiritual equal, and so, for him, Catherine's decision to marry Edgar is a sign of a kind of spiritual betrayal – a colossal act of 'theological *mauvaise foi*'[58] based on the mistaken belief that a move upward in class position is preferable to the authenticity of her relationship with Heathcliff.

> *Why* did you despise me? *Why* did you betray your own heart, Cathy? I have not one word of comfort – you deserve this. You have killed yourself. Yes, you may kiss me, and cry; and wring out my kisses and tears. They'll blight you –

---

[54] Ibid.
[55] Ibid., 52.
[56] Eagleton, *Myths*, 103.
[57] E. Brontë, *Wuthering Heights*, 52.
[58] Eagleton, *Myths*, 101.

they'll damn you. You loved me – that what *right* had you to leave me? What right – answer me – for the poor fancy you felt for Linton? Because misery, and degradation, and death, and nothing that God or Satan could inflict would have parted us, you, of your own free will, did it.[59]

Heathcliff's speech is undeniably vicious, but, as Arnold Kettle points out, the 'brutality is not neurotic, nor sadistic, nor romantic'[60] but rather a moral and theological criticism of Catherine's actions. The contradiction that Catherine attempts to square is that between authenticity and acceptability but not simply in a material or social sense. Heathcliff excoriates her with language that echoes Scripture – here drawing on the rhythms and intonations of Pauline theology (specifically Rom. 8:38-9).[61] Catherine, in her marriage to Edgar, has chosen the values of class respectability and outward acceptable piety in contrast to the connection she shares with Heathcliff (as she forcefully tells Nelly earlier in the novel, 'he's more myself than I)'.[62] In effect, to return to the question posed by her father, she has decided to be 'good' in terms of respectability, rather than continue to refuse the value judgements in the way she did as a young child. Heathcliff's point is rather prophetic as her marriage to Linton does damn her – it casts her out again from the Heights and the moors where she is freest. The strictures of her Calvinistic upbringing have been exchanged for a gilded cage, and in a much-noted speech to Nelly, Catherine articulates this spiritual yearning for an existence marked by freedom.

> The thing that irks me most is this shattered prison, after all. I'm tired, tired of being enclosed here. I'm wearing to escape into that glorious world, and to be always there; not seeing it dimly through tears, and yearning for it through the walls of an aching heart but really with it, and in in it.[63]

The two speeches, quoted at length, are illustrative of the heterodox theological vision that Brontë puts forward, underpinned by an intimate and profound connection between Catherine with Heathcliff that is fulfilled in nature. Her yearning to 'escape' back into the natural realm highlights an important tension – that between nature and society, or, as it is otherwise framed, between an

---

[59] E. Brontë, *Wuthering Heights*, 175.
[60] Arnold Kettle, 'Emily Brontë: *Wuthering Heights* (1847)', in *The Victorian Novel: Modern Essays in Criticism*, ed. Ian Watt (Oxford: Oxford University Press, 1971), 209.
[61] 'For I am convinced that neither death, nor life, nor angels, nor rulers, nor things present, nor things to come, nor powers, nor height, nor depth, nor anything else in all creation, will be able to separate us from the love of God in Christ Jesus our Lord'.
[62] E. Brontë, *Wuthering Heights*, 87.
[63] Ibid., 174.

experience of freedom and the limitations of institutional religiosity. Catherine's desire to be 'half-savage, and hardy and free' is a reflection of her desire to exist outside of the confines of a society structured by restrictive religious practices, away from the civility and restrictive performative piety that marks her daily existence. To be away from that savage state is, for Catherine, to be trapped. Existing in the world she is, as the traditional Gothic heroine, imprisoned. Whereas the early Gothic heroines would be trapped in a deserted castle, Catherine is trapped (admittedly by her own choice) within the world of the text that deprives her of authentic existence. Her connection with Heathcliff is, supposedly, a more liberated mode of being, contrasted with the arid 'heaven' of marriage to Linton – an apparent paradise but one from which Catherine yearns to be thrown. As Tom Winnifrith suggests, Linton may have a vision of heaven and future salvation, but for his new partner it is just as stifling as that that she wishes to escape.[64] For as heaven divides her from the moors, her marriage divides her from the one with whom she feels the most profound connection. In the preceding speech, Catherine appropriates the language of Christian eschatology,[65] desiring a kind of Edenic return to the state of nature but also to an authentic kind of personhood. She wishes to be a 'girl again, half-savage and hardy and free . . . I'm sure I should be myself were I once among the heather on those hills'.[66] Eagleton claims that Catherine's and Heathcliff's relationship is 'projected into myth',[67] yet its more accurate to say that it is projected into a kind of paradisiacal soteriology – a vision of a heaven to come, where the idea of religious performance is replaced by a kind of radical freedom, where there is no need to spend time in chapels listening to overly long sermons, or limiting one's behaviour in the name of being 'good'.

If this idea of freedom is absent within the religious institutions and codes of belief depicted within the novel, it is in nature, specifically the open spaces of the moors, that an experience of this kind can be found. Catherine seeks to escape into the material world, away from the realm of religious knowledge, back to a 'communion with the universal other, the re-integration of the self into what has ceased to be "my world."'[68] Interpersonal connection with Heathcliff is inextricably bound up in connection with the natural world, which is a more

---

[64] Winnifrith, *The Brontë's and Their Background*, 68.
[65] See 1 Cor. 13:12: 'For now we see in a mirror, dimly, but then we will see face to face. Now I know only in part; then I will know fully, even as I have been fully known'.
[66] E. Brontë, *Wuthering Heights*, 134.
[67] Eagleton, *Myths*, 109.
[68] Marsden, *Emily Brontë*, 137.

authentic and spiritually compelling mode of existence than the haunted and limited life at the Grange. Theologically speaking, this places Brontë within the more heterodox theological tradition of writers such as Schleiermacher, whereby religious experience is not found in 'previous knowledge'[69] of the divine but here in the uniting of the individual self with the universal splendour of nature. True religion, then, is not the pieties of Joseph or the acting out of a certain set of culturally approved behaviours but rather is 'a phase of consciousness in which differentiation of subject and object has not yet occurred'.[70] Brontë complicates this with the relationship of Catherine and Heathcliff within the wider scheme of nature. Catherine specifically describes her relationship with him through the language of eternity and images of nature: 'my love for Heathcliff resembles the eternal rocks . . . a source of little visible delight but necessary. Nelly, I *am* Heathcliff'.[71] The infinite, which in Schleiermacher's terms may or may not have the name God attached to it, is, for Catherine, found in her relationship with Heathcliff. However, such a phase of consciousness, such a unity of self with the infinite is presented as impossible as Catherine dies shortly after giving birth, shattering the potential for any kind of reunion with Heathcliff and thus, any possibility of connection with that infinite other which may be termed God. Rather than embracing the divine presence the novel consistently problematizes the idea of reaching it – Lockwood even goes so far as to ignore Nelly's question on the happiness of the dead in heaven, finding it 'somewhat heterodox',[72] here echoing the sacrilegious theology of heaven expressed by Catherine. Even death then is not a means of accessing heaven but rather a kind of exile – another casting out. If, in the relationship with Heathcliff there is something of the infinite, then after her death Heathcliff is trapped in his own hell – namely, separation from Catherine. 'Where is she?' he asks Nelly: 'not *there* – not in heaven – not perished . . . Catherine Earnshaw, may you not rest as long as I am living . . . do not leave me in this abyss, where I cannot find you!'[73] Catherine 'can be located only by reference to where she is not',[74] becoming a spectral presence, a paradoxical ghost who violates the realist framework of the novel, suggesting a 'lifting of the veil between worlds'.[75] Catherine becomes another ghost through

---

[69] Friedrich Schleiermacher, *The Christian Faith* (London: T & T Clark, 2016), 17.
[70] Reardon, *Religion in the Age of Romanticism*, 35.
[71] E. Brontë, *Wuthering Heights*, 88.
[72] Ibid., 179.
[73] Ibid., 181.
[74] Marsden, *Emily Brontë*, 138.
[75] Ibid., 139.

the text – a spectral force that fractures the easy separations between presence and absence and, more importantly between life and death. By her death she has, in effect, rendered Heathcliff as unable to fully live. Yet, this spectral presence becomes reported at second or third hand – usually through dreams or visionary experiences that allows them to sit, albeit uneasily, within the realist framework of the novel that these moments of spectral haunting threaten to disrupt.[76] This absent presence ensures that Heathcliff and Catherine can never be conclusively separated but also never finally reunited. Even at Catherine's grave when Heathcliff wishes to embrace her one final time, her spectral haunting ensures that this cannot take place:

> I was on the point of attainting my object, when it seemed I heard a sigh from some one above, close at the edge of the grave, and bending down . . . There was another sigh, close at my ear . . . I knew no living thing in flesh and blood was by – but as certainly as you perceive the approach to some substantial body in the dark, though it cannot be discerned, so certainly I felt that Cathy was there, not under me, but on the earth.[77]

It seems then, that at the moment of reuniting with Catherine's physical form, the spectre of Catherine's paradoxical presence and absence maintains an infinite deferral between the two. In the 'shadow' of Catherine's ghost, Heathcliff's own involvement in the physical world begins to dwindle, leaving him barely able to remember to eat or drink.[78] The world is both made into a Gothic abyss emptied of her presence and, at the same moment, 'a dreadful collection of memoranda' that consistently suggest the lost Catherine.[79] In a sense, the two consistently struggle to escape the world of restrictions that is marked by a religiosity and a distinct lack of grace, for a more authentic mode of being that reconnects both human subject with one another and the absent divine. However, ultimately the two fail to do so, yet the novel constantly holds open the possibility that such a relationship, a restoration between individuals and God is possible. Yet, despite what critics such as Eagleton argue, this possibility is not found in the relationship between Catherine and Heathcliff.

---

[76] Ibid. As Andrew Smith points out, this tension highlights the ways in which the Gothic has become part of the ostensibly non-Gothic forms of writing (in this case, the realist novel) once again closely tying together theology and the Gothic. See Andrew Smith, *Gothic Literature* (Edinburgh: Edinburgh University Press, 2007), 75.
[77] E. Brontë, *Wuthering Heights*, 309.
[78] Ibid., 344.
[79] Ibid., 345.

The loving equality between Catherine and Heathcliff stands, then, as a paradigm of human possibilities which reach beyond, and might ideally unlock, the tightly dominative system of the Heights.[80]

The optimism here feels misplaced, as the reading, so grounded as it is in strictly materialist terms, has no space for the idea of something as non-materialistic as theological inflected Calvinism or the possibility of grace, which can disrupt the world entirely ordered by those precepts. For, despite what Eagleton might claim, it is not the relationship between Heathcliff and Catherine that unlocks the dominative system of the novel but rather between Hareton and young Cathy. At the close of the novel, the two reach a 'tentative convergence'[81] – which Eagleton frames in terms of a synthesis between 'labour and culture, sinew and gentility'.[82] What allows such a synthesis to occur is not simply a co-mingling of nature with society but rather by some attempts at grace and forgiveness. Gilbert and Gubar describe her as the ideal Victorian woman, who has so well absorbed the 'lessons of patriarchal Christianity'[83] that she is able piously to forgive Heathcliff and Linton for their various sins. At the same time however, she is also haughty and dismissive, seemingly deeply aware of her class position, which emerges in her early treatment of Zillah. Not for nothing does Nelly describes her as possessing a 'propensity to be saucy, and a perverse will'.[84]

Yet, even so, Cathy's behaviour should not be dismissed as solely the product of a kind of bourgeois conditioning – a range of acceptable behaviours that she is too dutiful to challenge, as Heathcliff recognizes her as a threat – not just economically but spiritually too. He recoils from her, asserting that 'I'd rather hug a snake'[85] abusing her as a witch and a slut. This is, as Gilbert and Gubar point out, behaviour that makes sense, from a certain point of view, as 'besides threatening his present position, Catherine II's union with Hareton reminds Heathcliff specifically of the heaven he has lost'.[86] The physical resemblance to the dead Catherine 'tells Heathcliff not so much that Catherine endures as that she is both dead and fragmented'.[87] Once again, ghosts proliferate even in the world of the living and Heathcliff becomes doubly haunted – haunted by

---

[80] Eagleton, *Myths*, 103.
[81] Ibid., 118.
[82] Ibid.
[83] Gilbert and Gubar, *Madwoman*, 299.
[84] E. Brontë, *Wuthering Heights*, 203.
[85] Ibid., 294.
[86] Gilbert and Gubar, *Madwomen*, 300.
[87] Ibid.

Catherine's absence which traps him in hell and haunted by her presence in the form of Cathy. Yet, Cathy does not just serve as another spectral presence of the absent Catherine but also a sign of a potential future world not structured by the paradigms of violence, vengeance and retribution. Yet, at the same moment, without this world structure and without the tempestuous Heathcliff/Catherine pairing, the possibility of redemption that Hareton and Cathy embody would be impossible. As Hillis Miller asserts:

> What has intervened by the end of the novel to make possible the milder love of Hareton and the second Cathy? What has intervened is the love affair of Heathcliff and the first Cathy. The love of Hareton and the second Cathy appears to be possible only because Heathcliff and the first Cathy have broken through life into death.[88]

While without the relationship between Catherine and Heathcliff, Hareton would not need to be made into a gentleman in the first place, what this misses is Ingrid Geerken's point that 'regret is essentially generative of narrative'.[89] Catherine and Heathcliff's relationship is marked by regret – a failure to connect with one another and to reunite religious belief with theological experience. Only when the second Catherine has, like the Psalmist, walked 'through the shadow of death'[90] (in the case the death of Linton) can she begin to educate Hareton, teaching him to read and take possession of the Heights. As Gilbert and Gubar similarly note, it is only after the confrontation with the Miltonic Devil figure of Heathcliff that the two can build their new world, marrying on New Year's Day.[91] However, to extend the argument somewhat further, the relationship is not simply a marriage that carries with it an echo of social betterment. Cathy does not simply educate Hareton, but she rather draws him into a kind of existence that is not structured by religiosity and violence in the first place. If Catherine and Heathcliff's relationship is fundamentally marked by the tensions between religion and theology, Cathy and Hareton represent a possible future whereby religion and theology may be brought back into a kind of harmony, though tellingly that harmony does not involve a church or any other form of institutional religion. The book though resists any kind of closure, riven by a series of contradictions between the other and the subject, between nature and society and ultimately between divine absence

---

[88] Miller, *Disappearance*, 209.
[89] Ingrid Geerken, '"The Dead Are Not Annihilated": Mortal Regret in Wuthering Heights', *Journal of Narrative Theory* 34.3 (2004): 373–406.
[90] See Psalm 23, particularly verse 4.
[91] E. Brontë, *Wuthering Heights*, 359.

and presence. 'Every critic must leave the book in the awareness of not having reached a conclusion, and it will keep attracting new ones who find that the same applies to them.'[92] Thormählen's point is not merely a source of critical frustration but a product of the resistance to theological closure that run throughout the novel as a whole. Heathcliff, like Catherine, may die – fading into nature, where Catherine 'persists in every cloud, in every tree'.[93] He is found in his room, with open windows, and while the grumpy old hypocrite Joseph might claim that the 'th' divil's harried off his soul', his dissolution into the paradise of nature, back to the spectral Catherine is assured. As Heathcliff expresses it, 'my soul's bliss kills my body' – for in the possibility of reuniting with Catherine, the body itself becomes merely something to be escaped. There are echoes here with the theological power of nature that so preoccupied James Hogg in Chapter 2 as, once again, it is in nature that the theological finds powerful, albeit unorthodox, expression. At the close of the novel, the Heights is left and Hareton and Cathy return to the Grange – a more suitable home for the young couple – leaving the rather tiresome Joseph and servants to ensure that the Heights remains standing. Yet this too is presented as an ambiguous kind of closure. The house will be left shut up, as Lockwood asks, 'For the use of such ghosts as choose to inhabit it?'[94] Yet, as Nelly asserts, she may 'believe the dead are at peace: but it is not right to speak of them with levity'.[95] Despite the apparent success of Hareton and Cathy in establishing a new kind of relationship, the dead, it seems, are still a powerful presence within the novel. The little boy who spots Heathcliff and a woman wandering the moors 'hints at the powerful disruptive possibilities they represent'.[96] The final scene, where Lockwood walks past Gimmerton Kirk, adds to the ambiguity. While Catherine and Heathcliff have been reunited in death and a new Adam and Eve have taken over the Grange, restoring it for the future, the church is still empty and now physically decaying.

For Hillis Miller, 'the church is still deserted because it is unnecessary',[97] rendered irrelevant by the peaceful love of Cathy and Hareton. Yet, though the church itself is fractured and decaying, it still stands – suggesting that while a certain kind of institutional religion may have become neglected, it too is not beyond the bounds of renewal and resurrection. While John Maynard makes

---

[92] Thormählen, *Brontës and Religion*, 142.
[93] Gilbert and Gubar, *Madwomen*, 301.
[94] E. Brontë, *Wuthering Heights*, 359.
[95] Ibid., 360.
[96] Gilbert and Gubar, *Madwomen*, 305
[97] Miller, *Disappearance*, 211.

the point that it 'is inner experience replacing institution, ritual, and myth as the location of the sacred'[98] this misses that it is the very concrete relationship of Hareton and Cathy that has made the Kirk increasingly irrelevant.[99] While the church lies decaying and empty, the living is still at Wuthering Heights, not the local chapel. At the same time, there is a clear sense that the new world the two symbolize is deeply contingent, bound up as it is in the 'the three headstones on the slope next the moor'.[100] While Lockwood 'wondered how any one could ever imagine unquiet slumbers, for the sleepers in that quiet earth', this carries a deep sense of irony, for Lockwood knows all too well just how unquiet those buried in the earth may be. The Gothic text consistently asserts that the dead may rise once again and disturb the living. Those who have been reunited with the infinite cannot be assumed to be safely isolated or externalized away from the living, for as Lynne Pearce points out, the novel speaks of a deeply held 'resistance to the finality of death'.[101] The romantic sublimity of the ending, redolent with a grace that sublimates what is past and 'cancels out history',[102] is, at the same, riven with a sense of fragility – the ending of the novel is not a triumphant eschaton but one reached in the deeply Gothic awareness that the past can emerge unexpectedly into the present – often violently – and the ghosts of the dead cannot be distinguished easily from the ones who are still living. Existence is lived in awareness of its contingent nature – Hareton and Cathy at the end of the novel must 'brave Satan and all his legions'[103] but must do so through continuation, through life together, not through the strictures of institutional religion and public performances of acceptable religious behaviour. Rather than a simply religious allegory then, the text functions as a site for the Gothic elements within it to destabilize the boundaries between the religious and the secular, between the sacred and the profane and most crucially between the ghosts of the past and the life of the present. It is this question, of how one must live, that forms the crux of the theological concerns of Charlotte Brontë's *Jane Eyre*.

---

[98] John Maynard, 'The Brontës and Religion', in *The Cambridge Companion to the Brontë's*, ed. Heather Glen (Cambridge: Cambridge University Press, 2003), 193.

[99] It's striking that Nelly admits towards the end of the novel that while the Kirk has no minister, Joseph now attends the 'Methodists' or Baptists' place', (315), suggesting that while the Kirk has fallen into disrepair, the local population has moved to a new kind of religious practice, marked (in the case of Methodism) by a deliberate attention to both study of scripture and fellowship with others.

[100] E. Brontë, *Wuthering Heights*, 360.

[101] Lynne Pearce, *Romance Writing* (Cambridge: Polity Press, 2007), 108.

[102] Alison Milbank, *Daughters of the House: Modes of the Gothic in Victorian Fiction* (London: Palgrave Macmillan, 1992), 146.

[103] E. Brontë, *Wuthering Heights*, 360.

Jane Eyre as social theology

With the claim in the title to biography and a strong concern with the place of the individual within society, *Jane Eyre* is explicitly concerned with the ways in which society is and should be arranged. The ways in which society is constituted and the means for individual expression are decidedly moral and theological concerns (or, at the least, have certainly been questions with which religious institutions have been explicitly concerned) but also the inherently political nature of these questions links the text to the wider history of Gothic writing, which has a long critical investment in articulating political fears and anxieties.[104] Here, the question of theological criticism of *Jane Eyre* is more precisely understood as a question of political theology – the interaction between theology and the wider society within which believers exist. This, of course, is not simply a question of belief, or of institutionalized practice (attending church services for example) but, as with the criticism of institutional religion laid out in *Wuthering Heights*, entails a wider set of discourses and behaviours linked to the question of social and subjective behaviour removed from the institutions of religious adherence. Thus, this section will examine the ways in which Jane's experiences of navigating the various moments of enclosure and escape form part of an explicitly theological struggle towards a kind of subjective liberation and an expression of authentic Christian life. This process occurs within the generic convention of the women in the Gothic house or castle, and so, like *Wuthering Heights*, its religious and theological points cannot be disentangled from the Gothic means by which they are communicated. The novel profoundly critiques the culture of accepted, conventional religiosity (particularly in the character of the Rev. Brocklehurst), and as such the early critical reviews attacked *Jane Eyre* for its supposed anti-Christian nature. Brontë herself clarifies her own position in the preface to the second edition from December 1847:

> Conventionality is not morality. Self-righteousness is not religion. To attack the first is not to assail the latter. To pluck the mask from the face of the Pharisee is not to lift an impious hand to the Crown of Thorns ... men too often confound them: they should not be confounded.[105]

---

[104] For a discussion of this, especially with regard to the early Gothic novel, see Robert Miles, 'Political Gothic Fiction', in *Romantic Gothic, An Edinburgh Companion*, ed. Angela Wright and Dale Townshend (Edinburgh: Edinburgh University Press, 2016), 129–46.
[105] Charlotte Brontë, *Jane Eyre* (London: Penguin Deluxe Editions, 2009), 3–4.

Yet, as with *Wuthering Heights*, the text puts forward a scathing critique of both the institutionalized religion and the authoritarianism to which religious leaders within those traditions are prone – particularly in the figure of the Reverend Brocklehurst. That erect 'black pillar'[106] of a man with his fairy-tale appearance of a great nose and large prominent teeth is a ghoulish monster figure that questions Jane on the nature of hell and how to avoid it. Brocklehurst serves as a figure of the kind of Gothic theology that divides the world into a deceptive material reality and a danger-filled potentially damnatory spiritual realm – which possesses greater truth status than the world the individual inhabits.[107] This scene and Jane's assertion that to avoid the pit of fire all she must do is not die[108] can easily be read as a combination of childish naivety with Brontë's own satire of the Calvinistic and annihilationist theology espoused by evangelicals such as Brocklehurst (similar to the kind of discourses analysed extensively in Chapter 2).[109] However, while a compelling though simplistic reading, it ignores much of the rest of the scene and indeed the ways in which Jane's own theology changes and develops throughout the novel. What is striking about this confrontation between childish subjectivity and Gothicized hyper-Calvinist threat is the way in which Jane manages to articulate a theological response to Brocklehurst's intimidating rhetoric. Questioned on Scripture, Jane tells the reverend that her favourite parts of Scripture detail both liberation and eschatology. She picks the prophetic books of the Old Testament, the theodicy of Job, 'a little bit of Exodus' and the histories of Israel detailed in Samuel, Chronicles and Kings as well as the eschatological revelation. The choice of books here is deeply striking, as Eyre (a dispossessed, orphan unwelcome in the Reed family) is drawn to Scripture that reflects her own feelings of injustice and crucially offers up hope for a radical transformation of the world. This canon within the Bible tends towards prophetic and liberatory expressions of faith as opposed to the books Jane is expected to voice approval of by Brocklehurst. For Jane, the Psalms, so beloved by Brocklehurst, are 'not interesting',[110] used as they are to inculcate an acceptable evangelical 'infant piety'[111] in children who claim that they would rather have verses to learn than gingerbread. In response, Jane is

---

[106] Ibid., 33.
[107] Once again, see Chapter 2 for a more in-depth discussion of this kind of Calvinistic thought.
[108] C Brontë, *Jane Eyre*, 34.
[109] The similarities between the Calvinism of Robert and Brocklehurst reinforce the idea of the Gothic interest in Calvinistic theological ideas.
[110] C. Brontë, *Jane Eyre*, 35.
[111] Ibid.

told she has a wicked heart, a propensity for deceit and that she is a liar, destined to have her 'portion in the lake burning with fire and brimstone'.[112] 'Elected' to Lowood School, Jane is left a book containing 'an account of the awfully sudden death of Martha G – a naughty child addicted to falsehood and deceit'.[113] What is at stake in the conversation between Brocklehurst and Jane is not simply a satire of a singular religious vision – no matter how cutting that satire may be. Rather, what is presented are two distinct although ambiguously defined theological traditions – on the one hand is the evangelical Calvinist tradition that Brocklehurst exemplifies, this being well established, and socially powerful, aimed at teaching outward displays piety over sincere religious expression, conditioning a certain kind of class hierarchy and enforcing a strict category of acceptable behaviour.[114] Jane, on the other hand, seems drawn to a less dominant, 'minor' theological tradition – one that emphasizes overcoming injustice and the restoration of correct relationships between individuals and between societies and God. The reference to Genesis and Exodus, detailing creation, the first covenant between God and his people, their enslavement and, crucially, their liberation, is a Scriptural referent for the concerns of the text as a whole. Gilbert and Gubar note that *Jane Eyre* is a work permeated by angry, *Angrian* fantasies of escape-into-wholeness'[115] consistently drawn to themes of imprisonment and escape, and finding in its ending a muted, though hopeful response to the enclosing force of Victorian patriarchy. To reformulate the argument in a familiar piece of Gothic rhetoric, the castle from which the Gothic heroine must escape is nothing less than the systemic, hegemonic theo-political structure that underpins the world of the novel as a whole. It is this 'model of liberation rather than of defiance and revenge'[116] that Milbank draws attention to, while exploring the ways in which Brontë uses the theme of liberation as a 'plot of erotic provocation'.[117] This acknowledgement of the themes of escape and liberation

---

[112] Ibid., 36.
[113] Ibid., 37.
[114] Jane's aunt tells Mr Brocklehurst that she wishes Jane to be 'brought up in a manner suiting her prospects ... to be made useful, to be kept humble'. (*Jane Eyre*, p. 36.). For a discussion of the ways in which this conflicts with theological understandings of God, see the discussion of *Wuthering Heights*, earlier.
[115] Gilbert and Gubar, *Madwoman*, 336.
[116] Alison Milbank, 'Doubting Castle: The Gothic Mode of Questioning', in *The Critical Spirit and the Will to Believe: Essays in Nineteenth Century Literature and Religion*, ed. David Jaspers and T. R Wright (London: Palgrave Macmillan, 1989), 104–20, 105.
[117] Milbank, *Daughters of the House*, 11.

and Brontë's more general awareness of a 'sexual and often supernatural world'[118] make clear that the theology of the novel is concerned both with the eschatology of the oncoming Kingdom of Heaven, as well as the immediate practices of 'how to do justice, and to love kindness, and to walk humbly with your God'.[119] In other words, the text establishes an opposition between Jane's sociopolitical theology and the theological institutions that, while ostensibly non-political, seek to control her and reinforce strict social hierarchies and class privileges.[120] However, to complicate things further, both of these issues are bound up in one another – the expectation of the coming Kingdom and its imminent *parousia* is directed towards not just the long expected and long hoped for New Heaven but importantly a New Earth as well. As the novel's final line of 'Amen! Even so, come Lord Jesus'[121] implies, such a project is both still ongoing at the novels close and still to come.[122] In this sense then, Jane's response to Brocklehurst, that she 'must keep in good health and not die',[123] articulates a vital theological point – it is simply not enough to avoid hell through displays of piety, but authentic Christian faith must consistently work and live towards liberation rather than submission. Such a struggle towards liberation is juxtaposed throughout the novel with various theological and political systems of belief that seek to constrain and restrict behaviour in the name of piety and respectability. These systems operate upon the basis of an eschatological expectation of heaven at the expense of the life here on earth, or a lifetime of service that demonstrates an acceptable kind of religious behaviour.

In her move to Lowood, Jane encounters the 'physically maladroit but theologically adept Helen Burns',[124] who sees the relationship between life and

---

[118] Elaine Showalter, *A Literature of Their Own: British Women Novelists from Brontë to Lessing* (Princeton: Princeton University Press, 1977), 104.

[119] See Micah 6 particularly verse 8.

[120] For all their personal failures and their hypocrisies, the Reed family are seen as the very model of propriety and respectability by figures such as Rev Brocklehurst.

[121] C. Brontë, *Jane Eyre*, 453

[122] There is some critical debate around this last line – critics such as Kevin Mills see it as giving a rather spiritual conclusion to what is a very earthly book. By contrast, Simon Marsden argues there is a tension between Jane's description of her marriage with language drawn from Genesis and this quote from Revelation. Frankly, I find Marsden's Hegelian argument unconvincing as it seems to establish an uneasy divide between Heaven and Earth, or rather between creation and paradise, that neither Genesis or Revelation would support – after all, it is in Genesis where God walks in the garden with Adam and Eve, and in Revelation God once again dwells with his people in the new Earth. See Kevin Mills, *Approaching Apocalypse: Unveiling Revelation in Victorian Writing* (Lewisburg: Bucknell University Press, 2007) and Simon Marsden, 'The Earth No Longer a Void: Creation Theology in the Novels of Charlotte Brontë', *Literature and Theology*, 25.3 (2011): 237–51.

[123] C. Brontë, *Jane Eyre*, 34.

[124] Milbank, *Daughters of the House*, 147.

death as simply a matter of 'organic development'[125] that must be passed through to reach the sublimity of paradise. Passive in life, Helen simply accepts what seem to Jane to be intolerable injustices. As Helen argues,

> We shall put them off in putting off our corruptible bodies; when debasement and sin will fall from us with this cumbrous frame of flesh, and only the spark of the spirit will remain . . . perhaps again to be communicated to some higher being than man – perhaps to pass through gradations of glory, from the pale human soul to brighten to the seraph![126]

While there is much here that Jane silently accepts, there is a denial of the flesh – of the body specifically – that is simply unacceptable to such a materialist individual like Jane, who cannot abandon her concerns with justice and the ways in which she is treated. Faith, or rather more specifically, salvation, is not simply the mechanistic process by which the soul leaves behind the body to attain paradise but rather must be *worked* through as Paul outlines in Phil. 2. 'Work out your own salvation with fear and trembling, for it is God who is at work in you, enabling you both to will and to work for his good pleasure.'[127] Later on Helen goes further still in creating a false separation between spirit and flesh (echoing the rhetoric of Brocklehurst) as a means of ensuring she accepts her present material condition. Jane, Helen argues, thinks 'too much of the love of human beings; you are too impulsive, too vehement', in the light of the injustices of the world. Such an attitude is a mistake 'when life is so soon over and death is so certain an entrance to happiness'.[128] Helen's argument, which 'calmed' Jane, is mixed with 'an alloy of inexpressible sadness',[129] which seems to have no identifiable source but stems from a recognition of the insufficiency of Helen's argument, that privileges the potential future reward of paradise at the cost of material injustices in the immediate present. The idea of a paradise beyond death functioning as a kind of spiritual freedom for the oppressed seems one that Jane is ill at ease with – too practically minded to find 'justice to come' as a satisfactory idea. Even at the point of death Helen craves the company of another person – begging Jane to stay with her, suggesting that even Helen herself does not entirely ascribe to this idea of abandoning the physical world for the world beyond.

---

[125] Ibid.
[126] C. Brontë, *Jane Eyre*, 60.
[127] Phillipians 2 v 12–13.
[128] C. Brontë, *Jane Eyre*, 71.
[129] Ibid.

Also, while at Lowood, Jane encounters the other systemic theological belief that aims at restricting and limiting her behaviour and self in the form of Brocklehurst's sanctimonious disavowal of the body (in contrast to Helen's disavowal of the material conditions of wider society). Commenting on the food at Lowood, Brocklehurst tells the teachers that

> Should any little disappointment of the appetite occur, such as the spoiling of a meal . . . the incident ought not be neutralised . . . a judicious instructor would take the opportunity of referring to the sufferings of the primitive Christians; to the torments of martyrs; to the exhortations of our blessed Lord himself, calling upon his disciples to take up their cross and follow him . . . .Oh madam, when you put bread and cheese, instead of burnt porridge, into these children's mouths, you may indeed feed their **vile bodies**, [my emphasis] but you little think how you starve their immortal souls.[130]

Where the spiritual Helen Burns argues that the material conditions of existence are a mere distraction to an oncoming theological paradise, Brocklehurst sees the material conditions and specifically the body as inherently sinful and a site for the performance of piety.[131] Both of these arguments are designed to enforce individual passivity and acceptance of the wider state of affairs. They are, in a sense, both Gothic discourses, one which focuses upon the mortification of the body as a site of corruption, in the case of Brocklehurst's theology (if not his practice as his own family remains well-fed and well taken care of), whereas Helen Burns sees the world as irredeemably corrupted and something from which one must escape. Furthermore, both of these perspectives demand an adherence to a particular conception of truth. Non-conformance to a particular set of acceptable behaviours is met with extreme disciplinary procedures. In the case of Jane, who refuses to accept the notion of her aunt as virtuous, this leads to her being branded, publicly, a liar. Such a label seems, for Brocklehurst at the least, to be a major issue – he labels Jane 'worse than many a little heathen who says its prayers to Brahma', placing her below the colonial Other that missionaries sought to bring into the Christian empire. He calls upon her teachers to 'punish her body to save her soul – if, indeed, such salvation be possible'.[132] Jane's sin, as it were, is not simply that she has apparently lied, but that her insistence upon the truth of what she believes is a violation of the ideas that

---

[130] Ibid., 64–5.
[131] As Brocklehurst himself puts it at one point, 'my mission is to mortify in these girls the lusts of the flesh'. C. Brontë, *Jane Eyre*, 66.
[132] C. Brontë, *Jane Eyre*, 68.

undergird Brocklehurst's wider theological beliefs. After the intervention of the beneficent and appropriately named Miss Temple, Jane settles into the routines and structures of Lowood, but Helen – her theological double of a sort – passes away. She tells Jane, 'when you hear that I am dead, you must be sure and not grieve', for 'by dying young, I shall escape great sufferings'.[133] Yet, for Jane, this death is not an escape but a waste of potential and an affront to her rather more materialist understanding of faith. Years after Helen's death she rewrites her friend's memorial, adding the inscription to her grave of *Resurgam* – I shall rise, affirming both Helen's entry to paradise and the resurrection of the dead that the flesh-denying Helen Burns refuses to accept. Just as with *Wuthering Heights*, the distinction between the Gothic and the theological is not easily maintained, as Jane predicts a Gothic return from the grave for Helen Burns.[134]

In these encounters with both Helen and Brocklehurst Lowood School ultimately proves to be another source of constraint and enclosure, as gazing out onto the natural world, Eyre chafes against the restrictions that has been imposed upon her once more. 'I desired liberty; for liberty I gasped; for liberty I uttered a prayer . . . for change, for stimulus . . . "Then I", I cried, half desperate, "grant me at least a new servitude!"'[135] Once again, the theological emphasis is geared towards the work of Christian living (notably not the work to attain salvation but rather the dutiful work that emerges because of salvation rather than for it) – the scriptural referent is to Mt. 25. Searching for new work, Jane seeks the answer given in scripture: 'well done, good and trustworthy servant, you have been faithful with a little, I will put you in charge of many things – enter into the joy of your master'.[136] Like the Gothic heroine trapped in the castle, Jane seeks to assert her own subjectivity, but the escape for which she wishes is, at this point in the narrative, simply an exchange of one kind of imprisonment for another rather than any kind of authentic assertion of selfhood.

Jane's move to Thornfield and subsequent courtship with Rochester seem to offer the possibility of both a radical liberation from her past and a vital equality with her newfound partner. Here, the theological influence of Helen Burns comes to the fore but articulated in the setting of a material condition – namely marriage to Rochester, as in the proposal scene in the orchard:

---

[133] Ibid., 83.
[134] In a sense then she becomes a kind of theological vampire, a figure resting uneasily in the grave until called forth again to a new kind of life. For more on the connections between the vampire and theology, see Chapter 5.
[135] C. Brontë, *Jane Eyre*, 87.
[136] See Matthew 25 v.23.

> I am not talking to you now through the medium of custom, conventionalities, nor even of mortal flesh; – it is my spirit that addresses your spirit; just as if both had passed through the grave, and we stood at God's feet, equal as we are.[137]

Here, as Milbank claims, 'the sublime is no longer enough to effect equality in a novel in which the landscape is always owned by someone. The apocalyptic provision of the world beyond is all that can make possible communication as equals.'[138] Though Milbank's point here is well taken, the language of an eschatological apocalypse should not elide material conditions. The language is apocalyptic but at the same moment is grounded in a marriage proposal. Only through the medium of marriage *as sacrament* can there be a true equality between the two – as Jane seems to recognize with her honesty and call for Rochester to see her as she truly is. Yet, of course, the true impediment to their union is revealed in the figure of Bertha and Jane is forced to leave, repeating the motif of enclosure and escape. There can be no kind of sacramental marriage while Bertha is still living – in the aftermath of Bertha's discovery, once again Eyre turns to the language of theology, reinforcing the idea that the novel presents marriage not simply as an economic arrangement but as a sacramental idea. As Jane tells Rochester, 'Do as I do; trust in God . . . believe in heaven . . . I advise you to live sinless, and I wish you to die tranquil.'[139] Rochester offers her a marriage but one that is not theologically valid – she insists upon keeping 'the law given by God',[140] refusing a marriage that would not only be a sham but would be sinful. Rochester, despite being able to 'bend her with my finger and thumb'[141] is unable to prevent her leaving.

This ongoing conflict between faith and freedom reaches its height in the interactions between Jane and St John. Somewhat surprisingly, many of the critical works on the novel focus on the relation between Bertha and Jane,[142] when in fact; the 'mad-woman in the attic' is a fairly minor character in the

---

[137] C. Brontë, *Jane Eyre*, 253.
[138] Milbank, *Daughters of the House*, 147.
[139] C. Brontë, *Jane Eyre*, 317.
[140] Ibid.
[141] Ibid., 318.
[142] This is somewhat unsurprising given the impact of Jean Rhys's *Wide Sargasso Sea* – a definitive list is impossible, but some examples include Alexandra Nygren, 'Disabled and Colonized: Bertha Mason in Jane Eyre', *Explicator* 74.2 (2016): 117–19, Paul J. C. M. Franssen, 'Another Possible Source for Bertha Mason in Jane Eyre', *Notes and Queries*, 58.1 (2011): 88–9, Julia Sun-Joo Lee, 'The (Slave) Narrative of "Jane Eyre"', *Victorian Literature and Culture*, 36.2 (2008): 317–29, as well as Valerie Beattie, 'The Mystery at Thornfield: Representations of Madness in Jane Eyre', *Studies in the Novel* 28.4 (Winter 1996): 493–503.

book, in contrast to St John, who occupies a substantial section of the novel.[143] After leaving Thornfield, with little clue of where to go, the journey that Jane undertakes is framed as something akin to a pilgrimage – 'God must have led me on', as Jane expresses it.[144] St John, with his name referencing both St John the Evangelist and the St John of Revelation, functions as both a theological and emotional counterpoint to both Brocklehurst and Rochester but, as Thormählen points out, his name highlights his own theological flaws. 'Neither John Reed nor St John Rivers is ever capable of genuine love for a fellow human being. The former indirectly kills his mother, and not even the latter shines as a son.'[145] Despite this, he is the one who takes in Jane, provides her with the companionship she desires and the useful employment that, for her, is so desperately necessary. He promises what Rochester cannot – namely a marriage grounded in devotion to God, and good Christian duty with the promise of missionary work in the empire. Jane faces another type of imprisonment in the Gothic castle, but unlike the lascivious or suspect villains of the earlier Gothic, the imprisonment here is grounded upon the highest possible justification. St John's theology functions as both the means for justifying Jane's submission at the cost of her agency, and justifying involvement in the colonial exercise of empire building. It is a theological request that seeks both the violent domination of the individual and to participate in the violence of dominating far off nations.[146] Strikingly however, Jane does not deny St John's request on the grounds of its imperialistic and colonial nature but simply because it would not be right for her to do so – suggesting that even the practical Jane Eyre's theological sympathies do not extend beyond a certain sphere. Her theology then, while rather more astute than St Johns, still suffers from a number of limits and lacunae.

However, it is through the figure of St John that Brontë works her most subtle theological critique. While more conventionally attractive than Rochester (Jane specifically notes his 'Athenian mouth and chin')[147] he is crucially lacking in the most important theological value – namely love. Jane herself notes this, observing that while he is a great orator, capable of thrilling the heart and astonishing

---

[143] For a somewhat polemical take on this issue, see Laurence Lerner, 'Bertha and the Critics', in *Nineteenth Century Literature*, 44.3 (December 1989): 273–300.
[144] C. Brontë, *Jane Eyre*, 322.
[145] Thormählen, *Brontës and Religion*, 207.
[146] The link between theology and colonialism comes into great importance in Chapter 5 in connection to horror in the late 1800s as the empire becomes increasingly vulnerable and functions as a source of cultural anxiety.
[147] C. Brontë, *Jane Eyre*, 345.

the mind, 'neither were softened'.[148] There is a sense of theological tragedy for St John, for while he may be conscientious and zealous, he has not found 'the peace of God that passeth all understanding'. As his own sister puts it, 'it is right, noble, Christian; yet it breaks my heart'.[149] As a result, listening to St John, as with listening to the young Helen Burns, produces 'an inexpressible sadness'.[150] However, unlike Helen, who denies the world in order to achieve the goal of heaven, St John denies himself, in order to work for the glory of God in the world. Yet, for all of his dedication, there is an 'absence of any patent love for God and his Son'.[151] St John speaks of his desire for 'the destiny of . . . anything other than a priest',[152] before his 'powers heard a call from Heaven to rise . . . a missionary I resolved to be'.[153] St John then does not pursue the call of missionary work out of a sense of Christian love but rather out of an attempt to resolve the conflicts with his self-confessed 'human weakness',[154] that he fails to integrate into his overall theological understanding. For St John, missionary work is the specific end of the ways in which religion has developed his own original qualities – meaning that his faith, rather than emerging from his own dependence on grace, comes forth because of his personal commitment to a specific kind of religious practice. For a clergyman, particularly an evangelical, dedicated to proclaiming the *evangel* or good news, there can be no greater failure than to be what he himself confesses he is – 'a cold, hard man',[155] who has supressed his own emotional and spiritual nature in the service of a strict religious order.

In this respect then, the reasons for the basic incompatibility between Jane and St John become clearer as well as the reasons for why St John's offer of missionary partnership proves to be so tempting. Offering Jane the opportunity to 'enlist under the same banner'[156] (in a typically militaristic bit of evangelical terminology, considering St John's colonialist mission), he seeks to give Jane 'a place in the ranks of His chosen'.[157] In response, Jane asks whether, if she is truly qualified 'will not [her] own heart be the first to inform?'[158] Quite arrogantly and with typical patriarchal nerve, St John responds that if Jane's own heart

---

[148] Ibid., 353.
[149] Ibid., 357.
[150] Ibid., 353.
[151] Thormählen, *Brontës and Religion*, 208.
[152] C. Brontë, *Jane Eyre*, 362.
[153] Ibid.
[154] Ibid., 363.
[155] Ibid., 376.
[156] Ibid., 402.
[157] Ibid.
[158] Ibid.

remains silent, he 'must speak for it'.[159] As Thormählen argues, Jane is a far better evangelical theologian than St John, aware that no Christian can speak for another's calling from God – St John commits the sin of spiritual pride – 'arrogance in a peculiarly literal sense'.[160] It is not the offer of missionary work that divides Jane and St John (this commitment to productive labour, in and of itself, is probably what connects them most deeply) but rather the idea that St John can master Jane's soul. Such a martyrdom, as Jane herself admits, would be 'monstrous'.[161] While Jane admits his greatness, she adds to this that 'he forgets, pitilessly, the feelings and claims of little people in pursuing his own large views'.[162] St John in his theological arrogance, comes close to a type of Gothic villain who seeks not just to imprison the Gothic heroine but rather more seriously, seeks to possess her very soul and calling before God.

Thus, as with *Wuthering Heights*, the novel puts forward a stern critique of a specific kind of institutional religion and practice, but unlike Brocklehurst or the cantankerous old Calvinist Joseph, St John is not entirely condemned – although in practical terms both St John and Brocklehurst share a great deal of common ground. St John provides the impetus for a new, remade and redeemed Lowood, but at the same time, given St John's propensity for a repression of the heart (in contrast to Brocklehurst's own repression of the flesh) the two are often uncomfortably similar. After Jane refuses his marriage proposal, he preaches from Rev. 21, once again drawing upon the apocalyptic language of eschatology that forms the crux of a type of theological threat that aims to ensure Jane's submission:

> 'He that overcometh shall inherit all things; and I will be his God, and he shall be my son. But', was slowly, distinctly read, 'the fearful, the unbelieving ... shall have their part in the lake which burneth with fire and brimstone, which is the second death'. Henceforth, I knew what fate St. John feared for me.[163]

After her condemnation to the hell of Lowood School was interrupted by the heaven of her time with Rochester, once again Jane is confronted with the apocalyptic language of hellfire and eternal death. The threat of eternal damnation, coupled with what is admirable about St John, produces a profound effect, a deep and powerful impulse to forsake the world and to heed the call of

---

[159] Ibid., 403.
[160] Thormählen, *Brontës and Religion*, 209.
[161] C. Brontë, *Jane Eyre*, 406.
[162] Ibid., 417.
[163] Ibid., 418.

God, presented in a series of short, staccato phrases. 'Religion called – Angels beckoned – God commanded . . . all here might be sacrificed in a second.'[164] In this moment, Jane comes closer than at any point of the novel to finally accepting the theology of those like Helen Burns, who spurn their own agency for the greater glory of God. Such is St John's oratorical ability and theological powers of persuasion that his desire to control Jane can only be thwarted by a seemingly divine (or, at the least, supernatural) revelation. From a theological point of view, St John makes the categorical error of assuming the power of authority over Jane's own spiritual condition and attempting to reinstate the kind of spiritual submission she has consistently resisted. As Kathryn Swanson argues, 'whereas Rochester tried to force Jane to be his spiritual better half, St John attempts to become Jane's spiritual whole'.[165] Hearing the voice of Rochester, Jane responds that 'I am coming . . . Wait for me! Oh, I will come!'[166] She acknowledges that 'it was *my* time to assume ascendency . . . I mounted to my chamber; locked myself in; fell on my knees and prayed'.[167] Here, the power of female subjectivity is married to both theological language and practice – some critics identify this moment as a type of feminist assertion of selfhood[168] – that should be affirmed, and furthermore this is also a moment of theological significance. Freed from the constraining ideology of St John which seeks to erase Jane's subjectivity – what Swanson calls the 'sin of fusion',[169] that women under patriarchy are forced into – she is liberated by what seems to be a call from heaven that draws her back to the now blinded Rochester. Understood this way then, the logic of a binary opposition between Jane's theological convictions and desire for companionship and love can be subverted. In leaving St John she does not reject her religious beliefs or ideas – rather, read theologically her actions are 'consistently recognizable as a turning towards life, affirming her right to be loved with integrity and to love freely'.[170] Thus, it is not simply the systems of enclosure and limitations that can be seen as Gothic elements within the text but also the theological ideas which seek to force Jane into the sin of either idolatry or spiritual self-abnegation. In contrast to this kind of monstrous theology, Eyre

---

[164] Ibid., 419.
[165] Kathryn J. Swanson, 'A Liberative Imagination: Reconsidering the Fiction of Charlotte Brontë in the Light of Feminist Theology' (Unpublished PhD Thesis, University of St Andrews), 127.
[166] C. Brontë, *Jane Eyre*, 420.
[167] Ibid., 421.
[168] For examples, see Milbank, *Daughters of the House*, Showalter, *A Literature of Their Own*, and Hoeveler, *Gothic Feminism*.
[169] Swanson, *Liberative Imagination*, 121–31.
[170] Ibid., 131.

consistently clings to the ideas of God's provision and grace while refusing the theological logic that would imprison her once again.

The conclusion of the novel sees the two reunited – Jane, now sure of her selfhood, and economically independent could easily be read a model for escaping (or at the least, taming) the wild and patriarchal Byronic Rochester.[171] However, as previously argued such a position sets up an unnecessary binary between theological consistency and her marriage. What truly makes the reunion and marriage of the two possible is Rochester's 'voluntary subjugation to Divine authority'.[172] On her return, his 'heart swells with gratitude to the beneficent God of this earth just now'[173] and he confesses to a kind of conversion experience, beginning to pray, humbled by God and expressing the 'wish for reconcilement' that is the mark of repentance.[174] The union of the two in marriage must necessarily be coupled with a spiritual dimension to allow marriage to function as something more than another system of enclosure. At the close of the novel then, Brontë suggests that it is in the sacrament of marriage – lived 'entirely for and with what I love best on this earth',[175] that there can be a possible liberation and authentic Christian belief. Yet, this is not held up as an exclusive model – somewhat akin to *Wuthering Heights* the ending refuses absolute judgements. However, whereas *Wuthering Heights* insists upon the contingency and openness of the relationship between God and humanity, in the case of *Jane Eyre*, the ending is more akin to 'a balancing of the books' as Thormählen argues[176] – after all, the closing line is spoken in the expectation that God's judgement is, inexorably, coming. Jane has united her emotional and sexual desires with spiritual fulfilment in the sacrament of marriage, whereas St John remains, resolutely unmarried in the colonies, living out what remains of his life in service to a God that, for him, appears to be ever nearer to a second coming. Despite his theological hubris and his many other flaws, there is a deeply serious admiration for St John at the close of the novel. As DeLamotte writes,

> Brontë pays homage to the aspirations of souls that can find transcendence only through the search for a 'world elsewhere'. But Jane must find her fulfilment in the world, in fellowship with her 'kind'.[177]

---

[171] Such an argument being one made by Diane Long Hoeveler throughout *Gothic Feminism*.
[172] Thormählen, *Brontës and Religion*, 218.
[173] C. Brontë, *Jane Eyre*, 447.
[174] Ibid.
[175] Ibid., 451.
[176] See Thormählen, *Brontës and Religion*, 217–20.
[177] Eugenia C. DeLamotte, *Perils of the Night: A Feminist Study of Nineteenth Century Literature* (Oxford: Oxford University Press, 1990), 225.

Finally, then, both of these classic Gothic novels present two distinct critiques of theology. *Wuthering Heights* is a text wrought by the contingency of faith, a Gothic environment that reveals the fundamentally flawed nature of humanity and the impossibility of clearly separating the Gothic and the religious. The novel presents a staunch resistance to a vision of the divine as a Calvinist who eternally punishes before ending with a detailed examination of the ways in which grace functions as a means of breaking out of the patterns of sin. Theology in *Wuthering Heights* is a fragile and uncertain endeavour that can all-too-easily be shattered by the ghosts of the past. This awareness of the proximity of ghosts could potentially re-invigorate theology, but this is by no means guaranteed as the Gothic elements of the text make such certainty seem at best, tenuous. In the case of *Jane Eyre*, the inclusion of St John at the close of the novel may seem something of a strange choice when contrasted with the satisfied and sanctified life that Jane builds for herself. However, as Thormählen argues, the inclusion of St John serves to show the radical complexity of the Brontë's theological investigation.

> The mixture of extreme qualities that is St John Rivers thus illustrates the radical enquiry into religious thought, feeling and conduct which is so characteristic of all the Brontë works. It is in evidence, for instance, when Emily Brontë stands back from articulating a definite scenario for Catherine's and Heathcliff's afterlife and when Anne Brontë refrains from even suggesting whether Helen Huntingdon's hopes for her husband's ultimate salvation are likely to be fulfilled. The Brontë spirit of religious enquiry has always affected readers – even readers not fully aware that it was a religious challenge they were responding to.[178]

Still, the theological critiques that the Brontës provide highlight the extent to which orthodox presentations of Christianity were increasingly untenable – the Gothic text functioned as a space by which the fragility of Christian faith could be examined and possible imaginative solutions and reworking of theological ideas could be presented. However, as the nineteenth century advanced, the theological themes and concerns of the Gothic novel would become more urgent as the advancements of the fin-de-siècle would increasingly seek to provide a wholly materialist account of existence. Despite this, the theological persisted within the Gothic, moving further beyond the grounds of theological orthodoxy, while exposing the limitations of strict materialism. It is this productive tension that will be the topic of the final chapters, examining the ghost story before turning to the fin-de-siècle Gothic.

---

[178] Thormählen, *Brontës and Religion*, 219–20.

4

'Through a glass darkly'

Reading the Victorian ghost story theologically

Given the startling popularity of the Gothic, academic debates about its nature and definition have been a regular feature of the field of Gothic studies. Yet, what these claims to the end of the Gothic almost always acknowledge is the hybridity and resilience of the form. As the critics draw the curtain over the Gothic form, the possibility of return, of renewal, is always present. If the era of the classic Gothic form concludes with the publication of something like Charles Maturin's *Melmoth the Wanderer* (1820) it is also the beginning of an exponential growth in Gothic texts as it spreads from beyond its early generic formula to take on new, darker forms as the Gothic becomes found in almost all aspects of life. Jarlath Killeen points out that in the public imagination, the Victorian age is an unmistakeably Gothic one, with 'public respectability disguising private perversity'.[1] Such a conception goes some way to explaining the critical interest in the psychoanalytic in relation to the Victorian Gothic as critics sought to decode and bring to light the uncovered Gothic nature of this ostensibly respectable and straitlaced time. Coupled with the rise of popular scientific discourses, most famously with the cultural response to the work of Darwin, it is tempting to look at the Victorian age as one in which religion was replaced, or overwritten, with the repressed and the disturbing as the vision of the subject at the centre of a divinely ordered universe was overturned. This certainly provides a productive way to analyse the proliferation of supernatural fiction that appeared throughout the Victorian Gothic.

Yet, as Killeen takes pains to point out, this idea of the Victorian age is itself a product of a specific set of ideological and historical conditions. (See Kileen, particularly pages 3–12.) Work from a whole host of literary and historical

---

[1] Jarleth Killeen, *Gothic Literature 1825–1914* (Cardiff: University of Wales Press, 2009), 9.

researchers has shown the great complexity of the Victorian age and highlighted a key aspect to Victorian society and cultural production which much work on the Gothic has either missed or marginalized – namely, the role and function of Christian theology and religion. Despite the long-standing cultural idea of the nineteenth-century being marked by, in Matthew Arnold's words, the 'melancholy, long, withdrawing roar' of faith,[2] it was also the age of the Society for Psychical Research, spiritualism and séances, religious revival and theosophy. The nineteenth century saw also the start of the Gifford Lecture series and a whole range of theological debates as new approaches to faith and the Bible were keenly discussed. Not for nothing does David A Furgusson call the nineteenth century 'one of the most diverse and creative periods in the history of Christian theology'.[3] In addition, Mark Knight and Emma Mason make the point in their excellent study 'Nineteenth Century Religion and Literature' that the Victorian era was an intently religious one, seriously engaged with a range of theological and religious notions.[4] Christianity – contested though it was – remained a foundational discourse upon which much of Victorian life still rested. As Timothy Larsen argues in his work on the Bible, Christian belief and thought were seen as essential to Victorian life and society as well as being an indelible cultural influence.[5] This led to a critical examination and retelling of Christian faith, which arguably could be seen as resituating religious belief rather than undercutting it or seeking to negate it. Thus, rather than return to the constant reiteration of interiority or repression with the ghost being seen as a return of the uncivilized past into the present, taking a theological view of supernatural fiction allows for a critical engagement with the religious ideas within the text without reducing them to psychoanalytic discourses.

If, as Zoë Lehmann Imfeld claims, the ghost fiction of the Victorian age was haunted by an uncertain hope for a metaphysical revelation behind the empirical rationality of the world, then in the wake of post-secularity that same feeling of haunted-ness still lingers in the contemporary age.[6] As Simon Marsden points out in his work on the contemporary Gothic, the Gothic text is inescapably haunted by theology and so, even in the historical supernatural ghost story, the reader

---

[2] Matthew Arnold, 'Dover Beach', https://www.poetryfoundation.org/poems/43588/dover-beach, first accessed 15 October 2019.
[3] David A. Furgusson, *The Blackwell Companion to Nineteenth Century Theology* (Oxford: Wiley-Blackwell, 2010), xi.
[4] Knight and Mason, *Nineteenth Century Literature and Religion*.
[5] Timothy Larsen, *A People of One Book: The Bible and the Victorians* (Oxford: Oxford University Press, 2011).
[6] Imfeld, *The Victorian Ghost Story and Theology*.

might engage with not just the religious and theological ideas of a historical moment but an ongoing and unfolding imaginative theological discourse.[7] In J. Hillis Miller's landmark study the author expresses the fear of an absent God – that either divinity was gone, or simply inaccessible.[8] In contrast, a theological reading of the Victorian ghost story might show that as knowledge about the Victorians and critical interest in the theological renews, we might find in these texts a vision of the world that argues that beyond the veil of material reality is something more than just an absence but a strange and unexpected theological reality. Such a rethinking necessitates not just the spotting of theological semiotics within the supernatural Gothic text but also examining the ways in which there are spectral, haunted aspects to theology. Therefore, the first question to tackle is the issue of how to bridge the gap between theology and the Gothic – how best to draw together two disciplines with such varied terminology and critical registers. In Imfeld's study of the Victorian ghost story and theology, Imfeld argues that the ghost story opens a participatory space in which non-theological readers might be drawn into an encounter with theological ideas, realizing themselves as theological beings, rather than just materialist readers.[9] In a secular age theological claims are not easily understood and so, in the Gothic ghost story, wherein the supernatural does not require belief per se, but simply the admittance that supernatural encounters *could* be possible there remains the always-present possibility of theological encounter.

Thus, reading the ghost story theologically is not supposed to replace or overwrite secular critical methodologies but to emphasize that these texts, produced as they were in a context of great theological and religious tumult, are also engaged with a struggle over the nature and reality of religious ideas. Theology and horror are closely linked and a critical approach to the ghost story, which sidelines this aspect, misses much of what gives these texts their power. As Rudolph Otto notes in his *The Idea of the Holy*, fear has a distinct theological role.[10] For Kierkegaard, fear and dread are not simply affects produced by textual impact but are existential and theological states, which can fundamentally influence and shape human subjectivity. Thus, imaginative forms such as the supernatural Gothic tale are fundamentally bound up within the theological and

---

[7] Simon Marsden, *Holy Ghosts: The Theological Turn in Contemporary Gothic Fiction* (London: Palgrave Macmillan, 2018).
[8] Miller, *Disappearance*.
[9] See Imfeld, *Victorian Ghost Story*, especially Chapter One.
[10] Rudolph Otto, *The Idea of the Holy* (Oxford: Oxford University Press, 1958).

existential impacts of fear and dread. Finally, a word on method – the approach taken here is broadly historical, proceeding from early Victorian ghost stories to the latter half of the nineteenth century. However, such an approach can in no way claim to be exhaustive – the sheer volume of Victorian supernatural ghost stories would necessitate a multi-volume work, so the aim for this chapter is to provide a snapshot of sorts, that shows potential avenues for exploring the ways in which theology and this popular cultural forms interact.

Perhaps the most well-known of the Victorian ghost story writers, Charles Dickens would be an appropriate place to begin. Dickens, who popularized the link between Christmas time and the ghost story, making it both a hugely successful form and a vehicle for moral didacticism. In the 1835 short story 'The Story of the Goblins Who Stole a Sexton', Dickens rehearses many of the themes that would reach an apotheosis with the more famous *A Christmas Carol*. In the short story, an 'ill-conditioned, surly fellow' by the name of Gabriel Grub is visited by a cabal of goblins with the aim of correcting Grub's morose, antisocial character.[11] It would be easy enough to read this as a literary exercise in conformist bourgeois morality, with the aim of inculcating the correct degree of sociality in the readership. This would be entirely correct but missing something of the distinctly religious character of Dicken's text. It is deliberately set in an old Abby town and Grub is the sexton and gravedigger at the local churchyard. From the outset, Dickens establishes the idea that Grub's character fails to respond appropriately to the religious setting. 'Surrounded by the emblems of mortality', as Grub is, there is no reason for him to be a 'morose and melancholy man'. For Dickens then, good temperament is not simply a mark of good character but is also an outward sign of an inward faith appropriate to Victorian society.

After encountering a group of children and consoling himself with thoughts of their painful death, Grub finds himself in an unfinished grave. He is positioned as not just socially outcast but figuratively – and almost literally – dead. In his own words Grub occupies 'Brave lodgings for one, these, in holy ground!' It is here, while in the incomplete grave, that the spiritually dead Grub has a supernatural encounter with a 'strange unearthly figure, whom Gabriel felt at once, was no being of this world'. Mocking him, the goblin and the unseen voices form their own hellish parody of religious ecstasy as they sound like 'many choristers singing to the mighty swell of an old church organ' The

---

[11] All quotes taken from Charles Dickens, 'The Story of the Goblins Who Stole a Sexton', https://familychristmasonline.com/stories_other/dickens/gabriel_grub.htm [no page numbers], accessed 31 October 2019.

religious air of the setting reaches a crescendo with 'brilliant illumination within the windows of the church' and a host of goblins pour into the churchyard. What follows is a conversion experience of sorts, as the goblins show the 'man of misery and gloom, a few of the pictures from our own great storehouse'. Grub, and by proxy the reader, is shown the death of child with a family that knew the dead child 'was an angel looking down upon, and blessing them, from a bright and happy Heaven'. Whereas in *A Christmas Carol* Dickens would remain with the personalized scene of suffering, through the focus on the Cratchett family, here the story moves beyond the personal to take a wider view of the world, as the goblins show Grub a cross section of contemporary society and the ways in which suffering is perpetuated. Grub concludes that

> men like himself, who snarled at the mirth and cheerfulness of others, were the foulest weeds on the fair surface of the earth; and setting all the good of the world against the evil, he came to the conclusion that it was a very decent and respectable sort of world after all.

Had the text concluded here it would have been easy to dismiss this as a conversion from antisociality to more amiable character, but the narrative frames this as something far more profound. Awakening from his vision or dream, 'he could not bear the thought of returning to a place where his repentance would be scoffed at', and so Grub leaves his job and his disappearance becomes another aspect of faith. The rumour is that Grub has been taken away by the goblins is 'devoutly believed' until he returns some ten years later, 'ragged, rheumatic and contended'. What this move underscores is that Gabriel Grub's conversion is not simply a move into the social realm but is something beyond the concerns of day-to-day society. Dickens ends the short story with a didactic moral, a dire warning to his readers that they should beware drinking alone at Christmas lest they too end up like Gabriel Grub. Despite this, the text as a whole swings between a conversion narrative and a middle-class morality play, highlighting the extent to which the ghost story form exists in an in-between state, shifting back and forth from material reality to a supernatural beyond.

This state of indeterminacy, of an experience that *could* be true, is a recurrent theme throughout the Victorian ghost story. Amelia B. Edwards's 'The North Mail' from 1864 develops the ghost story in some interesting and suggestive ways for thinking through spectral encounters as a theological space. The short story opens by deliberately highlighting the potential truth status of the experience – 'the circumstances I am about to relate to you have truth to recommend them', begins the narrator.[12] There is not an attempt to create a literary sense of realism but rather to recommend possible truth that aims to imaginatively engage the reader without requiring a realist form or style. The story follows one James Murray who, twenty years ago while hunting in the far north of England, found himself caught in a snowstorm. Trapped by bad weather and increasing cold, the Murray's thoughts turn to issues of death: 'Death . . . how hard to die just now, when life lay all so bright before me'.[13] Interestingly, this line suggests that rather than read a ghost story as a return of the past; the spectral encounter can also be read as a response to the lost potential of the future. From a theological point of view, history has a particular teleology – namely an eschatological one, and here the narrator argues that a death in the midst of bad weather is not frightening on its own terms but because of what they may be deprived.

At the opportune time, an old man with a lantern comes into view. 'Thank God! was the exclamation that burst from my lips', but the older man is quick to remind the narrator that 'folks do get cast away hereabouts fra' time to time, an' what's to hinder you from bein' cast away likewise, if the Lord is so minded'.[14] Accompanying the taciturn older man to a house, the Murray is introduced to the master of the house, an elderly white-haired man who is presented as a cross between a scientist and theologian. The house is full of scientific apparatus and geological samples, but there is also an 'organ, fantastically decorated with painted carvings of medieval saints and devils'.[15] Murray and the host converse, and the topic of conversation shows a similar range, moving across practical science to mental philosophy. He passed on to that field that lies beyond the boundary line of even conjectural philosophy and reaches no man knows wither. He spoke of the soul and its aspirations, of the spirit and its powers; of second sight; of prophecy; of those phenomena which, under the name of ghosts, spectres and supernatural appearances, have been denied by the sceptics.[16]

Given his unorthodox and metaphysical interests, the master of the house has retreated from public life, serving a model for the ways in which the various challenges to theological truth were being contested at the time. Yet what is notable is the extent to which the text refuses to privilege one discourse over another – strict materialist science does not eliminate the supernatural and the ghostly but comprehensively fails to explain it. As the old master of the house

---

[12] Amelia B. Edwards, 'The North Mail', in *The Wimbourne Book of Victorian Ghost Stories, Vol II*, ed. Alastair Gunn (London: Wimbourne Books, 2018), 116.
[13] Ibid., 117.
[14] Ibid.
[15] Ibid., 120.
[16] Ibid., 122.

puts it, 'the world... grows hourly more and more sceptical of all that lies beyond its own narrow radius'.[17] Yet, despite this indictment of the flaws and limitations of scientific scepticism, the scientist-priest figure has not abandoned his scientific and experimental interests – Murray notes the range of scientific study that is clearly still on going. What this suggests, then, is the possibility of reading the ghost as a phenomenon of natural theology – beyond both divinely ordered revelation and outside of strict materialist scientism there remains an irreducible present metaphysical element, which cannot be wholly contained by either. Sent from the house to catch the late mail coach, Murray hears of an old accident wherein the coach left the road and four passengers were killed. Now late into the night, he finds his way to the coach and clambers aboard, noting the atmosphere of the coach 'was pervaded by a singularly damp and disagreeable smell'. The coach itself is in the throes of decay and Murray realizes that the passengers are 'no living men – that none of them were living men, like myself!'.[18] Flinging himself from the coach Murray awakens to find himself out of the supernatural and in a hospital, waited on by his wife. 'The surgeon found me in a state of raving delirium, with a broken arm and a compound fracture of the skull.' Here then the story could easily explain away the supernatural as a hallucination, but the final paragraph of the short story once again highlights the limits of strictly scientific explanation. Murray discusses his experiences with his surgeon, 'until we found we could discuss it with temper no longer, and then we dropped it'. The ultimate truth of the event cannot be decided and as Murray finishes his narrative, 'others may form what conclusion they please – I know that twenty years ago I was the fourth inside passenger in the Phantom Coach'.[19] The story as a whole exists in this interstitial space, between the limits of rationalized scientific explanation and the supernatural metaphysics that exists beyond that limit. The story serves as a microcosm of the secular, scientific and theological tensions of the day. The issue is not the absent supernatural, but that the supernatural is existent and inexplicable. Here then, we see the limit of seeing the ghost as a solely psychoanalytic discourse. The conversation between Murray and his surgeon at the close of the short story shows that viewing the ghost as simply a psychological affect is limited, and with a tendency to lapse into undecidability.

It is more than likely that writers who were believers at the time were familiar with the theological and spiritual impact of a ghostly encounter. Thomas Street

---

[17] Amelia B. Edwards, 'The North Mail', 122.
[18] Ibid., 128.
[19] Ibid., 129.

Millington's short story 'No Living Voice' (1872) shows the ways in which theologians and religious figures produced their own short fictions and used it as a space within which one could frame the ghost in more explicitly theological terms. The story opens in media res, a conversation between two gentlemen in a country house drawing room. One is asked whether 'you think, then, that it was really supernatural?' Mr Brown acknowledges, as the scientist-priest in the previous story did, that nature is infinitely strange and mysterious, 'we can scarcely speak of anything that happens as beyond it or above it'.[20] Faced with the offer a ghost story, Mr Browne's audience make explicit the mechanism at work – that the ghost stories potential truth claims function as an exercise in faith of sorts regarding a theological or non-material reality. The crowd promise that they will 'give it a respectful hearing, *implicit belief* and unbounded sympathy' (emphasis mine). Furthermore, the text itself rejects a solely psychological understanding of ghost experience, as the audience to Mr Browne's story promise to discount their psychological and sceptical theories and simply accept the possibility of what will be recounted.

The story unfolds when Mr Browne is in Rome during Holy Week – this context is a call back to the traditional Gothic novels of the late eighteenth and early nineteenth century that saw Europe as a place of exotic spiritualism and dangerous Catholicism (in contrast to the sober Protestantism of England). However, it seems the story refuses the anti-Catholicism that Diane Long Hoeveler would call the Gothic Ideology. Mr Browne is taken seriously as a Catholic pilgrim who, after a long day wandering through the countryside collecting 'relics from the ruins of the old Pelasgic fortresses' ends up at an old dilapidated inn. There he is awakened by the 'groaning of one in anguish and despair, but not like any mortal voice . . . a long, loud hollow protracted groan . . . which seemed to stop my breath and paralyse my limbs'. Fleeing the inn, Mr Browne is found by the local chief of police who explains that the inn is a haunt for bandits (here the old Gothic tropes about Italy continue themselves). The police and Mr Browne return to the inn and discover in the room below where Mr Browne slept a patch of uneven bricks. Here, the unfortunate innkeeper confesses that the body of his son is buried beneath the floor. Wounded in a fight he was taken to the house and as there was 'neither doctor nor priest, and in spite of all we could do for him he died'. Importantly for the innkeeper the hauntings and strange sounds heard at night are only solvable through theological means. As the innkeeper puts it, 'let him alone now, or let a priest first be sent for;

---

[20] All quotes taken from Thomas Street Millington, 'No Living Voice', http://gutenberg.net.au/ebooks 06/0606111h.html, accessed 31 October 2019. No page numbers.

he died unconfessed, but it was not my fault; it may not be yet too late to make peace for him'. It turns out that the innkeeper and son used to kill visitors and rob them. Mr Browne realizes that the son had lived long enough to repent his deeds and had 'urged his father to bring the confessor to his bedside . . . his prayers were disregarded, and his dying admonition were of no avail'. Thus, the ghost here is not malevolent but is a theological virtue – the ghost of the son haunts the inn to stop his father from committing further murders and thefts.

Here, in the final section of the story Mr Browne continues his religious journey and comes across a mendicant friar collected coins for the dead in purgatory. Mr Browne admits that 'I did not believe in purgatory, not in supplications for the death; but I dropped a piece if silver into that box . . . my prayer went up to heaven in all sincerity, – *Requiescat in pace*!' In the case of Millington's short story, it is possible to see the theological reading of the ghost rendered in more explicit terms. The ghost encounter is a positive religious experience – something literally life saving in the case of Mr Browne, and the text ends with a reinforcement of a particularly Gothic theological moral – namely that the dead are not simply gone, absent but are capable of impacting and acting in the world. Framed in religious terms, it could be said that the dead do not rest peacefully, particularly (the text argues) when denied the sacramental rites which only religious orders can provide. The ghost is laden with religious meaning, not simply a kind of theoretical heresy or simple conversion narrative but a form which can be used for religious ends of greater complexity than the religious conversion narratives with which the chapter began.

However, the ghost text is not simply a case of increasing religious complexity as the nineteenth century moves on. Richard Marsh's 'A Set of Chessman' from 1890 serves a good example of the ways in which theological and religious ideas can become generic features of the form.[21] Following a chess enthusiast who buys an exquisite set of chess pieces, which were owned by the chess fanatic M. Funichon. Funichon had recently died during a game of chess. Taking the set, the narrator ends up playing a game of chess with his morose flatmate, St Servan. Beginning their game, the two men realize that neither of them are playing in their usually styles and that there seems to be some force influencing the moves they decide to make. The narrator seems to take the possibility of the set having some form of spiritual influence with remarkable pragmatism – 'curiosities nowadays

---

[21] Richard Marsh, 'A Set of Chessmen', in *The Wimbourne Book of Victorian Ghost Stories, Vol. 5*, ed. Alastair Gunn (Kindle edition, no page numbers) (London: Wimbourne Press, 2017).

do fetch such fancy sums – and what price for a ghost? They appeared to be automatic chessman, automatic in a sense entirely their own'. As the game goes on the presence of the ghostly presence becomes harder to ignore. Finger marks appear on the two player's wrists, yet in contrast to the previous story, which would see the intervention of the spectral on the physical world as something positive here the reaction is more mixed. The narrator maintains a calm interest, whereas St Servan is deeply unsettled for explicitly religious reasons. 'Believe – in ghosts! In what then, do you believe? I, Monsiuer, am a religious man'. Here then, the ghost is not something which can be explained within religious or theological ideas but seems to exist entirely outside of it. St Servan can only conceive of the ghost as some kind of demonic or anti-theological phenomena that has to resisted. In contrast to his austere religious flatmate, the narrator treats the ghost an entirely natural phenomenon. In the first appearance of the ghost, the narrator seeks to experiment on the range of the ghost, testing its strength and trying to test whether it can offer some physical or audible sign of its presence. After this first encounter, the narrator mentions the possibility of communicating with the Psychical Research Society (a clear reference to the Society for Psychical Research, founded in 1882 under the leadership of Henry Sidgwick). The narrator sees this as a huge commercial opportunity and the experimental and scientific approach is a chance to exert power and control over supernatural phenomena: 'I almost began to hug myself on the possession of a ghost, a ghost too, which might be induced to perform at will.' Returning to his apartment which he shares with St Servan, he finds that his religious flat mate has returned with a priest and two acolytes who 'appeared to be holding some sort of religious service'. What they've done is grind the chess pieces into a powder, casting it into the fire. To the narrator's horror it turns out that St Servan and the priest have 'exorcised the demon'. The response of the narrator is one of horror 'they had ground my ivory chessman in the pestle and mortar, and then burned them in the fire'. The narrator is aghast that such a move would be made in 'the days of the Psychical Research Society! And they had cost me a hundred francs!' Here then, the ghost becomes something which must be explained but cannot be explained by the religious. Theology takes on a fundamentally conservative and oppositional tone – all that it can do here is seek to expel the supernatural and so the ghost encounter becomes caught between emergent scientific rationality (that Psychical Research Society) and an authoritarian religion that can make no place for the supernatural that exists in unexpected fashion. What this demonstrates is not a waning of religious faith or practice but perhaps a contraction of theological imagination that could only respond to the supernatural in certain set ways. In texts covered earlier in the chapter, the ghost encounter is bound up with sacramental theology, or serves as a spur for repentance and a renewed commitment to the ideological precepts of Victorian society, yet for Marsh it seems that the ghost is at best a good investment which can all too quickly be snatched away by the religious and short-sighted.

What this reflects is a concern expressed by Andrew Lang that, through overexposure, the ghost had become a 'purposeless creature', that no longer had any 'message to deliver'.[22] Yet in the same decade as Richard Marsh's story there also comes work from figures such as Margaret Oliphant, of whom M. R. James would write that 'The religious ghost story, as it may be called, was never done better than by Mrs Oliphant in 'The Open Door' and 'A Beleaguered City'.[23] 'The Open Door' follows the retired army officer Colonel Mortimer who, along with his young family, has taken the lease on Brentwood Manor. On the grounds are the remains of an older version of the property. Part of the ruin includes the titular door, which opens out onto nothing. For the Colonel it stands as a 'melancholy comment upon a life that was now over. A door that led to nothing'.[24] While settling in, the Colonel's son Roland becomes ill while riding home in bad weather. The doctor is summoned and suspects a hallucination or some kind of 'brain fever' and his father returns to his son. Roland, however, insists upon the supernatural reality of his experience, a response to which his own father seems to have little context for understanding and the idea of Roland having had a genuine supernatural encounter is something rather distasteful to the Colonel: 'My blood got a sort of chill in the my veins at the idea that Roland should be a ghost-seer; for that generally meant a hysterical temperament and weak health'.[25] In the words of the manor's servants 'the certainty that the place was haunted was beyond all doubt'[26] but to make a 'wark about ghosts' would be to open oneself for ridicule as even the 'minister and the gentry they just laugh in your face'.[27] The class discourse here is well worth highlighting as the middle and upper classes are keen to rationalize away the supernatural, while working-class communities are convinced of the metaphysical reality of the supernatural. Arguably this

---

[22] Andrew Lang, *Cock Lane and Common Sense* (Cambridge: Cambridge University Press, 1894), 95.
[23] M. R. James, *Some Remarks on Ghost Stories*, https://www.berfrois.com/2015/10/m-r-james-on-ghost-stories/, accessed 29 October 2019.
[24] Margaret Oliphant, 'The Open Door', in *The Virago Book of Ghost Stories*, ed. Richard Dalby (London: Virago Press, 2006), 91.
[25] Ibid., 99.
[26] Ibid., 102.
[27] Ibid., 103.

class divide reflects wider shifts in religious discourse, as the rationalistic theism of the middle classes was seen as an acceptable form of faith in contrast to the superstitious faith of the poor and working class (which was seen as both irrational and convenient, as it naturalized class positions and class hierarchies).[28]

The next evening the Colonel and his old batman Bagley go out to investigate the strange haunting noises that seem to have so effected Roland. The two hear again the ghostly voice calling for its mother, coming from the open door which leads nowhere. 'In the name of God, who are you' asks the Colonel of the mysterious voice, and yet immediately he wonders to himself whether to 'use the name of God was profane, seeing that I did not believe in ghosts or in anything supernatural'. The voice returns, yet the Colonel is quick to try and explain away the encounter as 'recollection of a real scene . . . I began to listen, almost as if it had been a play'.[29] The doctor too seeks to rationalize things away, as he dismisses the supernatural voices as nothing more than some 'trick of the echoes or the winds – some phonetic disturbance or other'.[30] Simson the doctor comes out and while again there is another supernatural encounter, the doctor himself admits that he does not believe anything to do with ghosts, underscoring the way in which Oliphant positions scientific rationalism as being its own form of faith – presented with undeniable evidence, the doctor still clings to the belief that there must be a reasonable and comprehensible cause behind things.

Unsurprisingly (and really rather wisely) the Colonel next calls for a minister, Dr Moncrieff, who is 'strong in philosophy, not so strong in Greek, strongest of all in experience'.[31] Moncrieff's reaction to the story of the Colonel is not to separate the natural and the supernatural (as the Doctor does), but instead Moncrieff insists upon both compassion and his own willingness to investigate the phenomena. Strikingly, the minister claims that he has no 'cut and dried beliefs on the subject',[32] in contrast to the Simson. It seems, then, that it is the minister of religion who more properly embodies scientific rationality as the narrative seeks to bring together supernaturalism and religious office. That evening, the colonel, Simson and Montcrieff go out again to explore the ruins of the old mansion. The minister carries a lantern, 'an old fashioned [one] with a pierced and ornamental top',[33] which is reminiscent of the lantern carried

---

[28] For more on this see Eagleton, *Culture and the Death of God*.
[29] Oliphant, M., 'The Open Door', 113.
[30] Ibid., 114.
[31] Ibid., 120.
[32] Ibid., 121.
[33] Ibid., 124.

by Christ in the famous William Holman Hunt piece, *The Light of the World* (1851–6) – a famous Victorian piece of religious art with which Oliphant's contemporary readers would no doubt be familiar. Montcrieff's encounter with the ghost is both far more personal and far more powerful as he names the ghost, Willie. This leads to the minister ordering the spirit away – 'if you will lie and sob and greet, let it be at heaven's gate, and no your poor mother's ruined door'.[34] The minister calls upon God; 'Lord, take him into Thy everlasting habitations'[35] and the ghost is gone. Strikingly, Montcrieff emphasizes the extent that religious or theological knowledge is essentially limited and contingent. Asked by the Colonel if he believes in purgatory, the elderly minister responds that 'an old man like me is sometimes not very sure what he believes. There is just one thing I am certain of – and that is the loving-kindness of God'.[36] From this point of view then, what is essential is not to understand the ghost (whether that understanding is framed in scientific or theological terms) but rather to show compassion towards them. The success of the exorcism-cum-redemption of Dr Montcrieff is constantly undercut by the attempts of the doctor Simson to explain the hauntings in terms of 'human agency', and the discovery of a small hole in which there is evidence of human lodging.[37] Yet, this revelation comes *after* the compassionate religion which sets the spirit to rest. The desperate drive of Simson to find a human agent underneath all things is entirely insufficient and can only look (at best) ridiculous when confronted by the religious supernaturalism of a haunting.

In conclusion, this chapter has sought to offer both an overview of nineteenth-century ghost stories and the ways in which religious and theological language, symbolism and theme shift as the form develops. The ghost story serves as site in which theological and religious ideas can be contested, challenged and explored, removed from the restrictions religious institutions. As seen, the ghost story can serve to be a moral conversion narrative that spiritually resurrects the antisocial to the life of good Victorian subjectivity. The ghost becomes a subject drawn into the emergent secularism of the Victorian age, and as many of the stories covered here have shown, the ghost can be a source of religious consolation or a phenomenon which draws one into both scientific and religious discourses as a liminal phenomenon which exists between those two fields. As

---

[34] Ibid., 126.
[35] Ibid., 126–7.
[36] Ibid., 128.
[37] Ibid., 131.

the ghost story proliferates, its religious elements and the supernatural seem to come into conflict, as to be a religious believer becomes something which is antithetical to the supernatural. However, as the final text covered shows, the tensions between scientific-materialist explanations of the supernatural and the religious understandings of it are not necessarily in conflict and can, in fact, be brought together by religiously engaged writers. As Zoë Lehmann Imfeld points out at the end of their study on the Victorian ghost story, 'the supernatural tale provides a space in which the non-theological reader can participate in the theological journey'.[38] Reading the ghost is to be reminded of the uncertainty, ambiguity and strangeness of the world – its sheer excess of meaning to which we, as theological readers, are invited to respond, even now generations after the texts were first published.

---

[38] Imfeld, *The Victorian Ghost Story*, 167.

5

The limitations of materialism

Fin-de-siècle Gothic, sin and subjectivity and the insufficiency of degeneration

The period of the fin-de-siècle is often theorized through a broad set of materialist non-theological discourses and critical practices classified as 'degeneration theory'.[1] This opening section will outline degeneration theory and the challenge it poses to theology before offering, in response, a theological reading of the fin-de-siècle Gothic. In brief, the common critical position is that in an era of ever-increasing technological sophistication, profound scientific successes, powerful British imperialism and the epistemic impact of works such as Darwin's *On the Origin of Species* (1859), *The Descent of Man and Selection in Relation to Sex* (1871), a more generally secular society emerged, and this secularism exerted a concomitant impact on cultural works. Crucially for the Gothic, within Darwinian thought was 'the spectre of its own inversion'[2] – not an evolution towards greater sophistication but rather a degeneration or biological reversion. As Edwin Ray Lankester's *Degeneration: A Chapter in Darwinism* (1880) argues, Darwinian natural selection had within it the potential to produce 'a gradual change in the structure in which the organism becomes adapted to less varied conditions of life'.[3] Lankester goes on to claim that this biological process could be seen in humanity as, for example, 'an active healthy man sometimes degenerates when possessed of the riches of the ancient world'.[4] A lack of moral behaviour, and even crime, could be explained in biological and strictly non-theological

---

[1] An exhaustive list is, due to space, impossible, but key studies include Hurley, *The Gothic Body*, as well as Andrew Smith, *Victorian Demons: Medicine, Masculinity and the Gothic at the Fin-De-Siècle* (Manchester: Manchester University Press, 2004), plus Kirsten MacLeod, *Fictions of British Decadence, High Art, Popular Writing and the fin-de-siècle* (London: Palgrave, 2006).
[2] Stephen Karschay, *Degeneration, Normativity and the Gothic at the Fin De Siècle* (London: Palgrave, 2015), 30.
[3] Edwin Ray Lankester, *Degeneration: A Chapter in Darwinism* (London: W.W. Norton, 1880), 32.
[4] Ibid.

terms.⁵ This was expanded in the work of criminal anthropologists such as Cesare Lombroso, who became famous for his theories of the born criminal, a figure explained by Kelly Hurley as someone

> Whose innate propensity for criminal behaviours could be explained by his atavism, or reversion to now latent characteristics that had been dominant in some earlier moment of the species-history.⁶

Thus, biological determinism becomes linked to ontology as the understanding of the nature of the human subject becomes framed in strictly non-theological terminology – theological concepts are perceived as increasingly superfluous – persisting in language but becoming increasingly emptied of content. Alternatively, where appropriate, theological language was simply mapped onto the emerging scientific discourses.⁷ Instead, in the fin-de-siècle, subjectivity becomes shaped by 'mere instruments of some ulterior, altogether impersonal evolution'.⁸ Existence, rather than operating on the divine preordination of God and heading towards a specific teleological end, was instead dictated by strictly materialist ideas of evolution and progress. Thus, the theological becomes either usurped by new rationalist ideas of human advancement or, in other cases, these discourses of evolution and progress form a kind of materialist theology – the transcendent, non-materialist ideas of Christian theology have been removed and replaced with materialist, scientific ideas. However, despite the ostensible secularity of the fin-de-siècle, the discourses of evolution and degeneration still retain theological notions of a specific end for humanity and the dangers of a possible fall into a state somehow below the level of human. This is true even if this is framed in the context of biology rather than theology – there is a kind of theological logic still at work even within the ostensible secular and scientific theories. This persistent theological presence goes some way in contributing to the consistency of religious belief at the time. As Owen Chadwick has argued in *The Secularisation of the European Mind in the Nineteenth Century*,

---

⁵ The extent of this shift can be seen when contrasted with the position of earlier thinkers such as Jeremy Bentham who argued in *The Principles of Morals and Legislation* (1781) that criminal action was the result of conscious motivation, based in the exercise of free will rather than any kind of biological predisposition.
⁶ Hurley, *The Gothic Body*, 92–3.
⁷ Simon Marsden makes a similar argument in his essay 'Nothing moved. Nothing was Seen, and Nothing was heard and nothing happened: Evil, Privation and the Absent *Logos* in Richard Marsh's *The Beetle*', *Gothic Studies*, 19.1 (May 2017): 57–72.
⁸ Terry Eagleton, 'The Flight to the Real', in *Cultural Politics at the Fin-de-siècle*, ed. Sally Ledger and Scott McCracken (Cambridge: Cambridge University Press, 1995), 16.

secularism, while an unsettling force for the church through the century, was not necessarily a negative issue for mainstream Christianity, with many religious figures arguing for a secular public and political sphere as a means for securing greater religious freedoms and opportunities for proselytizing.[9] Furthermore, as the work of Callum Brown shows, an increasingly secular society was not evidence of a marked decline in religious involvement – rather, the population growth in urban centres was coupled with an increased and sustained effort at evangelization.[10] As opposed to secularity or even science or the scientific method, the far more profound issue for Christian theology at the time was the broader issue of materialism. The work of Darwin, and to a greater extent that of popular Darwinian polemicists such as Thomas Huxley, provoked a stern challenge to theology,[11] proposing not just a scientific but a strictly materialist understanding of the world. As Huxley argued throughout *Evolution and Ethics: Delivered in the Sheldonian Theatre, May 18, 1893*, there was no conflict between evolutionary materialism and ethical judgements. Furthermore, his essay 'On the Physical Basis of Life' (1868) argued that 'the materialistic terminology is in every way to be preferred' and that any alternative, theological understanding of the world 'is utterly barren, and leads to nothing but obscurity and confusion of ideas'.[12] Unsurprisingly as a result, theologians increasingly turned to advancing the arguments of 'natural' theology, building upon earlier work from figures like William Paley, relying on reason and observations of the natural world to construct arguments about God.[13] With the undeniable cultural impact that discourses of degeneration had, Gothic narratives of the supernatural also

---

[9] Chadwick, *The Secularization of the European Mind in the Nineteenth Century*. As a side note, Shadi Hamid argues that Christianity could adapt to changing societal values as its founders never articulated a specific political vision for the organization of society and thus the faith was capable of shifting its relationship to the state in an era of secularization. In Augustinian terms, Christianity always saw the City of God as distinct and in many ways, separate from the City of Man. See Shadi Hamid, *Islamic Exceptionalism: How the Struggle over Islam Is Reshaping the World* (London: St Martin's Press, 2016).

[10] Brown, *The Death of Christian Britain*, 35–57.

[11] For an exploration of the impact of Darwinian thought on Christian theology, see James R. Moore, *The Post-Darwinian Controversies: A Study of the Protestant Struggle to Come to Terms with Darwin, 1870-1900* (Cambridge: Cambridge University Press, 1979).

[12] T. H. Huxley, 'On the Physical Basis of Life', http://aleph0.clarku.edu/huxley/CE1/PhysB.html, first accessed 14 February 2017.

[13] The Gifford Lectures, still one of the preeminent lecture series on Natural Theology in the world, first began in the period (from 1888) and were established by a bequest in the will of the Scottish jurist, Lord Adam Gifford. The Gifford bequest makes allowance for a series of public lectures on Natural theology and specifically asks that the lectures 'treat their subject as a strictly natural science . . . without reference to or reliance upon any supposed special exceptional or so-called miraculous revelation'. See http://www.giffordlectures.org/lord-gifford/willfirst accessed 14 February 2017.

increasingly reflected a more materialist understanding of phenomena.[14] Critics claim that as a result, the Gothic text becomes concerned with the condition of the subject framed in materialist terms often focused through the discourses of Darwinian evolution, criminology or anthropology. Kelly Hurley's landmark work *The Gothic Body* proposes that the fin-de-siècle Gothic enacts, almost obsessively, the 'ruination of the subject' replacing it with an 'abhuman' figure,[15] symptomatic of a broader metaphysical estrangement. Stephen Karschay follows Hurley's lead and links the Gothic fin-de-siècle more explicitly to the work of Nordau and Lombroso,[16] tracing the various disciplinary procedures at work, be they criminological, sociological and medical that sought to contain and police these degenerate figures.[17] In contrast to these theories, Robert Mighall sees the fin-de-siècle Gothic as staging the return of history into the present upon and through the bodies of 'savages, criminals and degenerates' that threaten the civilized present.[18] For Mighall, the late nineteenth-century Gothic shows the fear of 'going native', a reversion explained by reference to the criminologists and psychiatrists of the day.[19] Mighall's concern is instructive for contextualizing the fin-de-siècle Gothic and its criticism, highlighting a connection between the degeneration theory of Lombroso and the imperialism of the British Empire, which constructed a feared Other out of not just the degenerate criminal underclass but also the so-called 'lower races'[20] that the empire must civilize and bring to humanity. Stephen Arata notes that, just as with Lankester quoted earlier, the idea of degeneration serves as a kind of fin-de-siècle 'common-sense' (in the Gramscian understanding of the term) that 'mapped onto older paradigms of decline and fall from the Old Testament',[21] removing the need for theology in exploring the state of man in the present moment. Knight and Mason go further, arguing that by the time of *Jekyll and Hyde* 'religion has been translated

---

[14] Knight and Mason explore this in the work of George Eliot and Sheridan La Fanu where encounters with the supernatural are mediated through materialist understandings of cause and effect. See Mark Knight and Emma Mason, *An Introduction to Nineteenth Century Literature and Religion* (Oxford: Oxford University Press, 2007), 158–61.
[15] See Hurley, *The Gothic Body*, 1–2.
[16] See Max Nordau, *Degeneration* (New York: Appleton & Co, 1895) and Cesare Lombroso, *Crime, Its Causes and Remedies* (Boston: Little Brown and Company, 1899/1911).
[17] See Karschay, *Degeneration*, particularly the Introduction.
[18] See Mighall, *A Geography of Victorian Gothic Fiction: Mapping History's Nightmares*, (Oxford: Oxford University Press, 1999) both the Introduction and Chapter One.
[19] See Mighall, *A Geography of Victorian Gothic*, 139.
[20] See Hurley, *The Gothic Body*, 94.
[21] Arata, *Fictions of Loss*, 3.

into a veneer of bourgeois respectability that can no longer offer a meaningful distinction between the morality of Jekyll and his alter ego'.[22]

However, close reading of the Gothic texts of the period reveals profound, albeit marginalized and often latent, theological anxieties even in this era of scientific materialism. Drawing on a triptych of novels from the era, *The Picture of Dorian Gray* (1890), *The Strange Case of Dr. Jekyll and Mr. Hyde* (1886) and *Dracula* (1897), this section will argue that theological understandings of subjectivity, sin and evil offer new ways of conceptualizing issues of degeneration and decadence that expand the critical field and offer greater depth to Gothic studies and its approach to the fin-de-siècle text. Throughout these texts, I argue, there is a vacillation or movement between the fear of that which lies beyond the boundaries of accepted knowledge and at the same time a desire, driven by new discoveries, constantly to violate and redefine the limits of the 'acceptable'.[23] Jekyll's interest in transcendent medicine, Gray's desire for the height of aesthetic experience and the deviance of Dracula all demonstrate, to some degree, awareness of this vacillation between acceptability and the violation of normative boundaries. As Glennis Byron writes, 'as concerns about national, social and psychic decay began to multiply in late Victorian Britain, so Gothic monstrosity re-emerged'.[24] Yet, to consider these concerns without examining the theological discourses that inform them significantly reduces critical understanding of the scope and power of the narratives in question. While the scientific and materialist discourses of Huxley, Darwin and Lombroso detailed earlier were all undoubtedly influential and critically productive, the underlying questions regarding the status of humanity, the nature of morality and the ethical or moral norms of a cultural moment are all deeply informed by theological discourses and are thus productive sites of theological and critical inquiry. The fin-de-siècle Gothic text refuses to foreclose the theological nature of the fear of the time, while at the same time serving to highlight the necessary, painful and often impossible task of cultural, societal and individual change – what in theological terms is known as repentance. The theological scope of the fin-de-siècle Gothic is thus, like the texts themselves, constantly held in tension between multiple discursive positions: between the possibility of change and renewal and the possibility of falling into sin and corruption. Whatever change

---

[22] Knight and Mason, *Nineteenth Century Literature and Religion*, 176.
[23] Hurley labels this ambivalence to the natural sciences as one of the key markers of the fin-de-siècle Gothic text. See Hurley, *The Gothic Body*, 18.
[24] Glennis Byron, 'Gothic in the 1890s', in *A Companion to the Gothic*, ed. David Punter (London: Blackwell, 2000), 132.

may come can never be embraced as wholly positive – the transformations of the Gothic while undeniably new, are also horrifying. Just as with Darwinian natural selection, within every change is the threat or possibility of a degeneration or fall into something less than human. Rather than progress or perfectibility, change threatens to emerge as disaster – a regression destructive to both body and soul. In a cultural moment of increasing secularity, wherein the language of theology had been replaced by more evolutionary and criminological discourses, evil increasingly becomes something which culture lacks the appropriate vocabulary to describe. As Rowan Williams argues, 'secularism, as the necessary companion of modernity leaves us . . . [conceptually] bereaved; we are vulnerable because we have no way of making sense of the most deeply threatening elements of our environment'.[25] The fin-de-siècle Gothic embodies this impoverishment of language, resorting to the discourses of degeneration and corruption as moral language becomes emptied of theological content. Thus, a theological reading of these novels not just articulates the thematic content of the texts individually but serves to highlight something of the broader cultural moment – namely this sense of an inability to articulate evil as something other than a 'trivially emotive way of referring to what we hate or fear or just disapprove of'.[26] The fin-de-siècle Gothic is not just a collection of cultural and material anxieties around degeneration but rather serves to illustrate a moment where new secular discourses are revealed to be insufficient in describing metaphysical and horrific encounters.

Jekyll and Hyde – the law and the divided self: Fractured subjectivity and theology

Of the three novels under consideration, Stevenson's *Jekyll and Hyde* is most overtly concerned with scientific discourses, taking as its main character a medical doctor and scientist. The text follows a model of middle-class, bourgeois professional respectability in the figure of Dr Henry Jekyll, who through various chemical experiments manages to create a draught that allows him to take on the identity of the repulsive Mr Hyde and indulge in various immoral or hedonistic behaviours. Hyde's appearance, in contrast to that of the eminently well-thought-of Jekyll, is

---

[25] Williams, *Faith in the Public Square*, 11.
[26] Ibid.

'hardly human . . . something troglodytic',[27] and thus much criticism has focused upon physiognomic or racial and Darwinian discourses and the role class may play in the reading and construction of criminality.[28] Arata frames Hyde as embodying middle-class fear – the fears of both a criminal lower class and horror at the idle aristocracy that in the age of industrial revolution has fallen into the very worst kind of slothful corruption.[29] Of greater interest here, however, the critical prominence given to the division between Jekyll and Hyde and the subsequent discursive focus on categorizing and classifying Hyde's nature is the role of the divided self. The idea of a divided self is anathema to discourses of degeneration which would seek to explain subjectivity in terms of biology or evolution, yet the idea of a fractured or otherwise divided self is familiar and productive ground for the Christian theological tradition.[30] In the section of the text where Jekyll finally contributes directly to the narrative, from the opening, the presentation of subjectivity is clearly divided – a division which Jekyll himself seeks to minimize. While the 'worst of his [Jekyll's] faults' is presented as nothing more than a 'certain impatient gaiety of disposition' these run into conflict with his 'imperious desire to carry my head high'[31] – a desire perfectly in keeping with his public personae. As explored earlier (see Chapter 2) this stark division between the appearance of things and the spiritual reality that is unseen is a theme common to a certain tradition of Christian theology to which Gothic writing has repeatedly alluded to and found to be a productive source of cultural fear.[32] The split between what is seen and what is unseen (what in the broadly Calvinist tradition might be phrased as the spiritual vs. the flesh) lends itself, without much difficulty, to Jekyll's moral division.

> Many a man would have even blazoned such irregularities as I was guilty of; but from the high views I had set before me, I regarded them and hid them with an almost morbid sense of shame.[33]

---

[27] Robert Louis Stevenson, *Dr Jekyll and Mr Hyde and Other Stories* (London: Penguin Classics, 1979), 40.
[28] See Arata, *Fictions of Loss*, 33–4 as well as Stephen Karschay, *Degeneration, Normativity and the Gothic at the Fin De Siècle*, (London: Palgrave, 2015) 89–91, plus Julia Reid, *Robert Louis Stevenson: Science and the fin-de-siècle* (London: Palgrave, 2006).
[29] Arata, *Fictions of Loss*, 36.
[30] It has been a part of Christian thought throughout Scripture but gains the fullest articulation in the work of the apostle Paul. The nature of man (in the light of the revelation of Jesus Christ) was a recurring theme throughout early thought too – see particularly St Augustine's *Confessions of a Sinner*, trans. R. S. Pine-Coffin (London: Penguin Great Ideas, 2004).
[31] R. L. Stevenson, *Jekyll and Hyde*, 81.
[32] Particularly Calvinist discourses, which Stevenson was well acquainted with thanks to the influence of his nanny. See Jenni Calder, *RLS: Life Study of Robert Louis Stevenson* (London: Chambers, 1990).
[33] R. L. Stevenson, *Jekyll and Hyde*, 81.

Yet despite the use of the word 'shame' Jekyll goes on to claim that he is 'in no sense a hypocrite,'[34] but, rather, views both sides of his personality and their actions with complete sincerity. There is no lack of genuine feeling, either when Jekyll indulges his vices or practises his more respected virtues, indeed Jekyll goes so far as to practise and refine his doubled lifestyle. Thus, much critical work has been done exploring the nature of the connection between Hyde and Jekyll. Arata argues that Hyde is no anomaly but rather the very essence of bourgeoisie masculine behaviour.[35] However, even as Arata identifies the class discourses and latent misogyny that permeate this novel of professional men, and while this certainly serves to indict a certain presentation of middle-class professionalized bourgeois masculinity, this point does not necessarily approach the divide in subjectivity that Jekyll establishes as being foundational to his own sense of self. Arata's class analysis is essentialized to the level of ontology here, equating social standing with being. Whereas Lombroso equated biology with ontology, Arata makes the same mistake with class position. Rather than functioning as a social construct from a particular set of historical and material conditions, Jekyll's class position is claimed as the determining factor in his ontological status. Furthermore, this argument also relies upon ignoring or eliding the scope of theological language in the novel, claiming that language is, in the last instance, a marker of a certain class position, rather than demonstrating anything else. Rather than merely dismiss theological language as a sign of a class signification, theology must be engaged with upon its own terms.

Jekyll's admission of his own fundamentally divided nature, between the immoral and respectable sides of himself, coupled with the use of the term 'shame' and his secrecy throughout the text does challenge his own claim that he was in no way acting hypocritically. Despite the stated belief in his own integrity, the linguistic choices throughout the novel bespeak of an awareness of a normative ethical standard and his own violation thereof. He details certain 'indiscretions' in his youth, and furthermore, Jekyll is ostracized from much of the company he would normally keep further reinforcing the impression of the generalized ethical norm he has in some sense transgressed. From the opening of the novel, Jekyll is perceived by others as the very 'pink of proprieties'.[36] Yet Jekyll himself is glaringly absent from the opening of the text – the reader is left with the words and impression of other characters but little by way of direct interaction. He

---

[34] Ibid.
[35] See Arata, *Fictions of Loss*, 33–54.
[36] R. L. Stevenson, *Jekyll and Hyde*, 33.

becomes, therefore, the cause of, or catalyst for the plot through the traces that he has left behind – the most important of these traces being the will delivered to Mr Utterson, by which Jekyll's secret relationship with Hyde is exposed.[37] Utterson's first encounter with the mysterious Hyde is much quoted in criticism of the novel for the reference to Hyde's troglodytic appearance – Hyde becomes a figure for the concerns of atavism and degeneration thanks to the condition of his material body.[38] Yet what the degeneration critics miss is the fact that Utterson goes on to reference Hyde's appearance with theological language as well as the language of animalistic degeneration. Hyde's appearance is described as 'the radiance of a foul soul that thus transpires through, and transfigures its clay continent'.[39] The implication here is perfectly clear – exposure to Hyde's physical form is only a foretaste of the potential spiritual corruption that can be exerted upon those such as Jekyll. Furthermore, Utterson raises the possibility that Jekyll has, spiritually speaking, placed himself in danger, as Hyde's face bears 'Satan's signature' upon it,[40] and he is concerned that the presence of Hyde in Jekyll's life is explained through 'the ghost of some old sin'.[41] Here Utterson deploys theological language but it seems disconnected from any question of theological belief. Neither Utterson nor Jekyll exhibits any sincere religious commitment in thought or action. Utterson admits that he sees no need for religious belief to influence the behaviour of those he knows, preferring to 'let my brother go the devil in his own way'.[42] The theologically inflected language of sin and the devil he uses, has therefore been emptied of any theological referent, coming to stand in for ideas around class position, propriety and public respectability.[43] Utterson's use of this language suggests therefore that, at the end of the nineteenth century, not only does theological language now refer to a somewhat poorly defined moral ideal, but that there is no viable non-materialist language provided by the secular discourses the characters inhabit that would adequately encompass figures like Hyde. This brief aside on Utterson's part evidences the broader point made by Williams in *Faith in the Public Square* – Utterson is left conceptually

---

[37] The relationship between lawyer and client seems analogous to the secrecy and confidentiality of the confessional – one can imagine a more 'Catholic' writer could have written a similar tale with a priest in the role of discoverer.
[38] Discussed at length in Hurley, *The Gothic Body* (1996) and Arata, *Fictions of Loss*.
[39] R. L. Stevenson, *Jekyll and Hyde*, 40.
[40] Ibid.
[41] Ibid., 41.
[42] Ibid., 29.
[43] In a sense, this can be seen as a consequence of the theological/religious tension that so preoccupied Emily Brontë – for more on this, see Chapter 3.

impoverished by fin-de-siècle secular materialism and thus reaches back to a language of theology despite no longer professing any sincere theological commitment but merely the appearance of respectability.

While Jekyll may well indulge both sides of his nature, the terms in which this is presented reflect an awareness that his behaviour is in some sense, running contrary to the commonly accepted or normative moral standards within which he exists. His colleagues refuse to associate with him, because of his 'scientific heresy' and fondness for 'unscientific balderdash'.[44] The link here to *Frankenstein* is instructive, as while Victor Frankenstein was fascinated with the idea of overcoming death, Henry Jekyll is most concerned with overcoming the societal expectations that would shame him for his apparent moral failures. As a medical man, he is isolated from not just the material realities of a scientific community but whatever normative ethics might govern the practice of medical science against which he deliberately pushes in order to advance knowledge. Furthermore, the very first moment that he appears in the novel he is described as having 'something of a slyish cast'[45] about his appearance. Given the cultural impact of evolutionary and physiognomic discourses, this implies a certain degree of disingenuousness despite his class status and his treatment by others in the novel. However, the implication here should not be that Jekyll is personally responsible for this duplicity, but rather this hypocritical division of self is one produced by wider discourses. The scientific desire to push the boundaries of knowledge forms part of the normative standard of medical science, while scientific materialism (that to which Jekyll has devoted his life) lacks the power of moral or theological ideas to explain his moral propensity for 'duplicity'. It is this which encourages Jekyll's interests in the transcendent while at the same time viewing him with suspicion and doubt. The monstrosity of Hyde is not, therefore, a case of an individual's moral failing but rather a product of the operation of the materialist discourses of the fin-de-siècle. Hyde is not a monstrous presence that has come to disturb the genteel Jekyll; there is, in fact, no split or divide between the two on the level of ontology despite the critical attempts to divide the two, rather it is Jekyll himself who is the monster of the text.

Operating and existing in two separate spheres of life, Jekyll's division of his own self shares much in common with the Apostle Paul's description of a self divided between both moral and sinful activities or, in alternative phrasing,

---

[44] R. L. Stevenson, *Jekyll and Hyde*, 43, 36.
[45] Ibid., 43.

between the law and the flesh. In the Epistle to the Romans, Paul expands upon the nature of human subjectivity:

> For we know that the law is spiritual; but I am of the flesh, sold into slavery under sin. I do not understand my own actions. For I do not do what I want but I do the very thing I hate. Now if I do what I do not want I agree that the law is good. But in fact, it is no longer I that do it, but sin that dwells within me. For I know that nothing good dwells within me, that is, in my flesh. I can will what is right, but I cannot do it. For I do not do the good I want, but the evil I do not want is what I do.[46]

Stevenson's novella provides a secularized version of Paul's writing. In the work of Paul, the Law of God is perfect in its ability to reveal the fallen-ness of man – as Paul argues his knowledge of the sinful nature of his actions is revealed through the law. The Law of God reveals the actions of man to be what they are, and thus perfectly justifies divine judgement and the necessity of grace in the salvation of mankind. The law is for Paul the very basis of our shared condition of ontological sinfulness and is thus the basis of solidarity. If all have sinned, all are in need of salvation.[47] On the other hand, in *Jekyll and Hyde* there can be no such solidarity. Jekyll draws his knowledge of the nature of his own actions not from the law but from the public opinion and the potential for scandal that could emerge. Whereby in scripture, Paul's understanding of his actions leads to his realization of his dependence upon grace for redemption, Jekyll's realization of his actions leads to secrecy – to confess for Jekyll would not bring salvation but ultimately would only bring disaster. Furthermore, in this section of the Epistle, Paul frames in similar terms a comparable dilemma that is mentioned by Jekyll in his 'full account' section of the narrative but renders explicit what the degeneration theorists, referred to earlier, have left as merely implicit. Namely, it is a mistake to consider Jekyll and Hyde as separate or discrete individuals. Using sociological, criminological or evolutionary discourses that split the subjectivity of Jekyll away from Hyde inevitably allows for historicizing and materialist criticism.[48] However, the consequences of such a move whether intentional or not, is to fundamentally alter the ways in which ontology is understood as being

---

[46] See Rom. 7:14–19.
[47] For an excellent summary of this idea and its implications see Alan Jacobs, *Original Sin: A Cultural History* (London: Harper Collins, 2008).
[48] This is a common critical trend which emerges from the 'Victorian impulse toward scientific classification and a subsequent normalization of the possibilities - bodily, subjective, sexual - of human identity' (Hurley, *The Gothic Body*, 8). An excellent example of which is Richard von Krafft-Ebing's *Psychopathia Sexualis* (1886). In more modern criticism these materialist works are used as

presented within the text. To treat Jekyll and Hyde separately, as taxonomic categories that allow for insight into the anxieties of the age, effectively renders Jekyll as merely half – a subject rendered deficient by the intrusion of Hyde, or alternatively a subject that has become problematically corrupted by the arrival of Hyde's presence into consciousness. Throughout the novel, the correlations and areas of connection between Jekyll and Hyde are striking. Jekyll himself admits to Utterson that despite his own apparent reluctance to discuss the issue, he has 'a very great interest in Hyde',[49] a loaded reference to the fondness for duplicity that Jekyll claims has marked his life. Hyde also has huge freedom in Jekyll's home – with Jekyll giving explicit orders to servants and staff that Hyde is to be obeyed just as they do for Jekyll.[50] Furthermore, in the wake of the vicious murder of Danvers Carew, Hyde's murder weapon is discovered to be Jekyll's possession – given to Jekyll by Utterson himself.[51] When Hyde is eventually tracked down, the separation between Hyde and Jekyll becomes even more difficult to maintain. Despite residing in a particularly dingy quarter of Soho, the rooms Hyde rents are 'furnished in luxury and good taste', along the same lines of fashion enjoyed by Henry Jekyll.[52] For as has been already pointed out, Hyde is not some sort of supplement or add-on to Jekyll's moral self but is rather a product of the moral discourses that have informed the construction of this apparent model of moral respectability. Hyde is, quite literally therefore, an externalization and embodiment of the moral failings and tensions within Jekyll's own subjectivity. Rather than attempt to wrestle with any kind of theological introspection, an example of which is provided by Paul in the letter to the Romans,[53] Jekyll uses the tools of fin-de-siècle modernity to attempt to solve the problem once and for all. Rather than grapple with the tension of both law and flesh (to phrase the issue in Pauline terms) Jekyll simply prefers to forcibly externalize the tensions and moral failings which go so far in defining the nature of subjectivity. What is important to emphasize here is that there is no divided self – only a singular self, torn between the law and the desires of the flesh, or rather between the

---

the means to read the Gothic text – for examples Karschay uses Nordeau and Krafft-Ebing to read the works of Oscar Wilde. See Karschay, *Fictions of Loss* (2015), 71–84.

[49] R. L. Stevenson, *Jekyll and Hyde*, 44.
[50] Ibid., 41. For more on the spatial aspects of the novel see Linda Dryden, *The Modern Gothic and Literary Doubles: Stevenson, Wilde and Wells* (Cambridge: Cambridge University Press, 2003), particularly, 102–8.
[51] R. L. Stevenson, *Jekyll and Hyde*, 47–8.
[52] Ibid., 49.
[53] See Rom. 6–7 particularly 7:24, 'Wretched man that I am! Who will rescue me from this body of death?'

strictures of public opinion and personal morality. Thus, Jekyll is left riven by the need to aspire to 'exacting aspirations' while simultaneously being guilty of a 'profound duplicity of life'.[54] This duplicity of self is maintained not only through his actions but also through the lack of a theological vocabulary that allows him to articulate both wrongdoing and confession more generally.

Despite the constant references to the scientific and medical throughout the novel, the problem of the self is most clearly stated in theological terms. Jekyll wistfully wonders if each side of his self 'could but be housed in separate identities' as such a split would allow for his good half to proceed through life without further spiritual endangerment or moral trouble. Despite the critical notion of such desires being linked to evolutionary, sociological or criminological concerns, Jekyll frames it in the language of theology and salvation:

> The unjust might go his way, delivered from the aspirations and remorse of his more upright twin; and the just could walk steadfastly and securely, on his upward path, doing the good things in which he found his pleasure, and no longer exposed to disgrace and penitence by the hands of this extraneous evil.[55]

The scriptural allusions here are to the images of divine judgement – specifically ones mentioned in the Gospel of Matthew – the broad and narrow way of Mt. 7:13 as well as the division of the sheep and goats from Mt. 25: 31-46. Here Jekyll divides the world into the just and unjust, placing himself in the position of God. Even the arch historicist Robert Mighall acknowledges the signification of the 'theological path of righteousness and the notion of social betterment'[56] that the passage reflects. With this in mind, and given the comparison to the section of Romans, Jekyll's experiments function as an attempt to solve the theological dilemma experienced by Paul through the application of medico-scientific means. The eventual catastrophic failure of Jekyll's endeavour thus attains greater significance, as Stevenson's novel suggests that the application of these medical and scientific discourses could *never* satisfactorily contain or defeat Hyde. The externalization or splitting of subjectivity through the discourses of medical authority and modern science is doomed to fail in their quest to resolve the dilemma expressed in Rom. 7 and is heightened in Stevenson's novella. By framing Hyde in terms of evolution, criminology or biology, subjectivity is externalized once more. The common critical stance on the fin-de-siècle Gothic,

---

[54] R. L. Stevenson, *Jekyll and Hyde*, 81.
[55] Ibid., 82.
[56] Mighall, *A Geography of Victorian Gothic Fiction: Mapping History's Nightmares*, 147.

can only frame Hyde as a lingering problem that could or should be solved – the failure to do so being the true cause of the anxiety which gives rise to Stevenson's text. Thus, treating Hyde as an evolutionary, biomedical or criminological anxiety only risks repeating the doomed endeavour of Henry Jekyll himself – namely attempting to solve through historicist or scientific discourses what is, at root, a more metaphysical issue.[57] In effect, the realities of human nature ensure that all have the capacity for committing harm and a theological understanding of sin as intrinsic to human nature is not only necessary but allows for a broad solidarity between individuals.[58] A theologically inflected reading of the novel sees the split between the two as a concretizing of a pre-existing issue in the construction of subjectivity while problematizing the concept of evil. Furthermore, it is a theological reading that allows for an answer to the question posed by critics such as Hogle, who asks that 'surely we must wonder . . . why he [Jekyll] feels impelled to follow this course?'[59] Simply put, Hyde is an embodiment of the fallen condition that affects all people regardless of the scientific discourses of which he is ostensibly a product.

Furthermore, Hyde is consistently framed in terms that present him as both simultaneously human and less than human, he gives an 'impression of deformity without any malformation',[60] as Utterson expresses it after their first meeting, and this is reinforced through the references to his ape-like appearance and gnome-like stature. He is throughout the novel both present and absent – a recurrent figure often only partly glimpsed, hiding in doorways or skulking through the most dangerous and depraved parts of London.[61] As Zoë Lehmann Imfeld expresses it, 'the ghost-story demon is given its horror because it cannot be . . . it is at once impossible and recognisable'.[62] Hyde is both ontologically lacking and somehow perverse, and thus can be read within Augustinian terms. The two foundational premises which the Augustine argument rests upon are

---

[57] As Reid articulates it, 'Stevenson attributes degeneration to modernity's attempts to stifle the savage elements which have survived in the modern psyche'. Yet despite this insight, the metaphysical implications are not engaged with, remaining as a purely psychological insight ignoring the theological language of the novel and the long history of theological engagement with precisely this point. See Reid, *Robert Louis Stevenson: Science and the fin-de-siècle*, 98.

[58] Once again, see Jacobs, *Original Sin*.

[59] Jerrold E. Hogle, 'The Struggle for a Dichotomy: Abjection in Jekyll and His Interpreters', in *Dr Jekyll and Mr. Hyde after One Hundred Years*, ed. William Veeder and Gordon Hirsch (Chicago: Chicago University Press, 1988), 161.

[60] R. L. Stevenson, *Jekyll and Hyde*, 40.

[61] Utterson's tongue in cheek remark that 'if he shall be Mr. Hyde, I shall be Mr. Seek' highlighting the extent to which Hyde remains ontologically speaking, rather difficult to pin down.

[62] Imfeld, *The Victorian Ghost Story*, 29.

first an ontological *lack* – there is something missing from Hyde which, while some may be unable to clearly articulate, those who come across him seem very aware of. Evil is best understood not as an existing thing but rather as an absence – a privation of something that should in ordinary circumstances, be present.[63] Second, Augustine's theory of evil extrapolates an anthropological conclusion for the human subject from this first premise – namely evil involves a *perversion* of the Imago Dei in its effects upon the individual.[64] Throughout the novel, Hyde is described in these terms, as somehow less than human, smaller and more animalistic than the urbane Jekyll. Despite this, upon describing Hyde's appearance on his first discovery of the shift between these two aspects of his subjectivity, Jekyll mentions Hyde's stunted nature and troglodytic appearance as being nothing like his own. However, gazing at Hyde's reflection in the mirror he is 'conscious of no repugnance', for '*this too was myself*'[65] (my emphasis). Despite the descriptive markers that externalize Hyde and attempt to establish a clear separation between him and Jekyll, this moment of self-revelation adds credence to understanding Hyde as expressing the perversion and privation of Jekyll's ontology; a theological disaster framed in scientific terms. The two figures are not separable but rather serve as an exposition on the nature of man's ontological flaws.

The text itself provides much evidence for this understanding of Jekyll and Hyde's complex intertwining as being a theological issue that has been understood in materialist terms, namely degeneration theory. What this suggests is that the writing on degeneration carries within it an under-acknowledged theological logic (particularly in contemporary criticism which seeks to make use of writers such as Nordau). Nordau himself writes that a key marker of degeneration is, 'the being constantly occupied with mystical and religious questions, an exaggerated piety etc.'.[66] Such a point seems to hold for Henry Jekyll as after the murder of Sir Danvers Carew, Hyde disappears and 'a new life began for Dr Jekyll'.[67] This life entails not just a reconnection with friends but piety too, for as the novella explains, 'while he had always been known for charities, he was now no less distinguished for religion'.[68] Sadly, such a pattern of repentance and

---

[63] For an example of how privation theory may interact with literary work, see Mark Knight, *Chesterton and Evil* (New York: Fordham University Press, 2004).
[64] For perhaps the finest introduction to the Augustinian approach and the contemporary merits of the argument, see Mathewes, *Evil and the Augustinian Tradition*.
[65] R. L. Stevenson, *Jekyll and Hyde*, 84.
[66] Nordau, *Degeneration*, 22.
[67] R. L. Stevenson, *Jekyll and Hyde*, 56.
[68] Ibid.

charity proves unsustainable. As a result, one of Jekyll's few friends, the more scientifically and medically orthodox Dr Lanyon sustains a fatal shock – the issue that causes it is 'accursed' and when pressed, Lanyon begs 'in God's name, go, for I cannot bear it'.[69] The shock Lanyon suffers is not just the discovery of the true nature of the connection between Jekyll and Hyde but also the failure of normative medico-scientific discourses to provide a satisfactory response to the fracture in subjectivity that Jekyll's work has, quite literally, made flesh. What ultimately kills Lanyon is not the discovery of Hyde and Jekyll as one person, but rather the truth that within him there are the same fractures, moral failing and depravities as reside within Henry Jekyll. In effect, the materialist procedures by which degeneration and depravity are safely taxonomized and externalized are revealed to be insufficient. As is revealed later in the text within Lanyon's own record of events, he observes the connection between Jekyll and Hyde not in the coolly dispassionate language of medical science but rather in a state of religious inflected terror. He is warned by Hyde that his 'sight will be blasted by a prodigy to stagger the unbelief of Satan'.[70] Despite Lanyon's retort that he hears 'with no very strong impression of belief', he consents to stay and witness the transmutation of Hyde into Jekyll:

> He put the glass to his lips and drank at one gulp . . . and as I looked, there came, I thought a change – he seemed to swell – his face became suddenly black, and the features seemed to melt and alter . . . and at the next moment I had sprung to my feet and leaped back against the wall, my arm raised to shield me from that prodigy, my mind submerged in terror. O God! I Screamed, and O God! Again and again.[71]

Despite the fact that 'duality is presented in the story as both a kind of illness',[72] Lanyon's encounter, and the subsequent realizations that this experience carries, finds no other language to express itself than that of theology. His letter recording the events end with a bleak note that 'I saw what I saw, I heard what I heard and my soul sickened at it'.[73] In addition, Jekyll's take on the argument between him

---

[69] Ibid., 57.
[70] Ibid., 79.
[71] R. L. Stevenson, *Jekyll and Hyde*, 80.
[72] Colin Davis, 'From Psychopathology to Diabolical Evil: Dr Jekyll, Mr Hyde and Jean Renoir', *Journal of Romance Studies*, 12.1 (Spring 2012) http://go.galegroup.com.ezproxy.mmu.ac.uk/ps/i.do?p=AONE&u=mmucal5&id=GALE|A292992929&v=2.1&it=r&sid=summon&authCount=1#, first accessed 2 September 17.
[73] R. L. Stevenson, *Jekyll and Hyde*, 80.

and Lanyon, mentioned never directly, but in writing to Utterson again frames the issue theologically. As Jekyll speaks to Utterson,

> You must suffer me to go my own dark way. I have brought on myself a punishment and a danger that I cannot name. If I am the chief of sinners, I am the chief of sufferers also.[74]

Despite the general critical insistence upon the concretizing[75] of Hyde as a medical and scientific breakthrough, within the text the emergence of Hyde is framed as a moment of horrific theological revelation. The disingenuous Henry Jekyll goes so far as to tell the reader of his narrative that he 'will not enter deeply into this scientific branch of my confession',[76] as he recasts his scientific quest into a theologically inflected revelation of the 'doom and burthen of our life'.[77] Jekyll implicitly references scripture in his articulation of his attempt to bring forth Hyde – 'plucking back that fleshly vestment, even as a wind might toss the curtains of a pavilion'.[78] The scriptural referent here is Mt. 27:51, whereby at the moment of Christ's death the curtain that separated the Holy of Holies from the rest of the temple was not simply plucked aside but torn in two. In an echo of the crucifixion, Jekyll seeks to go beyond the limits of physical human nature, but where Christ's transcendence is both suffering and sacrificial, reuniting God with fallen mankind through the atonement of the cross, Jekyll's suffering is for reasons of ego.[79] Rather than seek to reunite God to man through substitutionary atonement, Jekyll's moment of pushing aside the veil fundamentally divides man from himself. Just as with Christ on the cross, Jekyll's first dose of the formula inflicts a 'horror of the spirit that cannot be exceeded at the hour of birth or death'.[80] Yet, as Christ rises to glory, Jekyll rises as Hyde, a figure he labels as 'alone in all the ranks of mankind', a figure of 'pure evil'.[81] The formula he discovers, Jekyll claims, is 'neither diabolical nor divine, it but shook the doors of the prison house of my disposition; and like the captives of Philippi, that which stood within

---

[74] Ibid., 58.
[75] I hesitate to use terms such as 'the creation of Hyde' for reasons that, thanks to the previous argument, I trust to be somewhat self-evident.
[76] R. L. Stevenson, *Jekyll and Hyde*, 83.
[77] Ibid.
[78] Ibid., 82.
[79] Here Henry Jekyll can be linked to the hubris of another Gothic scientist, Victor Frankenstein, who, like Jekyll wishes to go beyond the materialist constraints of the physical world, but lacks the theological understanding to comprehend the extent of his own egoistic hubris.
[80] R. L. Stevenson, *Jekyll and Hyde*, 83.
[81] Ibid., 85.

ran forth'.[82] Yet despite the scriptural allusion here, Jekyll falls far short of the mantle of the Apostle Paul he lays claim to. Unlike Paul, Jekyll's 'virtue slumbered; my evil, kept awake by ambition, was alert and swift to seize the occasion'.[83] Once again, the text repeatedly links Hyde's rise and dominance to Jekyll's own moral or theological passivity. His fondness for undignified pleasure and an aversion to the dryness of a life of study that is required of a doctor[84] are long-standing factors that Jekyll has no metaphysical or theological resources to deal with, and thus it comes as no surprise when Jekyll describes his increasing vulnerability to Hyde as a 'falling into sin'.[85] Jekyll's lack of pious aspiration is what he blames for Hyde's ontological fallen-ness but from a man who has from his earliest memories practised both moral and theological hypocrisy and duplicity this should come as no surprise and is consistent with Jekyll's disavowal of his own moral responsibility. The final pages of Jekyll's full statement of the case go into some detail to explain Jekyll's attempts to reconcile between the disparate parts of his own subjectivity. Hyde and Jekyll become entwined in terms of their living arrangement, their class position and even their finances[86] as Jekyll goes out of his way to ensure that he 'might enter on that of Edward Hyde without pecuniary loss'.[87] What noticeably fails for Jekyll is any attempt to reform his, and Hyde's, behaviour. In the wake of the murder, Jekyll frames his actions as an act of repentance and conversion. Taking his draught, 'Henry Jekyll, with streaming tears of gratitude and remorse, had fallen upon his knees and lifted his clasped hands to God'.[88] Once more the novella refers to the veil as Jekyll's sense of self was 'rent from head-to-foot',[89] and what follows is described in terms of spiritual torment. With prayers and tears, Jekyll seeks to undo his own experimentation and reunite his subjectivity into a coherent whole through the appearance of penitence and renewed moral action. Yet, despite his recommitment to the markers of positive morality, his acts of charity and his 'labour to relieve suffering',[90] Hyde proves irresistible. As Milbank writes, Jekyll seeks to solve the division of self 'not through acceptance

---

[82] Ibid. The scriptural reference here is to Acts of the Apostles 16:16-40, where an earthquake frees the apostle Paul and Silas from a jail cell, yet despite what Jekyll claims, neither run forth, but stay where they are to save their jailer from committing suicide after losing his prisoners.
[83] R. L. Stevenson, *Jekyll and Hyde*, 85.
[84] Ibid.
[85] Ibid.
[86] For more on this, see Kirsten Guest, 'Jekyll and Hyde Inc: Limited Liability, Companification, and Gothic Subjectivity', *Victorian Literature and Culture*, 44.2 (June 2016): 315–29.
[87] R. L. Stevenson, *Jekyll and Hyde*, 86.
[88] Ibid., 91.
[89] Ibid.
[90] R. L. Stevenson, *Jekyll and Hyde*, 92.

of Christ's imputed righteousness, but by an avoidance of [genuine] penitence.'[91] After a few brief months of propriety and outwardly respectable behaviour, it was 'as an ordinary secret sinner that I at last fell before the assaults of temptation.'[92] The passage sets up a telling paired opposition between the secrecy of Jekyll's 'sin' and the public attempts at atonement. Jekyll's response to his theological blunder in concretizing aspects of his own subjectivity is revealed as woefully insufficient. The discourses of science may have motivated his initial experiments, but it is through theology that Jekyll articulates the impact that Hyde asserts. While the work of degeneration theorists has conceptualized Hyde as an abhuman subject or the re-emergence of a more barbaric past into the civilized present,[93] a theological understanding of the novella and of degeneration more generally adds greater depth to critical understanding of the text. Rather than see Hyde as an aberration or addition to subjectivity, a theological understanding of degeneration presents Hyde as an inextricable part of modern subjectivity itself. Hyde the monster is not a figure which has returned from the past, or an expression of devolved humanity – rather, the horror of the text flows from the notion that Hyde expresses an aspect of modern subjectivity that cannot be easily or safely externalized away and the discourses which have attempted this begin to fracture and break down.

In a novella so preoccupied with the scientific taxonomies of the fin-de-siècle these discursive techniques are revealed as being utterly inadequate to deal with the fundamental fracture in subjectivity detailed in Romans by Paul. At the close of the text, Jekyll, having finished the last of his scientific elixir, realizes that it is 'the last time, short of a miracle, that Henry Jekyll can think his own thoughts and see his own face.'[94] What this neglects is the reality – Jekyll is not being replaced by an external force but is simply unable to maintain a coherent subjectivity that aligns with the normative standards and discourses of his cultural moment. The techniques and discursive practices which shape his being – medical training, class position and bourgeois morality – fail to resolve this division between the different aspects of his self, and thus, by implication are revealed as insufficient on a systemic level, for not just Henry Jekyll but all. Removing a theological or metaphysical awareness from criticism and analysis of the text serves only to continue the same error that dooms Henry Jekyll.

---

[91] Milbank, 'Covenanter Gothic', 98.
[92] Ibid.
[93] See Hurley, *The Gothic Body* and Mighall, *A Geography of Victorian Gothic: Mapping Histories Nightmares* (Oxford: Oxford University Press, 1999) respectively.
[94] Stevenson, *Science and the Fin-De-Siècle*, 96.

As Fred Botting acknowledges, these scientific theories only serve to 'expose the instability of the dualities that frame cultural identity'.[95] Degeneration, understood theologically, is not simply a historical concern or the product of the barbaric past re-emerging but something inextricably bound up with the nature of human subjectivity itself. Thus, any attempt to externalize it or concretize it through the discourses of materialism, no matter how sophisticated those discourses may be, is doomed to failure.

The realization of this failure is what kills off the conventional, orthodox and religiously sceptical Dr Lanyon in a moment of sheer theological terror, but the realization contained within the text extends further still. To recognize the failure of scientific, medical or criminological discourses in dealing with evil is to recognize that Jekyll and Hyde embody the 'Christian paradox of evil as both nothing and something'.[96] Thus, with the failure of the scientific and medical discourses to safely externalize and separate Hyde from Jekyll the reader too is challenged by the ontological connection between the two figures. Stevenson's novella is not something the reader simply observes, as in the manner of a scientific exercise but becomes something that demands participation on the part of the reader. As Imfeld argues, we participate in a 'theological anthropology' through which we come to learn more not just about the ontology of Jekyll but of ourselves – an imaginative exercise, which fundamentally alters the way in which we view the self. In a letter written to a friend, Stevenson shows great awareness of the impact of this ontological paradox and its effect upon the reader in reference to another great literary exploration of evil, Fyodor Dostoyevsky's *Crime and Punishment*:

> Many find it dull: Henry James could not finish it: all I can say is, it nearly finished me. It was like having an illness. [Henry] James did not care for it because the character of Raskolnikoff was not objective; and at that I divined a great gulf between us, and on further reflection, the existence of a certain impotence in many minds of to-day, which prevents them from living in a book or character, and keeps them standing afar off, spectators to a puppet show. To such I suppose the book may seem empty in the centre; to the others it is a room, a house of life, into which they themselves may enter, and are tortured and purified.[97]

---

[95] Fred Botting, *Gothic* (London: Routledge, 1995), 91.
[96] Imfeld, *Victorian Ghost Story*, 30
[97] The letter shows that the novel exerts such an impact that Stevenson makes a mistake on the title of the novel in question. See Bradford A. Booth and Ernest Mehew, *The Letters of Robert Louis Stevenson, Volume Five, July 1884-August 1887* (London: Yale University Press, 1995), 221.

Stevenson's acknowledgement that those who participate within the horror novel as readers may find it a traumatic experience, a site of torture but also potential purification or redemption. Despite the grim end reached by Henry Jekyll, the novella still offers the potential for change, for redemption even if the experience of it is sometimes painful. This possibility, however, requires a willingness to engage and participate within the theological nature of the text, and not, as Stevenson writes, stand afar off. Despite the bleak note that Jekyll's statement ends upon, the theological framework of the novel and the metaphysical questions it provokes in its reader do offer some modicum of hope. Through participation – that necessary act of entering the 'room' that Stevenson referred to, one may move beyond degeneration. The challenge of the text is to take seriously the theological point that subjectivity cannot be easily resolved into a coherent whole within solely materialist terms.

Oscar Wilde, decadence, sin and *The Picture of Dorian Gray*

If Stevenson's novella exposes the limitations of medical or scientific discourses to adequately construct a coherent subjectivity as well as emphasizing the divide between private sinfulness and public appearance, then Wilde's novel *The Picture of Dorian Gray* (1890) presents not a failure of subjectivity but a turn inward towards narcissism – the subjective obsession with aesthetic appearance. Wilde's only novel, it details the life of a young aristocratic man known for his physical beauty who falls into vice and amorality. After sitting for his portrait, the young Gray, enamoured with his own beauty, trades his soul for immortality. As he indulges his own narcissism and aesthetic sensuality, the painting shows the corruption of his soul in its representation of his face, while his own physical form remains entirely unchanged. Wilde's novel works as an examination of the relationship between aesthetics and being as well as imaginative exploration of Augustinian privation theory. In contrast to Stevenson's grotesque Hyde, Wilde presents a monster whose deviancy is caused by his extreme narcissism, a 'decadent Gothic subject whose beauty is the wellspring of horror'.[98] Initially a theological approach to the novel may seem something of an anachronism – while tinged with supernaturalism the Gothic aspects of the novel 'would be

---

[98] Dryden, *The Modern Gothic*, 114.

quite ludicrous if introduced to Henry's drawing room society'.[99] In fact, Joyce Carol Oates has argued that the novel and particularly the character of Dorian is generally rather 'secular' and whatever supernatural element the novel contains is rather vague:

> Is the devil responsible? But does the devil exist? Hell is hardly more than theoretical to Wilde, and heaven is equally notional; when Dorian is attracted to the Catholic church it is primarily for the sake of exotic ritual, ecclesiastical vestments, and other somewhat ludicrous treasures of the church, which Wilde delights in cataloguing. The consequences of a Faustian pact with the devil are dramatized, but the devil himself is absent.[100]

Rather more frequently, the novel is categorized as 'decadent writing' – part of a trend of aesthetic practice in fin-de-siècle art and literature marked by an insistence upon the autonomy of art, disgust with the prevailing bourgeois utility and a seeking after rare and intense sensations.[101] Given the primacy given to the aesthetic throughout the novel, a critical focus upon the text as a decadent work is hardly surprising.[102] From a theological perspective, Wilde's novel pairs well with Stevenson's novella with regard to the duel ideas of Augustinian privation theory – however, whereas with *Jekyll and Hyde*, the reader is allowed to see this ontological privation and perversion embodied in the figure of Hyde, Wilde's text presents perversion and privation within fundamentally aesthetic terms.[103] If, in the case of Stevenson, the aesthetic is an expression of the ethical – Hyde's appearance being an expression of the state of his being – Wilde subordinates ethics to the realm of the aesthetic. The preface to the novel makes this abundantly clear using Wilde's famous epigrams. No artist has any 'ethical sympathies', for this is an 'unpardonable mannerism of style'.[104] Rather than any kind of mannerism, then, the role of the artist is to create beautiful things, to produce pleasurable sensations in the viewer, to reveal art and obscure themselves in the process. What is neatly ignored in Wilde's as-ever

---

[99] Joyce Carol Oates, 'The Picture of Dorian Gray: Wilde's Parable of the Fall', *Critical Inquiry* 7.2 (Winter, 1980): 424.
[100] Ibid.
[101] See Kirsten MacLoed, *Fictions of British Decadence* (London: Springer, 2006) as well as David Weir, *Decadence and the Making of Modernism* (Massachusetts: University of Massachusetts Press, 1995).
[102] MacLoed goes so far as to claim that *The Picture of Dorian Gray* is the first British decadent novel. See MacLoed, *Fictions of British Decadence*, 79.
[103] In itself, this ties the work to wider issues around Wilde's body of work, especially as he made his public debut as a 'professor of aesthetics'. See Robert Mighall's introduction to Oscar Wilde, *The Picture of Dorian Gray* (London: Penguin Classics, 2000).
[104] Wilde, *Dorian Gray*, 3.

witty phrasing is the ethical implications of this approach when the subject of art is not an image but an individual. This kind of reduction of the individual to the image is broadly in line with privation theory more generally. Thought and language are made into tools for the artist and vice and virtue become mere grist to the mill of aesthetic experience. It is this subordination of the subject to aesthetics that can be read as functioning as a type of privation of being. Thus, the following section will read Wilde's novel in Augustinian terms, reflecting upon it as not simply a decadent novel but as an example of the potential risks involved in aesthetic experience as the basis for moral action and indeed, any kind of moral judgement. This section also engages with the historical context and criticism around aesthetics, particularly the work of Walter Pater, given his influence on Wilde's own thinking.

From the opening of the novel, the character of Dorian Gray first appears as his own image – the painting that so captivates Lord Henry Wooten, being worked on by Basil Haywood. Gray is introduced as a 'gracious and comely form', his portrait being praised as the best thing that Basil has ever done.[105] Gray is physiognomic perfection, and through this first encounter with him in the text, there is no trace of any engagement with Gray as an individual but merely as *image*. Wilde here ironically reverses the equivalence between positive aesthetics and personal quality, where the good equals the beautiful and vice versa.[106] Dorian might be beautiful, but Henry hopes that his intellect or internal life does not match his outward appearance. Henry refers to him as nothing more than a 'beautiful, brainless creature'.[107] The character of Dorian is rather a mere objet d'art – a motive for aesthetic reflection and an instrument of the artist himself. Indeed, in a telling moment, Basil admits his fear of exhibiting the work – 'I am afraid that I have shown in it the secret of my own soul'.[108] Gray thus becomes a mere accident or motive for Basil's own aesthetic endeavours, reified into serving a means to an end – Dorian becomes an image from which Basil can experience aesthetic pleasure. Here then, subjectivity becomes reduced to the image, to be 'varnished, framed and sent home'.[109] The image of the subject becomes static, and for all its beauty, it involves a necessary dehumanization of

---

[105] Ibid., 6.
[106] This was discussed in more detail in relation to Frankenstein's creature and the De Lacy family in Chapter 1 – the creature's appearance is equated with his moral quality and it is this which causes the De Lacy family to act so violently towards him.
[107] Wilde, *Dorian Gray*, 7.
[108] Ibid., 9.
[109] Ibid., 29.

the individual – a privation of all that Gray may become in order to maintain and create the single unchanging aesthetic marvel of his self.

Strikingly, the first section of the novel provides evidence for both a privation of Gray's ontology and a perversion of his being. Gray's first in-person appearance in the novel shows him in remarkably straightforward, almost naive terms. He is 'wonderfully handsome . . . there was something in his face that made one trust him at once', Henry notes.[110] His being equates to his aesthetic appearance too – 'one felt that he had kept himself unspotted from the world', a moral tabula rasa that appeals to the rather more predatory and amoral Henry. It is in the conversation with the older, worldlier Henry that a crucial point emerges – while frequently labelled a 'decadent text' Wilde's novel initially presents a *kind* of degeneration – in this case, that of the body in old age, as a disaster to be averted. Wooten's speech on the subject, a kind of aestheticized memento mori proves to be a powerful temptation for Gray:[111]

> The common hill-flowers wither, but they blossom again. The laburnum will be as yellow next June as it is now. In a month, there will be purple stars on the clematis, and year after year the green night of its leaves will hold its purple stars. But we never get back our youth. The pulse of joy that beats in us at twenty becomes sluggish. Our limbs fail, our senses rot. We degenerate into hideous puppets, haunted by the memory of the passions of which we were much too afraid and the exquisite temptations that we had not the courage to lead to.[112]

To live, argues the urbane Wooten, is to experience change and ultimately loss of that which he holds to be most valuable – namely beauty, pleasure and desire. Yet what Wooten misses (or rather artfully elides) is the extent to which pleasure in and of itself can all too often revert to selfishness. The 'passions' that Wooten speaks of are necessarily bound up in relationship with another – passion is, after all, passion *for* someone, even to consume the Other for the gratification of the self. Yet here, Wooten reduces it to the feeling itself, robbing the aesthetic of the relational aspect which infuses it with meaning. Gray's response upon first sighting the portrait seems aware of both the reduction of his self to the image

---

[110] Ibid., 19.
[111] For more on this see Karschay, *Degeneration*, 171–2.
[112] Wilde, *Dorian Gray*, 25.

and the sense of loss that such a reduction entails, yet at the same time it is also what provokes the Faustian bargain he immediately seeks to strike:

> How sad it is! Murmured Dorian Gray, with his eyes still fixed upon his own portrait. How sad it is! I shall grow old, and horrible, and dreadful. It will never be older than this particular day in June . . . If it were only the other way! If it were I who was to be always young and the picture that was to grow old! For that – for that – I would give everything! Yes, there is nothing in the whole world I would not give! I would give my soul for that![113]

Once again, and as with Jekyll, Dorian seeks the means to sacrifice the invisible (namely his soul) for the promise of permanent aesthetic perfection. In a sense, Gray is perfectly correct – the progression of age and of bodily vulnerability is terrible, yet, quite arguably, abundantly necessary for the development of being. Human finitude may well seem a grave injustice (in fact to see it this way does presuppose a theological framework of some kind) yet without an awareness of it as a reality to be confronted, Gray lapses into a highly aestheticized antinomianism – where his beauty becomes a means by which to live outside of any type of moral law and free of consequence. Without an awareness of our own finitude, the possibility for meaningful moral and theological reflection and action become limited – Gray retreats from the positive possibilities of the world towards the realm of the purely disinterested aesthete whereby being (whether one's own or another) becomes secondary to sensation and appearance.[114] Gazing at his own image, 'like a nineteenth century Narcissus'[115] Gray begins his descent into introspection, egotism and hedonism. It is through the pursuit of the aesthetic that Gray develops as a degenerate, it is through his fear of what he may become that he becomes monstrous. He reaches the point whereby his name becomes a byword for the scandals produced through his sensation seeking. He becomes, in Halberstam's terms 'a Gothic dandy' – representing simultaneously 'too much and too little, excess and paucity'.[116] Such dualism is in keeping with Augustinian approaches to evil; as Ewan Fernie points out, 'evil as selfishness expresses demonic negativity in the form of the self that is abstracted and alienated from the world'.[117] Dorian's hedonism then becomes

---

[113] Ibid., 27–8.
[114] For a more thorough exploration of the link between pure disinterestedness and ontological evil, see Eagleton, *On Evil* (2008). For a link between the removal of the subject from the status of being-in-the-world and the potential harm that emerges from this, see Chapter 1 on *Frankenstein*.
[115] Dryden, *The Modern Gothic*, 114.
[116] Halberstam, *Skin Shows*, 62.
[117] Fernie, *The Demonic*, 20.

an expression of his privation of being – an obsession with surface and artifice rather than any kind of genuine engagement with the life he encounters around him. Philosophically, the influence of Walter Pater seems clear here, and in a sense then the novel functions as an exaggerated and Gothicized application of Pater's aesthetics. In his work *The Renaissance: Studies in Art and Poetry* (1893), Pater writes that

> The aesthetic critic, then, regards all the objects with which he has to do, all works of art, and the fairer forms of nature and human life, as powers or forces producing pleasurable sensations. . . . What is important, then, is not that the critic should possess a correct abstract definition of beauty for the intellect, but a certain kind of temperament, the power of being deeply moved by the presence of beautiful objects.[118]

The issue here is not with the idea of art for art's sake – Pater's call (which Wilde undoubtedly would agree with) to a life of 'constant and eager observation'[119] would seem to lend itself to imaginative apologetics. Coupled with Vivian's point from *The Decay of Lying* – that art consists of the 'purely imaginative and pleasurable work dealing with what is unreal and non- existent'[120] – the links to a theological understanding of creation seem clear. However, the fundamentally problematic area of the Paterian aesthetic within *Dorian Gray* is the basis in *sensation* rather than anything else. Pater argues that aesthetics and aesthetic judgement should be based in the pleasurable sensations produced in the observation of the aesthetic object. Such an aesthetic idea goes some way to explaining the initial infatuation Gray experiences with Sybil Vane – her theatrical talents are enthralling, precisely because of the pleasure they induce. However, sensual pleasure in the aesthetic object is unreliable and perhaps even dangerous – as Kate Hext argues, the main problem being that Pater locates the ethical sensibility in sensual pleasure of the beautiful. This sensuality is something which can bypass reason, as Pater 'compares sensuality to being in service to a band of madmen'.[121] Gray's callous treatment of Sybil Vane reveals this mania with surface, with aesthetic appearances and sensation, over any kind of meaningful relationship. Discovering her acting in a rather run-down theatre

---

[118] Pater, *The Renaissance*, xxi.
[119] Ibid., 188.
[120] Oscar Wilde, 'The Decay of Lying', in *In Praise of Disobedience* (London: Verso Books 2018), 70.
[121] Kate Hext, 'At the Burning Point of Good and Evil: Aesthetics as Ethics in Walter Paters Aestheticism', in *Leeds Working Papers, Victorian Ethics*, ed. Nathan Uglow (Leeds: Leeds Centre for Victorian Studies, 2008), 50–60.

in a less than respectable part of London, he enthuses about her to Henry that she is 'all the great heroines of the world. She is more than an individual . . . my God Harry, how I worship her!'[122] Yet what Dorian is enamoured with is the pretence and artifice of performance that produces pleasure rather than anything about Sybil herself. After taking his friends to the theatre she performs in, and finding her performance rather curiously uninspired, he goes backstage to confront her.

> You used to stir my imagination. Now you don't even stir my curiosity. You simply produce no effect. I loved you, because you were marvellous, because you had genius and intellect, because you realised the dreams of great poets and gave shape and substance to the shadows of art . . . without your art you are nothing. What are you now? A third-rate actress with a pretty face.[123]

What she becomes is not an aesthetic object that produces pleasure but rather something which demands a response from him. Encounters between individuals operate on a different level of feeling than that of subject and object – while Dorian may observe her as an object and experience aesthetic enjoyment, relationships between individuals are far more complex things and laden with many other feelings aside from aesthetic pleasure. As Sybil moves from being *objectified* to being *subjectivized* she becomes something other than an aesthetic phenomenon and demands from Gray, a degree of recognition. Confronted with Sybil's genuine declaration of feeling – confronted by her true self as it were, Gray responds with vicious invective. As Halberstam writes, 'it is precisely when the boundaries between the spheres of art and life are too dearly drawn that desire, for Dorian, disappears.'[124] In fact, Halberstam does not carry this argument far enough, thanks to the insistence, first planted by Wooten, upon separating desire from the constituting ontology from which it is produced. It is not simply that Dorian's desire for Sybil vanishes when she stops performing for him as an aesthetic object, it is a more fundamental ontological conflict: between private being and authentic desires. Sybil's 'mistake' is to believe that theatre is a mask for life. Dorian's response is revealing of his own fear of authentic being and shows the extent to which more genuine expressions of feeling – an exercise that often carries with it pain rather than pleasure – is something with which he is unable to comprehend. Without the art (his own pleasing aesthetic appearance)

---

[122] Wilde, *Dorian Gray*, 54.
[123] Ibid., 85.
[124] Halberstam, *Skin Shows*, 63.

he fears that Sybil will discover that he too, is nothing. That evening Sybil Vane commits suicide and the first traces of cruelty appear on Dorian's portrait.

Gray, on hearing of her death is wracked with guilt, and in the company of Lord Wooten – the one who has tempted Gray into indulging in aesthetics – exclaims that 'Harry, Harry it is terrible'.[125] Yet at the encouragement of his friend and mentor he is persuaded to view her death again in aesthetic and distinctly dehumanizing terms. She becomes a figure of art, an object rather than individual. As Harry argues:

> You must think of that lonely death in the tawdry dressing room simply as a strange fragment from some Jacobean tragedy . . . the girl never really lived, and so she has never really died . . . . Mourn for Ophelia . . . cry out against heaven because the daughter of Brabantio died. But don't waste your tears over Sybil Vane. She was less real than they are.[126]

Once again, at the price of subordinating ethics to aesthetics Dorian ends up forgetting his remorse and even his guilt for his culpability, scorning her for her commonplace life.[127] In a telling moment Gray is informed of the results of the inquiry into Vane's death and turns away, thinking 'how horribly real ugliness made things'.[128] Reality and aesthetic beauty have little in common with one another – especially if it is solely the pleasurable sensations upon which aesthetics are judged. In the aftermath of Sybil Vane's death Gray's experiments in narcissistic hedonism accelerate. Yet despite this, Dorian's privation of being does not detract from his aesthetic appeal. He remains ageless and beautiful, embodying the paradox of Augustinian understandings of evil, that for all its negation and privation, it retains an attractive glamour. Gray indulges himself in what Dryden labels, 'self-conscious malevolence . . . a Gothic tendency toward the weird and uncanny'.[129] Such a tendency is well known through theological writings – Fernie (referring to Augustine's *Confessions*) specifically mentions evil's demonic appeal and this further ties Gray's marked Gothicism to the tradition of theology in understanding evil:[130]

> If the crime of theft, which I committed that night as a boy of sixteen was a living thing, I could speak to it and ask what it was that, to my shame, I loved

---

[125] Wilde, *Dorian Gray*, 96.
[126] Ibid., 100.
[127] Ibid., 106.
[128] Ibid., 120.
[129] Dryden, *The Modern Gothic*, 135.
[130] See Fernie, *The Demonic*, 13–14.

> in it . . . It was not the pears my unhappy soul desired. I had plenty of my own, better than those, and I only picked them so that I might steal. For no sooner had I picked them than I threw them away, and tasted nothing in them but my own sin, which I relished and enjoyed. If any part of those pears passed my lips, it was the sin that gave them flavour.[131]

Whereas Augustine has a self to lose, the sense of the novel is that perhaps Dorian no longer has a self to be destroyed – rather he has become the embodied image. He forms a type of empty signifier – his aesthetic appearance has become, in a way, all that he is. As a result, Dorian's privation of being becomes more markedly visible in the painting, which becomes essentially an image or reflection of his true self. Hiding it away from public view, it becomes a source of his pleasure to stand and observe the spread of the degradation of his own being. He becomes 'more and more enamoured of his own beauty, more and more interested in the corruption of his own soul'.[132] In a neat twist upon the old Gothic convention of the haunted mirror, the portrait allows him to see 'himself' – he becomes the perfected aestheticized body, while his soul becomes increasingly degraded. Gray literally comes to embody the division between the aesthetic and moral that the novel maintains and the toll of such a division is revealed through the portrait. His own aesthetic consistency and enduring attractiveness to others serves as both a symptom of his ontological privation while at the same time maintaining a sense of appealing glamour to his person. The novel repeats the phrase that 'he had always the look of one who had kept himself unspotted from the world', as well as this, his wealth and beauty are presented as a kind of purity that rebukes the suspicions of others.[133] Despite the shame, scandal and hedonistic passions he indulges in, which dog his reputation throughout society, he is still possessed of a 'strange and dangerous charm'.[134] It seems to be this appealing glamour to Dorian Gray that leads to the outlandish claim from Halberstam that Gray is 'rewarded with longevity'[135] despite Gray's own admission that he 'looked on evil simply as a mode through which he could realize his conception of the beautiful'.[136]

If Wilde's hierarchy of the aesthetic over the ethical does seem to be the root of both the privation and the perversion of Gray's being, this serves to not only

---

[131] St Augustine, *Confessions*, 15–16.
[132] Wilde, *Dorian Gray*, 124.
[133] Ibid.
[134] Ibid., 136.
[135] Halberstam, *Skin Shows*, 64.
[136] Wilde, *Dorian Gray*, 140.

expand the depths to which *The Picture of Dorian Gray* serves as an exploration of evil but also shed new light upon decadent writing generally as a source of potential theological significance. Read within Augustinian terms (or to express it another way, as a Gothic example of Paterian aesthetics), Wilde's novel and the character of Dorian in particular reveal the prevalence of a lack of theological articulation in the era of fin-de-siècle secular materialism. It would seem, then, the theological challenge presented by the text is to find a way to respond to the evil of Gray without being seduced by the glamour of his decadence. For such a theological challenge to be met would require a synthesis of the aesthetic with the theological in order to reconcile the split that Gray so appealingly embodies and proves so fatal to the more Calvinist Henry Jekyll. As Basil states at the beginning of the novel, in an aside referring to Dorian, 'the harmony of soul and body . . . we have in our madness separated the two and have invented a realism that is vulgar, an ideality that is void'.[137] This telling aside goes some way to articulating the theological problem, yet the novel does provide a few clues for where such a synthesis may occur – namely through an incarnational and confessional theology. The few direct references to any kind of theology through the novel are distinctly Catholic in nature. Gray's attraction to Catholicism is, like Wilde's own attraction, initially on the level of aesthetics.[138] The attraction of the religion is its rites, vestments and 'the allure of its ritual and costume, not its renunciation'.[139]

> It was rumoured of him that he was about to join the Roman Catholic communion; and certainly the Roman ritual had always great attraction for him. The daily sacrifice . . . stirred him as much by its superb rejection of the evidence of the senses as by the primitive simplicity of its elements and the eternal pathos of the human tragedy that it sought to symbolize.[140]

The daily sacrifice of the Eucharist is contrasted to the sacrifices of pagan religion and Christ as saviour is corporeally absent, yet theologically present. Thus, Christ forms the opposite of Dorian, a corporeally present but spiritually void subject. This awareness of Christ as present in spirit but not in body is what makes the ritual seem so moving, and as Gray explains, the sacrament of

---

[137] Ibid., 13.
[138] For a detailed exploration of Wilde as a queer theologian and his own interest in Roman Catholic practice and theology, see Frederick Roden, *Same Sex Desire in Victorian Religious Culture* (London: Palgrave Macmillan, 2003), particularly Chapter 5.
[139] Roden, *Same Sex Desire*, 140.
[140] Wilde, *Dorian Gray*, 128.

the Eucharist is precisely what can bridge the divide between the material and aesthetic and the immaterial or spiritual:

> He loved to kneel down on the cold marble pavement, and watch the priest, in his stiff flowered dalmatic, slowly and with white hands moving aside the veil of the tabernacle, or raising aloft the jewelled lantern shaped monstrance with that pallid wafer that at times, one would fain think, is indeed the '*panis celetis*,' the bread of angels, or robed in the garments of the Passion of Christ, breaking the host in the chalice, and smiting his breast for his sins.[141]

Christ is here as both sign and revealed presence – the veil is moved aside and the pallid wafer is transformed into the bread of heaven. Receiving communion is an essentially embodied activity – it involves kneeling, consuming host and responding verbally but these gestures go beyond mere pleasurable aesthetic posturing. Sign and symbol combine and point to something greater than themselves and all of this is mediated through another body – that of the priest. In the Eucharist, the divide between aesthetic materiality and spirituality is overcome and both body and soul are united before God and with the other congregants. Yet Dorian seems unable to grasp the essentially communal and public nature of sacraments. In contrast to Jekyll who seeks a kind of public confession of his sins if only to exonerate his own standing, Dorian finds the prospect of public confession deeply terrifying. He acknowledges the portrait as a record and moral ledger of the state of his own soul yet refuses to allow Basil to exhibit it, for fear of what might be seen there. He is drawn to another sacramental tradition of Catholicism – namely confession, but once again, he recoils from it. He might 'long to sit in the dim shadow' of the confessional booth but never does and it remains 'black and impenetrable'.[142] Throughout the narrative, public confession is, as Knight and Mason note, continually 'held out to the reader'[143] but always deferred and turned away from – another temptation to which Gray does not, and cannot, yield. Thus, the reader is left with a vision of a closed, closeted confessional, from which nothing can be heard and nothing redeemed. This contrasts markedly to the high value that Augustinian thought has placed upon the idea of a public confession.[144] Ultimately, it seems that Dorian, and fin-de-siècle aestheticized culture, 'struggles to comprehend the sacramental quality of language as public'.[145] As Catherine

---

[141] Ibid.
[142] Ibid.
[143] Knight and Mason, *An Introduction to Nineteenth Century Literature and Religion*, 205.
[144] Hence Augustine's most well-known work, *Confessions*.
[145] Knight and Mason, *An Introduction to Nineteenth Century Literature and Religion*, 205.

Pickstock argues, language is typically 'construed as innocuous decoration', an image or 'adornment' of a prior frame of the 'real'.[146] By contrast Pickstock claims the 'liturgical city' is 'avowedly semiotic'.[147] Thus, rather than functioning as signs that conceal or adorn the real, these 'signs are both things and figures or signs – of one another and of that which exceeds appearance'.[148] Theological language is also communal, passed on to others 'and itself constitutes the offering and the consummation of the citizen's subjectivity as a "living sacrifice."'[149] This inability to grasp the essentially public nature of confession and faith more widely is a key to the novel more generally. As with Jekyll, in a society where the Law of God has been replaced by the rule of public opinion and appearance, the question simply becomes 'why confess at all?' Public confession would once again not involve any kind of group solidarity and redemption but would irredeemably corrupt the image of Dorian Gray in the eyes of those who behold him. As the self has been subordinated to the image (which in Wilde's work becomes the only kind of true ontological nature) confession would destroy the image and reveal the fundamentally empty and privated character of what lies beneath it. It is, then, extremely telling that it is only behind closed doors that Dorian Gray's portrait is finally exposed to Basil Haywood, who sees the extent of Dorian's spiritual decay – how 'the leprosies of sin are eating'[150] him away. Basil, the priest figure who through his mediation of the aesthetic form has inspired Dorian, attempts a spiritual rather than aesthetic intervention.

> 'Pray, Dorian, pray', he murmured. 'What is it that one was taught to say in one's boyhood? "Lead us not into temptation. Forgive us our sins. Wash away our inequities." Let us say that together. The prayer of your pride has been answered. The prayer of your repentance will be answered also. I worshipped you too much. I am punished for it. You worshipped yourself too much. We are both punished.'[151]

As Roden argues, Basil attempts to spiritualize Dorian, 'He had worshipped Dorian's beautiful body instead of his soul. When Basil tries to rescue him, he is too late'.[152] His attempt to bring forth a public confession and some measure of

---

[146] Catherine Pickstock, *After Writing: On the Liturgical Consummation of Philosophy* (London: Blackwell, 1998), 169.
[147] Ibid.
[148] Ibid., 170.
[149] Ibid.
[150] Wilde, *Dorian Gray*, 150.
[151] Ibid., 151.
[152] Roden, *Same Sex Desire*, 145.

repentance from Dorian (which would, necessarily, involve a drastic change in behaviour and the culture he exists in more widely) is met with rage.

> An uncontrollable feeling of hatred for Basil Hallward came over him . . . the mad passions of a hunted animal stirred within him, and he loathed the man who was seated at the table more than in his whole life he had ever loathed anything. . . . He rushed at him and dug the knife into the great vein that is behind the ear . . . stabbing again and again.[153]

Unlike his callous dismissal of Sybil Vane, here Dorian is wracked with guilt in the aftermath of his murder and the blackmail he enacts to dispose of the body. Dorian seems willing to change his behaviour, but once again, the notion of a public confession strikes him as 'monstrous'[154] – in a society where the aesthetic is so highly prized, confession could be nothing but a complete catastrophe. At the close of the novel, instead of engaging in reformed behaviour Dorian seeks the destruction of his self. Like Christ's body in the sacrament of the Eucharist, his body is destroyed and yet transformed. Whereas Christ's transformation is public, a destruction of the body in order to give out to the many, Gray's own transformation is inward, private and monstrous. He is found with a 'withered, wrinkled and loathsome of visage,'[155] recognizable only through his jewellery. The possibility of confession and of the sacramental possibility of language is ultimately never permanently foreclosed, but Wilde shows the cost of refusing the sacramental possibility in language, and refusing the potential freedom of confession. Removed from a connection with authentic being, aesthetic desire is shown as a dangerous process, disastrously prone to a negation of being. Whereas in Wilde's novel the sacramental is a possibility that is ultimately unfilled, the final novel under consideration explores the potential for the sacraments and iconography of Christian theology for purification and redemption when confronted with evil.

Dracula, iconography, sacramentality and purification

Stoker's *Dracula* (1898) has had a colossal cultural impact and as such has produced a vast array of criticism. A complete and exhaustive list of all works is not possible here, but key texts include Christopher Frayling's historical

---
[153] Wilde, *Dorian Gray*, 151.
[154] Ibid., 211.
[155] Ibid., 213.

overview of the vampire[156] as well as Clive Leatherdale's *Dracula, The Novel and the Legend*.[157] A highly influential work is Nina Auerbach's magisterial survey of the vampire and the wider role it plays in culture, *Our Vampires, Ourselves*.[158] This 'textually dense' narrative and formally complex text has produced such swathes of criticism that Ken Gelder argues that there is no original text – to read the novel is to inevitably produce 'new' versions.[159] Despite the proliferation of critical work on the novel it is the theological criticism that has been most neglected, or if not ignored, then unnecessarily marginalized. Thus, the aim of the concluding section will be to re-examine and re-assert the role of theological discourses at work within the novel. As Christopher Herbert asserts, 'Restoring its religious motivation to view is bound to complicate its standing as an icon of radical fin de siècle modernity',[160] but it will also encourage a fresh engagement with theological issues around sacramentality, purification and the complex ways that theology is appropriated as a key stratagem with which to bring about Dracula's defeat. Some critics seem to bypass this aspect of the text, theorizing the novel and Dracula in particular, as a 'stereotypical anti-Semitic nineteenth-century representation of the Jew'.[161] Other critics seem to recognize that the text is frequently concerned with issues that are non-material yet a lack of theological engagement inevitably limits the critical work. Daniel Pick claims the novel is, at points, 'frozen between Victorian evolutionism and psycho-analysis',[162] without posing the seemingly obvious question of what may lie between those two – namely theological ideas around the nature of being and subjectivity. A frequent approach in the scholarship is to focus on the novel as an example of 'Imperial Gothic', seeing Dracula as a 'tempting figure around which

---

[156] Christopher Frayling, *Vampyres: Lord Byron to Count Dracula* (London: Faber & Faber, 1991).
[157] Clive Leatherdale, *Dracula, The Novel and the Legend* (Wellingborough: Aquarian Press, 1985).
[158] Nina Auerbach, *Our Vampires, Our Selves* (Chicago: University of Chicago Press, 1995). Other key works include Peter Haining and Peter Tremayne, *The Undead: The Legend of Bram Stoker and Dracula* (London: Constable, 1997); James B. Twitchell, *The Living Dead, A Study of the Vampire in Romantic Literature* (Durham, NC: Duke University Press, 1981) and although not directly related, Elaine Showalter's *Sexual Anarchy, Gender and Culture at the fin-de-siecle* (London: Virago Press, 1992) has been extremely important in discussions of gender and sexuality particularly with regard to the character of Lucy Westenra.
[159] Ken Gelder, *Reading the Vampire* (London: Routledge, 1994), 65. Gelder's point proves not just true of the Gothic but of theology more widely. The Gothic, as with Christian belief, is consistently being (re)read and reinterpreted, with 'new' versions being produced all the time.
[160] Christopher Herbert, 'Vampire Religion', *Representations* 79.1 (Summer 2002): 100–121 – though it is perhaps worth acknowledging that Herbert makes an equivocation between the fin-de-siècle modernity and secularity that should not necessarily be accepted without question.
[161] Halberstam, *Skin Shows*, 86.
[162] Daniel Pick, 'Terrors of the Night: Dracula and Degeneration in the Late Nineteenth Century', *Critical Quarterly* 30.4 (1989): 71.

the motif of invasion might be developed'[163] coming as he does from outside the British realm of control to the centre of the empire wielding considerable power, particularly economically. However, given the extent to which the power of the British Empire is bound up with Christian belief and justified through theological reasoning, an examination of a classic Imperial Gothic text without theological analysis is, at best, limited.[164]

On a theological level, the text presents itself as 'a solemn parable of what John Henry Newman called 'the warfare between the city of God and the powers of darkness'.[165] On first examination, the characters are explicitly religious when confronted with the supernatural powers of Dracula. Trapped in the castle with those 'women of the Pit', Jonathan Harker makes his audacious escape attempt, comforted by the fact that 'God's mercy is better than that of these monsters'.[166] This religious concern is not just an articulation of the text's characters – the reader need only look at the 'frequent echoing of biblical verses'[167] and scenic moments such as Quincy Morris's death at the novel's conclusion, bleeding from a Christ-like wound in the side, expiring in the arms of his friends as they let forth 'a deep and earnest Amen'.[168] The clear textual allusion to the *pieta* of Christian art as well as Morris's resurrection in the form of Mina and Jonathan's child shows how redemptive Christian associations form the backdrop for the defeat and negation of Dracula. Stoker himself seems to have been aware of the theological associations of the text, writing in a letter to Gladstone that, 'though superstition is fought in it with the weakness of superstition I hope it is not irreverent'.[169] Characters cross themselves, pray, wield crucifixes and communion wafers as well as Winchester rifles and for all the novel's fascination with modernity[170] it functions as a narrative deeply invested, albeit ambiguously so, in religious and theological discourse. However, the large amount of theological iconography present exists alongside folk medicine and superstitions such as

---

[163] William Hughes, 'A Singular Invasion: Revisiting the Postcoloniality of Bram Stoker's *Dracula*', in *Empire and the Gothic: The Politics of Genre*, ed. Andrew Smith and William Hughes (London: Blackwell, 2003), 91.
[164] For the link between Anglican belief and the British Empire, see Rowan Strong, *Anglicanism and the British Empire, c.1700-1850* (Oxford: Oxford University Press, 2007).
[165] Herbert, 'Vampire Religion', 101.
[166] Bram Stoker, *Dracula* (London: Penguin Classics, 2003), 61.
[167] Herbert, 'Vampire Religion', 100.
[168] Stoker, *Dracula*, 401.
[169] Quoted in William Hughes, *Beyond Dracula: Bram Stoker's Fiction and Its Cultural Context* (London: Palgrave, 2000), 15.
[170] Franco Moretti famously reads the novel sociologically, seeing Dracula as a model of capitalist predation. See Franco Moretti, 'The Dialectic of Fear', *New Left Review* 136 (November–December 1982), 67–85.

garlic, suggesting that there is a degree of fragility and even limitation on what theology may do alone.

Thus, the idea of the novel functioning as a relatively straightforward religious parable of good vs. evil is a position that should not be accepted uncritically. This argument usually focuses upon what is assumed to be a prevailing Catholicism within the text with some critics claiming that 'the novel's religious analogy is obvious' as 'Count Dracula is the figurative anti-Christ who promises eternal life through the ingestion of actual human blood'.[171] The error here is to assume that the concept of Eucharistic sacrifice is exclusively Catholic – while the two religious traditions would find differing elements of the text sacrilegious, it should not be ignored that Protestants would still recognize and abhor this corruption of the Eucharist. The religious elements of the text are historicized as a reaction to the decline of the strength of the church in the new Darwinism of Victorian England.[172] While giving valuable wider context, both perspectives are greatly hindered by a limited understanding of how religious ideas function in the text, and of theological thinking generally. Crucially, the combination of the Protestant and Catholic theological influences connects the Irish Protestant Stoker with Oscar Wilde as another theological influenced author who drew from both Protestant and Catholic theological semiotics. As Alison Milbank points out, Stoker had a bourgeois Protestant Ascendancy background 'similar to that of . . . Wilde'.[173] This Irish Gothic tradition not only situates Ireland as a site of Gothic barbarism and powerful superstition but also allows for figures such as Stoker and Wilde to offer themselves as the class 'to control its primitive force'.[174]

Turning to the text the evidence quickly problematizes this idea of a simple divide between either Catholic or Protestant, or religion and superstition. The religious imagery and iconography that the characters appropriate is an unexpected mix of Protestant and Catholic religious discourses. Importantly, it seems that symbolism can be extracted from a wider religious tradition and yet retain its efficacy. One of the first key moments of the narrative shows the blending of the two theological perspectives. Harker, travelling through the

---

[171] D. Bruno Starrs, 'Keeping the Faith, Catholicism in Dracula and Its Adaptations', *Journal of Dracula Studies* 6 (2004).
[172] See Herbert, 'Vampire Religion', 102.
[173] Alison Milbank, '"Powers Old and New": Stoker's Alliances with Anglo-Irish Gothic', in *Bram Stoker: History, Psychoanalysis and the Gothic*, ed. Andrew Smith and William Hughes (London: Palgrave, 1998), 12.
[174] Ibid., 13.

regions of both Eastern European superstition and orthodox theology, reveals his final destination, which draws the following reaction from a nearby observer:

> She then rose and dried her eyes and taking a crucifix from her neck offered it to me. I did not know what to do, for, as an English Churchman, I have been taught to regard such things as in some measure idolatrous, and yet it seemed so ungracious to refuse an old lady meaning so well.[175]

Here then, Harker, as a self-identified 'English Churchman', takes on the theological accoutrements of the Catholic and Orthodox churches out of a sense of 'grace'. This use of the religiously shaded word 'grace' casts serious doubt upon the idea that this represents the start of Harker's journey of conversion from Protestant to Catholic theology – rather, it seems that Harker's journey is not only geographical and temporal but spiritual as well. In the moment quoted earlier it is rather the combining of the two theologies – the foreign crucifix in the possession of the Protestant Harker – that both physically and spiritually protects him from Dracula. Harker himself comes to a similar realization when he first begins to be confronted with the true nature of Dracula:

> Bless that good, good woman who hung the crucifix round my neck! For it is a comfort and a strength to me whenever I touch it. It is odd that a thing which I have been taught to regard with disfavour and as idolatrous should in a time of loneliness and trouble be of help. Is it that there is something in the essence of the thing itself, or that it is a medium, a tangible help, in conveying memories of sympathy and comfort? Some time, if it may be, I must examine this matter and try to make up my mind about it.[176]

Harker's question raises interesting possibilities about the potential sacramental nature of Christian iconography that emphasizes the divide between Catholic and Protestant theologies. The object that to the English Protestant is to be regarded with disfavour comes to have some mysterious efficacy, though the source of its spiritual power remains a rather less important point than the fact that this power is a source of reassurance. However, the text is no simple paean to the powers of ecumenicalism, as it is when Dracula achieves his aim of transporting himself into the West that the complexity of the theological discourse becomes revealed. Stoker does not treat religion as a non-rationalist system in comparison to the prevalent scientific ideology of the day. Rather, the

---

[175] Stoker, *Dracula*, 11.
[176] Ibid., 35.

theological emphasis rests on the dangers that Dracula poses to the ordered systematized theology back in the 'civilized' world.[177] As Herbert notes, 'the evil Count is above all . . . an image of a terrible menace posed by the superstitious mentality to decent Christian existence'.[178] For evidence one only need to read Harker's thoughts on the risk of Dracula's arrival in England – 'where, perhaps for centuries to come he might, amongst its teeming millions, satiate his lust for blood'.[179]

Interestingly, it seems that the source of religious danger is from the wildness of the 'horseshoe of the Carpathians' and its 'people who are without religion, save superstition'.[180] What these two points highlight is the extent to which in the Age of British Imperialism, theology has become instrumentalized as both rational, homely belief, useful for upholding the virtues of capitalist exchange and empire, and at the same, a superstitious force that endangers the status of the British middle classes. The fin-de-siècle materialism of Stoker's novel is not opposed to religion (Harker for example makes frequent reference to God and faith) but rather the threat lies in religious faith that is not under the control and in the service of good Protestant patriarchs. Thus, it is not rational science that is the danger to religion but rather ordered religion – the religion of 'English Churchmen' as the text articulates it – manages to coexist with the science of the time as both of these ideologies are opposed to the uncontrolled superstition that Dracula embodies (which by this point in the development of the Gothic is not linked with Catholicism as it was with Matthew Lewis's *The Monk*).

The personification of this fusion of both religion and science within the text can most clearly be seen in the character of Van Helsing. Van Helsing is an open-minded Dutch doctor, part-exorcist, part-philosopher who is introduced as a physician to attend upon Lucy when she begins to fall prey to Dracula. Van Helsing is 'a philosopher and a metaphysician and one of the most advanced scientists of his day'[181] but functions as both doctor and priest, drawing upon scientific and superstitious techniques, from blood transfusions to garlic flowers. His language also serves this initially odd combination of 'nineteenth-century medical and scientific knowledge with vampirological lore drawn from

---

[177] Here Stoker shares much in common with William James, in his psychological investigations of religious belief. See William James, *The Varieties of Religious Experience* (London: Penguin Classics, 1985).
[178] Herbert, 'Vampire Religion', 101.
[179] Stoker, *Dracula*, 60.
[180] Ibid., 8.
[181] Ibid., 122.

superstition and ancient belief'.[182] This combination of both the materialist and the religious is expressed in one simple sentence: 'my thesis is this: I want you to believe'.[183] This is the language that fuses the theological and scientific into a singular whole poised against the influence of Dracula. The point Van Helsing makes is that confronting Dracula on the grounds of rational secularity is ineffective – to see this one only need turn to the failure of modern medicine that leads Seward to call in the services of Van Helsing in the first place. Rather, in dealing with the embodiment of superstition, Van Helsing tells Dr Seward that he must 'believe in things that you cannot'[184]– Seward must go beyond the ostensibly rational and the secular to understand the extent of the power and danger that the vampire poses. Essentially, Van Helsing challenges the doctor to re-examine the non-materialist discourses and fields of knowledge that have come to be considered as superstition. The character of Van Helsing essentially converts Seward from what William James called his 'medical materialism . . . a too simple minded system of thought' that cannot fully account for the reality of the vampire.[185] Seward's mode of thinking seeks to clearly demarcate the separation of what is scientific and what is religious, but Van Helsing's call to believe in that which he cannot highlights the extent to which such a separation is not necessarily clear or easy to maintain. Van Helsing's initial encounter with Lucy precedes very much as a doctor and patient. His first diagnosis is that she is not anaemic although 'there has been much blood lost',[186] and so Van Helsing's initial reaction is to look for a traditionally rationalist cause, 'this disease – for not all to be well is a disease – interest me'.[187] However, his response to the failure of the rational is an 'exclamation of horror, '*Gott in Himmel!*''[188]

From this point, Van Helsing's actions begin to reflect more theological language, and he begins to reject any attempt to classify Dracula with conventionally rationalist language – 'it is the fault of our science that it wants to explain all; and if it explains not, then it says there is nothing to explain'.[189] The implication is that there are certain limits to rationalist knowledge, and that beyond these limits is accessible only by priest figures such as Van Helsing. Dracula, the powerful figure of wild superstition, exists outside of these limits,

[182] Starrs, 'Keeping the Faith'.
[183] Stoker, *Dracula*, 206.
[184] Ibid.
[185] James, *Varieties*, 13.
[186] Stoker, *Dracula*, 125.
[187] Ibid.
[188] Ibid., 137.
[189] Ibid., 204.

and to contain and confront him, Van Helsing turns to a potent admixture of folkloric superstitions and practices as well as Christian theology and iconography. The use of garlic raises a quizzical response from Seward (perhaps still expecting a more rationalist method of treatment) that Van Helsing appears to be 'working some spell to keep out an evil spirit'.[190] Given his hidden knowledge at the real nature of Dracula, Van Helsing responds that 'perhaps I am'.[191] Yet this treatment proves insufficient, and so Lucy, left alone, can turn only to prayer – 'what am I to do? God shield me from harm this night . . . god help me!'[192] The churchyard where Lucy is buried serves as the geographical representation of this re-examination of the non-material discourses as characters have to travel to a traditionally sacred space to confront and contain that which the rational has no ability to fully comprehend and understand.

It is in then that comes the climactic scene as Lucy is staked and 'killed' for a second time. The scene contains a powerful visual of the modern world surrounding and completely defeating the vampiric force as well as exposing the vacuous argument that the novel can be reduced to a simple binary of good vs. evil. The character of Arthur has his 'true friends' around him, 'pray[ing] for you all the time'[193] as he 'strike[s] in God's name'.[194] Afterwards, the brutal and highly sexualized scene is followed by a 'holy calm', of which Lucy's now redeemed body forms the visible symbol. Arthur goes so far as to specifically thank Van Helsing for the theological service he has done – 'God bless you that you have given me my dear one her soul again.'[195] What is interesting to note is the clear association between Lucy's transformation into this 'wanton' version of herself and the Arthur's notion of her own damnation. While the vampire may herald a dangerously appealing and liberated sexuality, the expression of female sexuality is tightly bound up in the moral discourses of the day, and furthermore these policing discourses are riven with theological language.

Lucy appears as a sexually wild, voluptuous figure to the men who come to stake her, but the encounter in the churchyard is not simply a case of sexual repression meeting sexual liberation. Lucy's fiancé is 'now in the bitter waters. By this time tomorrow you will, please God, have passed them, and have drunk

---

[190] Ibid., 141.
[191] Ibid.
[192] Ibid., 155.
[193] Ibid., 230.
[194] Ibid.
[195] Ibid., 231.

of the sweet waters'.[196] Arthur's experience is not simply a sexual temptation but akin to baptism – an induction into a new violent theological reality. Rather than read this section of the novel as a fear of unleashed sexuality in itself, this sexual 'wantonness' is a symptom of the dangerous, extreme and superstitious religious force that vampires embody. Her death, then, is not necessarily a punishment for her sexuality but rather a form of highly violent and patriarchal spiritual warfare, curtailing the spread of Dracula's spiritual force in a brutal, yet effective manner using an act of physical violence not only to kill Lucy but to redeem her spiritually; freeing her soul and herself from Dracula's contamination. She is, by the scene's conclusion, 'not any more a foul Thing for all eternity',[197] but rather she is 'God's true dead, whose Soul is with Him!'[198] The staking of Lucy is a penetrative act of re-inscribing her body with the theological inflected discourses of holiness, purity and chastity. Lucy therefore is punished for her desire for all three men (all three are present at the churchyard) and at the same time 'redeemed'. Here then, the modern theology of these new crusaders shows just as much propensity for violence as the foe they seek to attack. Theology and the rites of Christian belief become the visible sign of the theological conflict. While the group do destroy a child-killing vampire, it should not be ignored that the prayers and appropriation of Christian iconography allow for the rites of purification to function as a performative justification of physical violence.

However, rather than see the novel in binary terms of theological righteousness combatting the spiritual darkness of the vampire, the text shows the ways in which theology can all too easily be used to provide a discursive framework for violence and domination. Those who stake Lucy co-opt the language of theology for their actions and in this the distinction between themselves and the work of Dracula becomes increasingly unstable. Throughout the novel, not simply in the character and redemptive death of Lucy, one can see Dracula's attempt to spread his influence in theological terms. The inmate of the insane asylum, Renfield, seems to be the clearest formation of how the perverted 'theology' of Dracula is articulated. With his constant displays of devotion and the quasi-scriptural references to the idea that 'the blood is life',[199] Renfield serves as a John

---

[196] Ibid., 227.
[197] Stoker, *Dracula*, 232.
[198] Ibid.
[199] A Scriptural referent here is to Levitical laws around sacrifices – consumption of blood is strictly forbidden, as it is through blood that the atonement of the Lord is granted, and life sustained. As all life ultimately belongs to the Lord, such consumption is an act of colossal spiritual arrogance and hubris.

the Baptist type figure, locked away 'as the best way of silencing his sacrilegious evangelism'.[200] He is the first person in the civilized contemporary world of fin-de-siècle London who theologizes Dracula. He refers to him as 'the master' as Dr Seward nervously 'thinks it is some form of religious mania which has seized him'.[201] The allusions are further strengthened when Renfield is overheard talking to Dracula:

> I am here to do your bidding master. I am Your slave and You will reward me, for I shall be faithful. I have worshipped You long and afar off. Now that You are near I await Your commands and You will not pass me by will You, dear Master.[202]

To separate this from the idea of a specific religious ideology is rendered impossible by Dr Seward's response, which neatly encapsulates the fundamental selfishness at work, 'He thinks of the loaves and the fishes even when he believes he is in a real presence'.[203] It seems then, when examined in combination with Lucy's reportedly grossly exaggerated desire for her fiancée, that the fundamental tenet of the vampire theology is one of extreme self-interest and self-gratification. Renfield enacts a kind of linguistic parody of religious language, using it for his self-interested ends and once again showing the fragility and corruptibility of theological discourse. It is for this reason that vampires are positioned as fundamentally opposite to a civilized modern world – in the civilized world of British imperialism, it is simply not possible to be as exploitative and self-interested as Dracula as it serves as both a societal and spiritual danger, threatening the theological justifications for the hegemony of empire. Renfield is contained within the asylum, limiting his potential to damage to society, both politically and theologically, and Dr Seward immediately highlights how self-involved this self-aggrandizing faith is:

---

[200] Herbert, 'Vampire Religion', 107.
[201] Seward claims that a religious mania is something that can be medically diagnosed. Once again, this links to the emerging field of psychology and in particular the work of William James. James specifically distinguishes between the 'ordinary religious believer' and those who have 'excessively pursued' the religious life which results in 'abnormal psychical visitations' (William James, *The Varieties of Religious Experience* (London: Penguin Classics, 1985) p. 6). There is, it seems, an appropriate amount of belief or religious faith that is psychologically dangerous to exceed. Thus, the novel further destabilizes the divide between religion and science in fin-de-siècle materialism.
[202] Stoker, *Dracula*, 113.
[203] Ibid. and a reference to Mt. 14 and Jn 6, the moments in the Gospels where Christ feeds thousands through a few loaves and fish. Seward's point is that Renfield's aims are remarkably base – concerned only with his physical desire for consuming, to the extent that he ignores the theological realities at play.

> How these madmen give themselves away! The real God taketh heed lest a sparrow fall, but the God created from human vanity sees no difference between an eagle and a sparrow. Oh! If only men knew![204]

Rather than encourage any kind of humility and value in others, Dracula (and thus all he influences) sees no distinction between people, dividing them into either prey or a threat. The eternal life he offers is a mockery of the sacrifice of Christ, as rather than shed blood for the sake of others Dracula is only capable of taking from those who worship or encounter him. Thus, Dracula's 'faith' involves a forcible taking from others – physically and spiritually for his own purposes. However, Dracula's actions are uncomfortably similar to those of Harker, Van Helsing and the rest who seek his destruction. While cloaked in the language of religion the language used throughout the novel is annihilationist – Harker calls on God to allow him to 'destroy that earthly life of him which we were aiming at'.[205] Further still, Harker seeks to 'send his soul for ever and ever to burning hell',[206] for Dracula's feeding on Mina. One of the heroes of the novel is, just as with Dracula, a force of great power, capable of using sophisticated systems and technologies for exploitation and domination. Through the appropriation of the language of morality and theology, violence is justified, made into something not just necessary but divinely approved. This divine sanction for violent retribution allows for a collective response to the emergence of the vampire. This notion of collective faith or common church widens the access to the necessary materials with which to further the fight against Dracula. In collective belief, the group wields crucifixes as well as guns, both of which, by this point in the narrative, are held up as products of civilized, fin-de-siècle society. This is due to the influence of Van Helsing whose exhortation to believe in what is beyond the material has encouraged the rest of the crew of light to utilize the power of the non-materialist (in this case crucifixes) alongside the technologies of the materialist age.

In other words, the fundamental sacrilege of the vampire is a perversion of the Eucharistic sacrament, whereas in the orthodox theology of the church it brings the many disparate parts of the body of Christ around the same table. Here Dracula is the one feeding on the many. The best example of this is shown in how both Mina and Renfield are treated in their encounters with Dracula. Mina's encounter with Dracula that 'Van Helsing misleadingly terms the

---

[204] Stoker, *Dracula*, 113.
[205] Ibid., 328.
[206] Ibid.

vampire's baptism of blood ... is given the form and discourse of a communion'[207] which shows how the vampire corrupts the sacraments of the church. Mina is forced into drinking the Count's blood, while her husband impotently stands and watches – reduced to both theological and material spectator. Dracula transforms her into the 'bountiful wine press' and his 'companion and helper'[208] through this ceremony. An orthodox theological understanding placed great emphasis on the Eucharist and the act of Holy Communion as a process of the transmission of the nature of Christ: here, the '*cordon sanitaire* between religious piety and superstition'[209] has been collapsed as Dracula blurs and corrupts the lines between the sacrament and sacrilege. As Girard points out, this religious impulse to separate the sacred and the sacrilegious 'is not dissimilar to that of medicine when suddenly confronted with an unknown disease',[210] that given Dracula's need for blood, further connects both fin-de-siècle science and a distinctly theological discourse. The conclusion to the Vampire Eucharist is how Dracula treats Renfield; savagely beating him to death, soaking him in the blood upon which Dracula feeds. The end point of the Vampire Eucharist, then, is not the spiritual sustenance offered in the sacrifice that the Christian Eucharist is based on, but rather Dracula forces Renfield into a sacrifice solely for his own ends – as soon as Renfield is no longer fit for Dracula's purpose, he is brutally disposed of. This physicalizing of the transcendent sacrament offers a vision of theology as a weapon and provides an uncomfortable similarity between the spiritual power of Dracula and the theological legitimacy of those who seek to confront him.

The important idea of collective faith and action lends credence to the notion that the confrontation with Dracula is a form of missionary evangelism. The group of Mina, Jonathan, Arthur, Quincy Morris and Dr Seward form around the charismatic leadership of Van Helsing. Together the group goes back from the civilized world into Transylvania. The group, now well armed in both the technological and spiritual sense,[211] return to the superstitious land in which the novel opened. Rather than an individual alone, the return to Dracula's homeland

---

[207] Noel Montague-Etienne Rarignac, *The Theology of Dracula, Reading the Book of Stoker as Sacred Text* (London: MacFarland and Co, 2012), 115.
[208] Stoker, *Dracula*, 306.
[209] Herbert, 'Vampire Religion', 110.
[210] René Girard, *Violence and the Sacred*, trans. Patrick Gregory (London: Bloomsbury Academic, 2013), 36.
[211] They go having experience with the effectiveness of the Host and crucifixes in dealing with Dracula as well as carrying weapons – the combination of physical weaponry and spiritual force proves to be highly potent.

is a collective endeavour. As one critic notes, 'Harker instead of being alone, unsure, and Protestant, he is now in a group, experienced, and quasi-Catholic'.[212] Stoker defines the journey back into the region as not simply a geographical journey, but rather a 'time-journey into a stratum of the European mind prior to the supposed conquering of pagan magical thinking by Christianity'.[213] The superstition of the area is defined anthropologically and in going back in to Dracula's own country the characters appropriate theological language of the crusades, thus framing the conflict as not just a religious quest but also a spiritual battle, in the tradition of the bloody past of Christian colonialism:

> thus are we ministers of God's own wish . . . he has allowed us to redeem one soul already, [the death and salvation of Lucy Westenra] and we go out as the old knights of the Cross to redeem more. Like them we shall travel towards the sunrise.[214]

Thus, as with the crusades of old, it is not simply a moral divide between Dracula and these new nineteenth-century crusaders but rather the journey of the group into the East and fight against Dracula represent the age of modernity in its struggle against pre-Christian superstitions. This is not simply a religious quest though, as Dracula's opponents always manage to utilize the technology and privileges of the modern world that Dracula cannot use. For example, the group manages to use the technologies of travel that Dracula does not, as Van Helsing explains that while Dracula travels by boat, 'It will take her . . . three weeks to reach Varna', the others can 'travel overland to the same place in three days'.[215] Not only do they take advantage of the industrialization[216] that modernity brings that advantages them over Dracula; they also make the conscious decision to go 'armed against evil things, spiritual as well as physical'. Just as the crusaders took arms, here the group adds 'Winchesters to our armament', and set out to defeat Dracula with not only the powers of heaven but with all the powers of the modern industrial age.[217]

---

[212] Kellie Wixson, 'Dracula: An Anglo-Irish Novel', in *Dracula: The Shade and the Shadow*, ed. Elizabeth Miller (Westcliff-on-Sea: Desert Island Books, 1998), 254.
[213] Herbert, 'Vampire Religion', 102.
[214] Stoker, *Dracula*, 341.
[215] Ibid., 345.
[216] For the connections between modernity and the figure of the vampire, see Stacey Abbott, *Celluloid Vampires: Life After Death in the Modern World* (Texas: University of Texas Press, 2009).
[217] Notably the group take Winchester rifles thanks to the American Quincey Morris, this incidental detail serves as both a material and theological link to the United States, itself a nation founded on the principle of theologically justified colonialism.

It is in the novel's conclusion that this synthesis of science, technology and religion is used most explicitly to finally bring about Dracula's death. The final religious mark is the scene where the men of the group swear to release Mina's soul back to God, kneeling before Mina and promising to kill her rather than allow her to fall victim to Dracula for eternity. The scene is laden with religious overtones that unsettle the characters and reinforce the sacrificial religious traits that Mina's character takes upon herself. As Dr Seward writes:

> How can I . . . tell of that strange scene, its solemnity . . . its sweetness. Even a sceptic, who can see nothing but a travesty of bitter truth in anything holy or emotional, would have melted to the heart had he seen that little group of loving and devoted friends.[218]

Mina, stricken with the taint of 'impurity', poses a danger to the entire group. As Girard notes, there is only one way to purify her infected blood – 'only blood itself – the blood, in short of sacrificial victims – can accomplish this task'.[219] This scene serves as not only a form of spiritual redemption for Mina, allowing her to sacrifice herself for the sake of others and thus achieve some form of redemption from Dracula but has a crucial role for the other characters. The men in this scene are commissioned by Mina, to go out to fight Dracula – 'What will each of you give? Your lives I know . . . Your lives are God's, and you can give them back to him.'[220] The scene finishes with Seward noting that the 'coming relapse from her freedom of soul' now did not seem so 'full of despair'.[221] In a sense, the group has been consecrated by Mina's sacrifice to go out and redeem the modern, civilized world from the vampire's influence. This point is further proven by Mina's note in her journal that 'we are truly in the hands of God', suggesting divine providence behind the actions of the characters out to destroy the vampire and thus behind the whole of the material, fin-de-siècle civilized society that they represent. What this implies is that there must be both the actions of the individual and the divine providence of God acting in combination with one another to control and defeat Dracula.

In conclusion, the theology of the novel and the ways in which the theology is enacted is a highly effective blend of both contemporary Protestant identity coupled with the ancient sacraments and iconography of the Catholic Church.

---

[218] Stoker, *Dracula*, 354.
[219] Girard, *Violence*, 39.
[220] Stoker, *Dracula*, 351.
[221] Ibid., 354.

As such, the use of theological sacraments and iconography is at best eclectic, mixing Catholic hosts with the detail of Protestant testimony narratives. Perhaps we mistakenly assume that this book, 'hybrid as it is of Gothic horror-mongering and religious earnestness will prove to be fully coherent in its thinking'.[222] Alternatively, this mix of the ancient and modern, the Catholic and the Protestant might be seen as attempting a type of syncretism. As Alison Milbank writes,

> Stoker used a demonic character to unite a disparate opposition. So, Dracula calls forth a union of Protestant word and Catholic sacrament, figured as modern and ancient modes of communication.[223]

However, the claims of syncretism do not seem totally convincing – functioning as an attempt to apply systematic definitions and dogmatic separations to an imaginative presentation of the role of sacramentality and iconography in dealing with an encounter with monstrous evil. Rather than this kind of theological literalism, the text is more hermeneutically fruitful than simply bringing together Catholic and Protestant traditions. Fundamentally, the novel shows that rather than being antagonistic, Christian theological discourses and modernity can be brought together to serve the same function in different ways. The rationalist and materialist ideology can only explain a small part of the nature of the vampire and must necessarily be paired with religion. The use of Christian iconography, sacraments and theology allows characters to find the means to 'engage the world beyond the self, whether of material or spiritual objects, as truly real'.[224] In effect, this means that the rational world of fin-de-siècle modernity could not defeat Dracula and thus without a religious or theological aspect to the civilized world, there would be no way for the individual characters to be capable of engaging with the irrational and spiritually powerful force that Dracula embodies. Through the technologies of modernity, the vampire can be fought, but it is through the iconography and sacraments of Christian thought that Dracula can be defeated. However, this relationship is not unproblematic, as within the novel, theology and the rites and symbols of Christian faith are not excused from violence but are weaponized, drawn into the culpability of violence and domination that Dracula embodies. Thus, not only does *Dracula* serve as an imaginative re-engagement with the nature and true theological significance of sacraments but also poses a profound challenge. If a sacramental theology can

---

[222] Herbert, 'Vampire Religion', 102.
[223] Milbank, 'Powers Old and New: Stoker's Alliances with Anglo-Irish Gothic'.
[224] Milbank, 'Apologetics and the Imagination', 33.

reinstate purity through violence, then the theologically aware reader is forced to confront the vulnerability of theology.

Finally, the fin-de-siècle Gothic text reveals itself to be theologically productive as well as highlighting the extent to which theological understandings of sin contribute to understandings of the Gothic in the light of degeneration theory's failure to properly engage with non-materialist discourses. Theological readings of the novels reveal the necessity of understanding degeneration in more than solely materialist terms, as discourses emptied of theological content leave understandings of these texts conceptually impoverished. At the same time, a theological understanding of these three texts reveals a greater complexity and conceptual richness that degeneration theorists, through their materialist biases, cannot help but miss. However, theology does not stand above, or separate from, the materialist discourses of degeneration, as throughout the fin-de-siècle Gothic, theology is instrumentalized in similar ways to degeneration theory into a tool of violence and imperialism, frequently used to justify colonial domination and class oppression in the name of God. Theological readings of these texts thus provide both much-needed depth to degeneration theory as well as a means by which understandings of evil and the supernatural find new expression outside of the strictures of Christian theology which becomes increasingly reliant on natural theology. The fin-de-siècle Gothic text functions not simply as the embodiment of materialist anxieties around the status of human subjectivity as these texts consistently resist simply materialist explanation. Criticism that rests upon the materialist ideas of degeneration theory, while beneficial ignores much of the theological content of these novels and is thus methodologically limited, unable to adequately engage with the non-material aspect of the Gothic that emerges during the fin-de-siècle. However, as *Dracula* clearly shows, the distinction between the material conditions of the fin-de-siècle and the theological elements are not necessarily clear– theology and theological anxieties are both produced by a particular set of historical and social conditions and are simultaneously a response to these conditions. Within *Dracula*, theology is both a part of the materialist, technologically sophisticated and imperialist society that battles the vampire, yet at the same time, the power of Dracula resides in his superstitious and theological nature. What these texts prove, through a theological reading, is that the Gothic text allows for an exploration of theological anxieties in new ways. As materialist discourses became increasingly widely accepted, there remains within the Gothic a strain of theological discourse which responds to the predominant materialist degeneration discourse of the cultural moment. Thus, despite the proliferation and widespread acceptance of degeneration discourses, even in a cultural era of ostensible secularity and materialism, and even within a technologically sophisticated and imperialist nation such as Britain, these materialist discourses alone are insufficient. Augustinian notions of privation and evil are not reducible to discourses of biological destiny or degeneration that were so prevalent in the post-Darwinian age. That said, the entanglements between theology and the materialist discourses of the fin-de-siècle Gothic render theology unstable and vulnerable – as much as a theological reading of these three texts may highlight the need for theological awareness (indeed it is essential in combatting Dracula, for example) it is all too easily co-opted and used to justify violence, misogyny and oppression. The challenge for criticism on the fin-de-siècle Gothic is to explore and engage the theological and non-material element of the language and themes of the text while interrogating the ways in which this language is complicit and bound up within ongoing violence and oppression.

Conclusion

Through the Gothic castle, back to theology

From beginning at a theological starting point from which to investigate the Gothic nineteenth-century novel, the conclusion returns to theology, having passed through the Gothic text. This book has argued that the nineteenth-century Gothic narrative expresses theological and imaginative concerns that have, thus far in criticism, remained either latent, under-acknowledged or ignored. Utilizing an imaginative apologetics, the texts have been read as expressing a variety of theological issues outside the strictures and limitations of conventional theology or orthodox religious practice, while at the same time seeking to remain aware of the historical and critical contexts that inform the text's production. What emerges from the preceding chapters is the ways in which theological readings can provide new insights into the Gothic novels studied, as well as contribute to the fields of both imaginative apologetics and Gothic studies more widely. The scope of the texts chosen has led to theological examinations of personhood and subjectivity, the tensions between religion and theology, political theology and the importance of sacramentality. Such theological content has thus far been given insufficient critical attention.

As argued in the introduction, if the Gothic novel is read as possessing a theological content, no matter how heterodox or ambiguous, this carries an implicit challenge to the wider field of theology. Within the Gothic, theology is held in ambiguous tension with the supernatural, yet, as Hughes points out, 'the conventional closures which characterise many Gothic works'[1] aim at a restoration of Christian morality and at fictionalizing a reassuring belief in the omnipotence and omnibenevolence of God. However, as argued throughout this book, the Gothic relationship to theology is not limited by narrative closure. Rather than read the Gothic novel as staging something as straightforward as a morality play or pious ethical allegory, the book has argued that, throughout the Gothic, closure is never final or ultimate as the texts consistently emphasize

[1] Hughes, *Beyond Dracula*, 14.

both the reality and the power of supernatural experiences alongside the role of theology. Thus, as Hughes writes, 'the Gothic retains a commitment to an ongoing ontological dialectic in which the credible and the orthodox are presented as relative rather than Absolute, if only for a time'.[2]

This relativity of the credible and realist alongside the orthodox, religious and supernatural insights of the Gothic novel revealed through this imaginative apologetic reading can and, indeed, must be worked back into the wider, ongoing and multifaceted development of Christian theology and practice. Furthermore, this persistence of the theological content of the Gothic novel and the productive readings generated through imaginative apologetics would seem to require a more theologically open aspect to Gothic criticism. As Geary argues, Gothic criticism has, through its history, generally seen the religious as something explicable in psychological terms – this he pins to the influence of Freud and his essay on the uncanny. 'Since the supernatural was but a covert means of exploring more forbidden themes of the self and the other, it no longer has a place in the post-Freudian world.'[3] However, solely psychological readings of the Gothic do not adequately explain the proliferation of theological and religious theme, imagery, trope and symbol that persist throughout the texts in question. With this in mind, the conclusion seeks to establish the ways in which the Gothic informs and challenges theological thought and, in addition, the ways in which imaginative apologetics may continue to inform and add to the ongoing investigation of Gothic literature in all of its forms. The challenge that emerges from the investigations in previous chapters is to articulate how and in what ways theology must respond to the insights generated from Gothic sources.

In her book on women writers of the nineteenth century, Rebecca Styler argues that 'it was necessary for these writers to create a literary theology because female writers were denied any formal theological role in the church and academy'.[4] While a promising starting point, Styler's argument does not necessarily extend to the writers considered here – while the Brontë sisters may fit Styler's model that certainly does not hold true for writers such as Hogg and Wilde (see Chapters 2 and 5, respectively). Rather, it seems that regardless of the theological position of the authors of the text, the Gothic novel can function as

---

[2] Ibid., 15.
[3] Geary, *Supernatural*, 127–8.
[4] Rebecca Styler, *Literary Theology by Women Writers of the Nineteenth Century* (Farnham: Ashgate, 2010), 1.

a space within which theological ideas are explored outside of the institutional boundaries of a religious denomination or the discursive boundaries of theology itself, embodying the tensions that Kutter Calloway and Barry Taylor refer to as a/theology.[5] Thus, rather than follow Styler and argue that these writers produced a 'Gothic theology' as a consequence of a lack of formal theological authority, the texts instead function as a way in which orthodoxy can be bypassed and the limitations of denominational acceptability can be ignored. However, it would be a mistake to consider the Gothic as a kind of 'repressed theology' as this steers too close to a psychoanalytic logic that could discount the theological within the texts. Rather, what is required is a more expansive view of theology that moves beyond the limitations and barriers of either religious practice, orthodoxy and denomination or the edges of a particular body of thought and scholarship. Such an attitude only serves to isolate natural theology from the culture in which it exists and thus restrict the ways in which theology and culture may profitably interact. As David Brown explains in the conclusion to his work *God in Mystery and Words*:

> The art, music, architecture, and literature referred to are essentially illustrative of a more fundamental thesis: that both natural and revealed theology are in crisis, and that the only way out is to give proper attention to the cultural embeddedness of both. Religion does not operate in isolation, and so theology and philosophy as it reflects on religion is equally incapable of escaping that wider influence, however much it may pretend otherwise.[6]

First, then, the theological reading of the Gothic contributes to theology by revealing the extent to which imaginative theology is culturally embedded – even within what would seem to be an ostensibly 'low' cultural form such as the Gothic novel. Crucially, this reinforces the point made by Milbank that the Gothic renders the familiar and mundane eerie and strange – and as a result, opens up onto the religious sense. Christianity, as Milbank writes, is 'not narrow but a vision that includes everything'[7] – not just the literature of Christian writers

---

[5] Kutter Calloway and Barry Taylor, *The Aesthetics of Atheism: Theology and Imagination In Contemporary Culture,* (Minneapolis: Fortress Press, 2019).

[6] Brown, *God in Mystery and Words*, 269. While Brown's point regarding a crisis may be open to contestation, there are two points worth adding – that the natural theology of writers such as Brown has done much to move theology beyond the point of crisis and furthermore, it is remarkable how little attention was given to this question through much of the history of Gothic criticism. Parenthetically it should be acknowledged that both Milbank and Brown are engaged in very different projects, yet the work the two have done had expanded the field of understanding for examining the ways in which culture and theology interact.

[7] Milbank, 'Apologetics and the Imagination', 44.

but the horrors and terrors of the Gothic novel are just as capable of leading upward to talk of God. The failure to acknowledge this seems to be both short-sighted and imposing a limit on where imaginative apologetics may turn for resources. In certain respects, it would seem that Brown's point about the crisis in theology shows that the suspicions of Coleridge over the Gothic's theological liminality, mentioned in the introduction, remain unresolved.

Here, then, we may begin to articulate the theological challenge within the Gothic novel a little more clearly – with the caveat that the readings given in the previous chapters, while generally Augustinian in tone, should by no means be considered as a comprehensive theological hermeneutic. Rather, it seems that the Gothic novel operates upon the same linguistic and imaginative ground as theology, while not necessarily sharing its commitments, or further still, opposing them completely. That said, the novels considered in the course of this book do operate upon the terrain of the theological, even if that is directed towards a non-theological or even atheist reader. The Gothic text uses much of the same language that makes talk of God (however conceived) possible in the first place. This inevitably has implications for both the theologian and the Gothic critic, as Imfeld writes:

> The supernatural tale provides a space in which the non-theological reader can participate in the theological journey. For the literary scholar, theological readings of the ghost story provide a recovery of a specific ontological vocabulary, and for theologians, they provide a reminder that the divine is there in the grotesque.[8]

The Gothic novel, with its accompanying monsters, violence and supernatural occurrences, serves as a fruitful site for theological engagement in terms that do not depend upon theological knowledge or even religious faith, and so should be seen as hugely valuable for any imaginative apologetic work. The Catholic philosopher William Desmond lays out the implications of this in striking terms:

> Why should only the faces of beauty show the divine, and not the faces of the repulsive? Startling us, sometimes monstrous faces seem truer masks of the divine, for even in the revulsion they call forth a reckless consent. The divine is there in the grotesque, disproportionate to our sense of finite harmony, shattering the concord of our finite measure of love. There is excess to the repulsive we cannot stand, but the ultimate stands with the monstrous too, and we must look

[8] Imfeld, *The Victorian Ghost Story*, 167.

at the monstrous differently to be with the ultimate differently. We need *agapeic* beholding of the beauty in the ugly, the eyes of God in the scabby countenance.[9]

The Gothic novel, then, challenges the theologian to find the revelation of God in the strangest, most violent and unexpected of places. Read theologically and imaginatively, it issues a test to the theologian – to look into the very darkest possible forms of narrative and culture and there discern the movement and action of God. In a secular age where religious faith is seen as no longer the easiest or perhaps even a defensible position, it seems that the Gothic novel possesses both a reach and an imaginative capacity that theology as a whole should not ignore. Thus, the work of continuing to draw both Gothic studies and imaginative apologetics together must continue. As mutually beneficial and productive partners, the two fields may continue to reveal the extent to which God is at work, in all places – even if those places are wholly unexpected, terrifying and unpredictable, challenging and unsettling to believer and nonbeliever alike. As Augustine wrote of God as the water which permeates every aspect of the sponge that is the world, there is always more to discover if the idea of universality is taken with its due seriousness.[10] Read with imaginative engagement and theological awareness, the Gothic novel is shown to be a part of this process. Even in the very darkest, most terrifying aspects of our culture and the world we share, we may, if we are willing to look carefully and with humility, find something of the nature of the divine, where it is most needed and most unexpected.

---

[9] William Desmond, *God and the Between* (London: Wiley-Blackwell, 2008), 197.
[10] Augustine, *Confessions*, 55–63. While this is a point made by Augustine in his Manichean phase, it serves to illustrate the crucial point that revelation about the nature of the divine can and indeed does emerge from sources that are outside of the Christian tradition.

Bibliography

Abbott, Stacey. *Celluloid Vampires: Life After Death in the Modern World*. Texas: University of Texas Press, 2009.

Abrams, M. H. *Natural Supernaturalism: Tradition and Revolution in Romantic Literature*. London: Norton, 1971.

Acosta, Ana. *Reading Genesis in the Long Eighteenth Century: From Milton to Mary Shelley*. London: Ashgate, 2006.

Adams, Hazard, Leroy Searle, ed. *Critical Theory Since Plato*. London: Wadsworth Publishing, 2004.

Adams, Marilyn McCord. *Christ and Horrors: The Coherence of Christology*. Cambridge: Cambridge University Press, 2008.

Allot, Miriam, ed. *The Brontës: A Critical Heritage*. London: Routledge, 1974.

Anderson, Cameron J. *The Faithful Artist: A Vision for Evangelicalism and the Arts*. Downers Grove, IL: InterVarsity Press, 2011.

Andrews, Stephen. 'The Ambiguity of Capacity, A Rejoinder to Trevor Hart', *Tyndale Bulletin* 45.1 (1994): 169–79.

Arata, Stephen. *Fictions of Loss in the Victorian Fin-de-siècle: Identity and Empire*. Cambridge: Cambridge University Press, 1996.

Astley, Jeff, David Brown and Ann Loades. *Problems in Theology: Evil – A Reader*. London: Continuum, 2003.

Augustine. *Confessions of a Sinner*, trans. R. S. Pine-Coffin. London: Penguin Great Ideas, 2004.

Baldick, Chris. *In Frankenstein's Shadow; Myth, Monstrosity and Nineteenth Century Writing*. Oxford: Clarendon Paperbacks, 1990.

Barth, J. Robert. *Romanticism and Transcendence: Wordsworth, Coleridge and the Religious Imagination*. Missouri: University of Missouri Press, 2003.

Beattie, Valerie. 'The Mystery at Thornfield: Representations of Madness in *Jane Eyre*', *Studies in the Novel* 28.4 (Winter 1996): 493–503

Bentham, Jeremy. *An Introduction to The Principles of Morals and Legislation*. http://www.earlymoderntexts.com/assets/pdfs/bentham1780.pdf, first accessed 6 June 16.

Bloom, Harold, ed. *Mary Shelley*. London: Modern Critical Voices, 1985.

Botting, Fred. *Gothic*. London: Routledge, 1995.

Bretherton, Luke. *Hospitality as Holiness: Christian Witness Amid Moral Diversity*. London: Ashgate, 2009.

Brontë, Charlotte. *Jane Eyre*. London: Penguin Deluxe Editions, 2009.

Brontë, Emily. *Wuthering Heights*. London: Penguin Classics, 2012.

Brown, Callum G. *The Death of Christian Britain: Understanding Secularisation 1800–2000*, 2nd edn. London: Routledge, 2009.
Brown, Charles Brockden. *Wieland and Memoirs of Carwin the Biloquist*, ed. Bryan Waterman. London: Norton Critical Editions, 2011.
Brown, David. *Discipleship and Imagination: Christian Tradition and Truth*. Oxford: Oxford University Press, 2000.
Brown, David. *God and Enchantment of Place: Reclaiming Human Experience*. Oxford: Oxford University Press, 2004.
Brown, David. *God in Mystery and Words: Experience Through Metaphor and Drama*. Oxford: Oxford University Press, 2011.
Brown, David. 'The Arts' Critique of Theology', delivered at the Ian Ramsey Centre - Humane Philosophy Project 2014–2015 Seminar. Available at https://www.youtube.com/watch?v=SgskbXGdHtI, first accessed 26 June 2017.
Brown, David. *Tradition and Imagination: Revelation and Change*. Oxford: Oxford University Press, 1999.
Brunner, Emil. *Natural Theology: Comprising Nature and Grace by Professor Dr. Emil Brunner and the reply No! by Dr. Karl Barth*. London: Wipf & Stock, 2003.
Buell, Larence, ed. *The American Transcendentalists: Essential Writings*. New York: Modern Library, 2006.
Bunyan, John. *The Pilgrim's Progress*. Oxford: Oxford University Press, 2003.
Butler, Judith. *Precarious Life: The Powers of Mourning and Violence*. London: Verso Books, 2004.
Butler, Marilyn. *Romantics, Rebels and Reactionaries: English Literature and Its Background 1760–1830*. Oxford: Oxford University Press, 1981.
Byron, Glennis, and Townshend, Dale, ed. *The Gothic World*. London: Routledge, 2013.
Calder, Jenni. RLS: *Life Study of Robert Louis Stevenson*. London: Chambers, 1990.
Callaway, Kutter and Barry Taylor. *The Aesthetics of Atheism: Theology and Imagination in Contemporary Culture*. Minneapolis, Fortress Press, 2019.
Calvin, John. *Commentary on John*, ed. J. I. Packer. Wheaton: Crossway, 1994.
Calvin, John. *Institutes of the Christian Religion*, trans. Henry Beveridge. Michigan: WM. B. Eerdman Publishing, 1998.
Chadwick, Owen. *The Secularization of the European Mind in the Nineteenth Century*. Cambridge: Cambridge University Press, 1975.
Chambers, Robert. *Traditions of Edinburgh: A New Edition*. Edinburgh: W&R Chambers, 1847.
Chesterton, G. K. *Charles Dickens*. Teddington: Echo Library, 2007 [1906].
Clarke, Michael M. 'Emily Brontë's "No Coward Soul" and the Need for a Religious Literary Criticism', *Victorians' Institute Journal* 37 (2009): 195–224
Clemens, Valdine. *The Return of the Repressed: Gothic Horror from the Castle of Otranto to Alien*. New York: SUNY Press, 1999.

Coleridge, Samuel Taylor. *Biographia Literia*. http://www.gutenberg.org/files/6081/6081-h/6081-h.htm#link2HCH0013, first accessed 5 September 2017.

Coleridge, Samuel Taylor. 'Review of Matthew G Lewis, *The Monk*', *The Critical Review* (February 1797): 194–200. http://www.english.upenn.edu/~mgamer/Etexts/coleridge.reviews, Online, accessed 24 July 2017.

Copjec Jean, ed. *Radical Evil*. London: Verso Books, 1996.

Cottom, Daniel. 'Frankenstein and the Monster of Representation', *SubStance* 28 (1980): 60–71.

Critchley, Simon. *Faith of the Faithless, Experiments in Political Theology*. London: Verso Books, 2014.

Davis, Colin. 'From Psychopathology to Diabolical Evil: Dr Jekyll, Mr Hyde and Jean Renoir', *Journal of Romance Studies* 12.1 (Spring 2012): 10–23.

Davis, Steve. *Emily Brontë: Heretic*. London: The Women's Press, 1994.

Davison, Andrew, ed. *Imaginative Apologetics: Theology, Philosophy and the Catholic Tradition*. London: SCM Press, 2011.

Davison, Carol Margaret. *Gothic Literature 1764–1824*. Cardiff: University of Wales Press, 2009.

Davison, Carol Margaret and Monaca Germana, ed. *Scottish Gothic: An Edinburgh Companion*. Edinburgh: Edinburgh University Press, 2016.

DeLamotte, Eugenia C. *Perils of the Night: A Feminist Study of Nineteenth Century Literature*. Oxford: Oxford University Press, 1990.

Desmond, William. *God and the Between*. Oxford: Wiley-Blackwell, 2008.

Dryden, Linda. *The Modern Gothic and Literary Doubles: Stevenson, Wilde and Wells*. Cambridge: Cambridge University Press, 2003.

Eagleton, Terry. *Culture and the Death of God*. London: Yale University Press, 2014.

Eagleton, Terry. *Myths of Power: A Marxist Study of the Brontës*. Basingstoke: Palgrave Macmillan, 2005.

Eagleton, Terry. *On Evil*. London: Yale University Press, 2008.

Edwards, Jonathan and Reiner Smolinski, ed. 'Sinners in the Hands of an Angry God. A Sermon Preached at Enfield, July 8th, 1741', (1741) *Electronic Texts in American Studies*, 54. http://digitalcommons.unl.edu/etas/54

Empson, William. *Milton's God*. London: Chatto & Windus, 1961.

Faflak, Joel. *Romantic Psychoanalysis: The Burden of the Mystery*. New York: State University of New York Press, 2009.

Fernie, Ewan. *The Demonic: Literature and Experience*. London: Routledge, 2013.

Fiddes, Paul. *Freedom and Limit: A Dialogue Between Literature and Christian Doctrine*. London: Palgrave, 1991.

Franssen, Paul J. C. M. 'Another Possible Source for Bertha Mason in Jane Eyre', *Notes and Queries* 58.1 (2011): 88–9.

Frye, Northrop. *Return of Eden: Five Essays on Milton's Epics*. Toronto: University of Toronto Press, 1965.

Geary, Robert F. *The Supernatural in Gothic Fiction Horror, Belief and Literary Change*. Lampeter: The Edwin Mellen Press, 1992.

Geerken, Ingrid. '"The Dead Are Not Annihilated": Mortal Regret in *Wuthering Heights*', *Journal of Narrative Theory* 34.3 (2004): 373–406.

Gelder, Ken. *Reading the Vampire*. London: Routledge, 1994.

Glen, Heather, ed. *The Cambridge Companion to the Brontës*. Cambridge: Cambridge University Press, 2003.

Gilbert, Sandra M. and Susan Gubar. *The Madwoman in the Attic: The Woman Writer and the Nineteenth-Century Literary Imagination*. London: Yale University Press, 1984.

Girard, René. *Violence and the Sacred*, trans. Patrick Gregory. London: Bloomsbury Academic, 2013.

Guest, Kirsten. 'Jekyll and Hyde Inc: Limited Liability, Companification, and Gothic Subjectivity', *Victorian Literature and Culture* 44.2 (June 2016): 315–29.

Guite, Malcolm. *Faith, Hope and Poetry: Theology and the Poetic Imagination*. London: Routledge, 2010.

Haining Peter and Peter Tremayne. *The Undead: The Legend of Bram Stoker and Dracula*. London: Constable, 1997.

Halberstam, Judith. *Skin Shows: Gothic Horror and the Technology of Monsters*. London: Duke University Press, 1995.

Hamid, Shadi. *Islamic Exceptionalism: How the Struggle over Islam Is Reshaping the World*. London: St Martin's Press, 2016.

Hart, Trevor. 'A Capacity for Ambiguity? The Barth/Brunner Debate Revisited', *Tyndale Bulletin* 44.2 (1993): 289–305.

Hauerwas, Stanley. *Unleashing the Scripture: Freeing the Bible from Captivity to America*. Nashville: Abingdon Press, 1993.

Herbert, Christopher. 'Vampire Religion', *Representations* 79.1 (Summer 2002): 100–121

Hoeveler, Diane Long. *Gothic Feminism: The Professionalisation of Gender from Charlotte Smith to the Brontës*. Liverpool: Liverpool University Press, 1996.

Hoeveler, Diane Long. *Gothic Riffs: Secularizing the Uncanny in the European Imaginary 1780–1820*. Ohio: Ohio University Press, 2010.

Hoeveler, Diane Long. *The Gothic Ideology: Religious Hysteria and Anti-Catholicism in British Popular Fiction, 1780–1880*. Cardiff: University of Wales Press, 2014.

Hoeveler, Diane Long and Deborah Denenholz Morse, eds *A Companion to the Brontës*. London: Wiley-Blackwell, 2016.

Hogle, Jerrold E., ed. *A Companion to the Gothic*. Cambridge: Cambridge University Press, 2001.

Hogg, James. *The Private Memoirs and Confessions of a Justified Sinner*. London: Wordsworth Classics, 2003.

Hopps Gavin and Jane Stabler, ed. *Romanticism and Religion from William Cowper to Wallace Stevens*. London: Ashgate, 2006.

Hughes, William. *Beyond Dracula: Bram Stoker's Fiction and Its Cultural Context*. London: Palgrave Macmillan, 2000.
Hurley, Kelly. *The Gothic Body: Sexuality, Materialism and Degeneration at the fin-de-siècle*. Cambridge: Cambridge University Press, 1996.
Huxley, T. H., 'On the Physical Basis of Life'. http://aleph0.clarku.edu/huxley/CE1/Phys B.html, first accessed 14 February 2017.
Inglis, Kenneth Stanley. *Churches and the Working Class in Victorian England*. London: Routledge, 2007.
Imfeld, Zoë Lehmann. *The Victorian Ghost Story and Theology: from Le Fanu to James*. London: Palgrave Macmillan, 2016.
Imfeld, Zoë Lehmann, Peter Hampson and Alison Milbank, eds *Theology and Literature After Postmodernity*. London: Bloomsbury Press, 2015.
Jacobs, Alan. *Original Sin: A Cultural History*. London: Harper Collins, 2008.
James, Henry. *The Turn of the Screw*. London: Dover Thrift Editions, 2000.
James, William. *The Varieties of Religious Experience*. London: Penguin Classics, 1985.
Jaspers, David, ed. *Postmodernism, Literature and the Future of Theology*. London: Palgrave, 1993.
Jaspers, David. *The Study of Literature and Religion, An Introduction*. London: Palgrave, 1992.
Jaspers David and T. R. Wright, ed. *The Critical Spirit and the Will to Believe: Essays in Nineteenth Century Literature and Religion*. London: Palgrave Macmillan, 1989.
Kafer, Peter. *Charles Brockden Brown's Revolution and the Birth of American Gothic*. Philadelphia: University of Pennsylvania Press, 2004.
Kant, Immanuel. *Religion Within the Boundaries of Mere Reason and Other Writing*, ed. Allan Wood and George di Giovanni. Cambridge: Cambridge University Press, 1998.
Karschay, Stephen. *Degeneration, Normativity and the Gothic at the Fin De Siècle*. London: Palgrave, 2015.
Kearney, Richard. *Strangers, Gods and Monsters*. London: Routledge, 2003.
Kelly, Joseph F. *The Problem of Evil in the Western Tradition: From the Book of Job to Modern Genetics*. Minnesota: The Liturgical Press, 2001.
Knight, Mark. *Chesterton and Evil*. New York: Fordham University Press, 2004.
Knight, Mark. *An Introduction to Religion and Literature*. London: Continuum Books, 2009.
Knight, Mark and Emma Mason. *Nineteenth Century Literature and Religion: An Introduction*. Oxford: Oxford University Press, 2006.
Lamm, Julia A., ed. *The Wiley Blackwell Companion to Mystical Theology*. London: Wiley- Blackwell, 2013.
Lankester Edwin Ray. *Degeneration: A Chapter in Darwinism*. London: W.W. Norton, 1880.
Lawrence, D. H. *Studies in Classic American Literature*. London: Penguin Classics, 1971.

Leavis F. R. and Q. D. Leavis. *Lectures in America*. London: Chatto and Windus, 1969.
Ledger, Sally and Scott McCracken, ed. *Cultural Politics at the Fin-de-siècle*. Cambridge: Cambridge University Press, 1995.
Lee, Julia Sun-Joo. 'The (Slave) Narrative of *Jane Eyre*', *Victorian Literature and Culture* 36.2 (2008): 317–29.
Lerner, Laurence, 'Bertha and the Critics', *Nineteenth Century Literature* 44.3 (December 1989): 273–300.
Levine, George and U. C. Knoepflmacher, ed. *The Endurance of 'Frankenstein': Essays on Mary Shelley's Novel*. London: University of California Press, 1979.
Locke, John. *The Reasonableness of Christianity as Delivered in the Scriptures*. London: Bibliolife DBA of Bibilio Bazaar II LLC, 1824.
Lombroso, Cesare. *Crime, Its Causes and Remedies*. Boston: Little Brown and Company, 1899/1911.
Loughlin, Gerard. *Telling God's Story: Bible, Church and Narrative Theology*. Cambridge: Cambridge University Press, 1996.
MacLeod, Kirsten. *Fictions of British Decadence, High Art, Popular Writing and the Fin-De- Siècle*. London: Palgrave, 2006.
Mathewes, Charles T. *Evil and the Augustinian Tradition*. Cambridge: Cambridge University Press, 2008.
Matthiessen, T. O. *American Renaissance: Art and Expression in the Age of Emerson and Whitman*. Oxford: Oxford University Press, 1941.
Marsden, Simon. *Emily Brontë and the Religious Imagination*. London: Bloomsbury Academic, 2014.
Marsden, Simon. 'Nothing Moved. Nothing Was Seen, and Nothing Was Heard and Nothing Happened: Evil, Privation and the Absent Logos in Richard Marsh's *The Beetle Gothic Studies* 19.1 (May 2017): 57–72.
Marsden, Simon. 'The Earth No Longer a Void: Creation Theology in the Novels of Charlotte Brontë', *Literature and Theology* 25.3 (2011): 237–51.
Marx, Karl. *Economic and Philosophical Manuscripts of 1844*. https://www.marxists.org/archive/marx/works/1844/manuscripts/labour.htm, first accessed 30 August 2017.
Mather, Cotton and Reiner Smolinski, ed. 'The Wonders of the Invisible World. Observations as Well Historical as Theological, Upon the Nature, the Number, and the Operations of the Devils (1693)', *Electronic Texts in American Studies* 19. http://digitalcommons.unl.edu/etas/19, First accessed 22 August 2016.
Mays, Milton A. '*Frankenstein*, Mary Shelley's Black Theodicy', *The Southern Humanities Review* 3 (1964): 146–53.
McCarraher, Eugene. *The Enchantments of Mammon: How Capitalism Became the Religion of Modernity*. Cambridge: Harvard University Press, 2019.
Milbank, Alison. *Daughters of the House: Modes of the Gothic in Victorian Fiction*. London: Palgrave Macmillan, 1992.
Milbank, John. *Being Reconciled: Ontology and Pardon*. London: Routledge, 2003.

Miller, Elizabeth, ed. *Dracula: The Shade and the Shadow*. Westcliff-on-Sea: Desert Island Books, 1998.

Miller, J. Hillis. *The Disappearance of God: Five Nineteenth Century Writers*. London: Oxford University Press, 1963.

Mills, Kevin. *Approaching Apocalypse: Unveiling Revelation in Victorian Writing*. Lewisburg: Bucknell University Press, 2007.

Milton, John. *Paradise Lost*, ed. Gordon Teskey. London: Norton Critical Editions, 2005.

Mishra, Vijay. *The Gothic Sublime*. New York: SUNY Press, 1994.

Monti, Anthony. *A Natural Theology of the Arts*. London: Ashgate, 2003.

Moretti, Franco. 'The Dialectic of Fear', *New Left Review* 136 (November–December 1982): 67–85.

Moore, James R. *The Post-Darwinian Controversies: A Study of the Protestant Struggle to come to terms with Darwin, 1870–1900*. Cambridge: Cambridge University Press, 1979.

Moore, Stephen D. *Literary Criticism and the Gospels: The Theoretical Challenge*. London: Yale University Press, 1989.

Newman, Beth. 'Narratives of Seduction and the Seductions of Narrative: The Frame Structure of *Frankenstein*', *English Literary History [ELH]* 53 (1986): 141–61.

Nordau, Max. *Degeneration*. New York: Appleton & Co, 1895.

Nygren, Alexandra, 'Disabled and Colonized: Bertha Mason in *Jane Eyre*', *Explicator* 74.2 (2016): 117–19.

Oates, Joyce Carol. 'Frankenstein's Fallen Angel', *Critical Inquiry* 10 (March 1984): 543–55.

Oates, Joyce Carol. '*The Picture of Dorian Gray*, Wilde's Parable of the Fall', *Critical Inquiry* 7.2 (1980): 419–28.

Ordway, Holly. *Apologetics and the Christian Imagination: An Integrated Approach to Defending the Faith*. Ohio: Emmaus Road Publishing, 2017.

Parreaux, Andre. *The Publication of the Monk; A Literary Event 1796–1798*. Paris: Marcel Didier, 1960.

Pater, Walter. *The Renaissance: Studies in Art and Poetry, The 1893 Text*, ed. Donald L. Hill. London: University of California Press, 1980.

Pearce, Lynne. *Romance Writing*. Cambridge: Polity Press, 2007.

Pelikan, Jaroslav. *The Christian Tradition: A History of the Development of Doctrine Volume Four, Reformation and Dogma 1300–1700*. Chicago, IL: University of Chicago Press, 1985.

Perry, Seamus, ed. *Coleridge's Notebooks: A Selection*. Oxford: Oxford University Press, 2002.

Pick, Daniel. 'Terrors of the Night: Dracula and Degeneration in the Late Nineteenth Century', *Critical Quarterly* 30.4 (1989): 71–87.

Pickstock, Catherine. *After Writing: On the Liturgical Consummation of Philosophy*. Oxford: Blackwell, 1998.

Price, Richard. 'A Discourse on the Love of Our Country': Delivered on November 4th, 1789, at the Meeting House in the Old Jewry, to the Society for Commemorating the Revolution in Great Britain. Dr Richard Price, D. D. LL. D. F. R. S. and Fellow of the American Philosophical Societies at Philadelphia and Boston 1789', *The Literary Magazine and British Review* 3.41 (December 1789): 455–6.

Priestly, Joseph. *The Doctrine of Philosophic Necessity Illustrated an Appendix to the Disquisitions Relating to Matter and Spirit. to Which Is Added an Answer to the Letters on Materialism and on Hartley's Theory of the Mind.* London, 1777.

Punter, David, ed. *A Companion to the Gothic*. London: Blackwell, 2000.

Punter, David. *The Literature of Terror: A History of Gothic Fiction (Two Vols.)* London: Routledge, 1996.

Rarignac, Noel Montague-Etienne. *The Theology of Dracula, Reading the Book of Stoker as Sacred Text*. London: MacFarland and Co, 2012.

Reardon, Bernard. *Religion in the Age of Romanticism*. Cambridge: Cambridge University Press, 1985.

Reid, Julia. *Robert Louis Stevenson: Science and the fin-de-siècle*. London: Palgrave, 2006.

Richardson, Samuel. *Pamela: or Virtue Rewarded*. Oxford: Oxford University Press, 2008.

Ricouer, Paul. *The Symbolism of Evil*, trans. Emerson Buchanan. Boston: Beacon Press, 1969.

Rigby, Elizabeth. 'Vanity Fair – and *Jane Eyre*'. *Quarterly Review* 84 (December 1848): 153–85. http://www.quarterly-review.org/classic-qr-the-original-1848-review-of-jane-eyre/ first, accessed 24 April 2017.

Roden, Frederick. *Same Sex Desire in Victorian Religious Culture*. London: Palgrave Macmillan, 2003.

Rousseau, Jean Jacques. *The Social Contract, Or, Principles of Political Right*. trans. G. D. H. Cole. Public domain. Available at https://www.ucc.ie/archive/hdsp/Rousseau_contrat- social.pdf, first accessed 7 August 2017.

Ruland, Richard and Malcolm Bradbury. *From Puritanism to Postmodernism: A History of American Literature*. London: Penguin Books, 1992.

Sage, Victor. *Horror Fiction in the Protestant Tradition*. London: Macmillan Press, 1988.

Schleiermacher, Friedrich. *The Christian Faith*. London: T & T Clark, 2016.

Schraam, Jan-Melissa. *Testimony and Advocacy in Victorian Law, Literature and Theology*. Cambridge: Cambridge University Press, 2000.

Schwartz, Regina. *Remembering and Repeating: Biblical Creation in Paradise Lost*. Cambridge: Cambridge University Press, 1988.

Sedgwick, Eve Kosofsky. *Between Men: English Literature and Male Homosocial Desire*. New York: Columbia University Press, 1985.

Sedgwick, Eve Kosofsky. *The Coherence of Gothic Convention*. London: Methuen Press, 1986.

Seed, David. '*Frankenstein*: Parable or Spectacle?' *Criticism* 24.2 (Fall, 1982): 327–40.

Shaftesbury, Anthony Ashley Cooper. *Characteristicks of Men, Manners, Opinions, Times, Volume 3*. Indiana: Liberty Fund Press, 2001.

Shelley, Mary. *Frankenstein*. London: Penguin Classics, 2012.

Shelley, Mary. *Frankenstein, 1818 Text*, ed. Marilyn Butler. Oxford: Oxford University Press, 1998.

Shelley, Mary. *Letters Written During a Short Residence in Sweden, Norway, and Denmark*. http://www.gutenberg.org/files/3529/3529-h/3529-h.htm, first accessed 19 May 2016.

Showalter, Elaine. *A Literature of Their Own, British Women Novelists from Brontë to Lessing*. Princeton: Princeton University Press, 1977.

Showalter, Elaine. *Sexual Anarchy, Gender and Culture at the Fin-de-Siècle*. London: Virago Press, 1992.

Simpson, Louis, *James Hogg, A Critical Study*. London: Oliver & Boyd, 1962.

Smith, Andrew. *Gothic Literature*. Edinburgh: Edinburgh University Press, 2007.

Smith, Andrew. *Gothic Radicalism: Literature, Philosophy and Psychoanalysis in the Nineteenth Century*. London: Palgrave, 2000.

Smith, Andrew. *Victorian Demons: Medicine, Masculinity and the Gothic at the Fin-De-Siècle*. Manchester: Manchester University Press, 2004.

Smith Andrew and William Hughes, eds *Bram Stoker: History, Psychoanalysis, and the Gothic*. London: Palgrave Macmillan, 1998.

Smith, Andrew and William Hughes. *Empire and the Gothic: The Politics of Genre*. London: Blackwell, 2003.

Starrs, D. Bruno. 'Keeping the Faith, Catholicism in *Dracula* and Its Adaptations', *Journal of Dracula Studies* 6 (2004): 13–18.

Stevenson, Robert Louis. *Dr Jekyll and Mr Hyde and Other Stories*. London: Penguin Classics, 1979.

Stoker, Bram. *Dracula*. London: Penguin Classics, 2003.

Strong, Rowan. *Anglicanism and the British Empire, c.1700–1850*. Oxford: Oxford University Press, 2007.

Summers, Montague. *The Gothic Quest, A History of the Gothic Novel*. London: Fortune Press, 1938.

Surratt, Marshall N. "'The Awe-Creating Presence of the Deity": Some Religious Sources for Charles Brockden Brown's *Wieland*', *Papers on Language & Literature* 33.3 (Summer 1997): 310–24.

Swanson, Kathryn J. 'A Liberative Imagination: Reconsidering the Fiction of Charlotte Brontë in the light of Feminist Theology'. Unpublished Doctoral thesis, University of St Andrews, 2017.

Tanner, Tony. *Scenes of Nature, Signs of Man*. Cambridge: Cambridge University Press, 1987.

Taylor, Alan. *American Colonies: The Settlement of North America to 1800*. London: Penguin, 2003.

Taylor, Charles. *A Secular Age*. London: Harvard University Press, 2003.

Thormählen, Marianne. *The Brontës And Religion*. Cambridge: Cambridge University Press, 2004.

Twitchell, James B. *The Living Dead, A Study of the Vampire in Romantic Literature*. Durham, NC: Duke University Press, 1981.

Uglow, Nathan, ed. *Leeds Working Papers, Victorian Ethics*. Leeds: Leeds Centre for Victorian Studies, 2008.

Vanhoozer, Kevin J. *Remythologizing Theology: Divine Action, Passion, and Authorship*. Cambridge: Cambridge University Press, 2010.

Varma, Devendra. *The Gothic Flame: Being a History of the Gothic Novel in England, Its Origins, Efflorescence, Disintegration, and Residuary Influences*. London: Morrison and Gibb, 1957.

Veeder, William and Gordon Hirsch, ed. *Dr Jekyll and Mr. Hyde after One Hundred Years*. Chicago: Chicago University Press, 1988.

Walton, Heather. *Literature and Theology: New Interdisciplinary Spaces*. London: Ashgate, 2011.

Walpole, Horace. *The Castle of Otranto: A Gothic Story*. Oxford: Oxford World Classics, 2008.

Ward, Graham. *True Religion*. Oxford: Blackwell, 2003.

Watt, Ian. *The Rise of the Novel*. London: The Hogarth Press, 1987.

Watt, Ian, ed. *The Victorian Novel: Modern Essays in Criticism*. Oxford: Oxford University Press, 1971.

Weir, David. *Decadence and the Making of Modernism*. Massachusetts: University of Massachusetts Press, 1995.

Wilde, Oscar. *In Praise of Disobedience*. London: Verso Books, 2018.

Wilde, Oscar. *The Picture of Dorian Gray*. London: Penguin Classics, 2000.

Williams, Anne. *Art of Darkness: A Poetics of Gothic*. Chicago: Chicago University Press, 1995.

Williams, Raymond. *Culture and Society 1780–1950*. London: Penguin Books, 1961.

Williams, Rowan. *Faith in the Public Square*. London: Bloomsbury, 2015.

Winnifrith, Tom. *The Brontës and Their Background: Romance and Reality*. London: Palgrave Macmillan, 1988.

Wittenreich, Joseph. *The Romantics on Milton*. Ohio: Case Western University Press, 1970.

Wright, Angela and Dale Townshend, ed. *Romantic Gothic: An Edinburgh Companion*. Edinburgh: Edinburgh University Press, 2016.

Index

absolutism 62, 63
Adam 31, 35, 37, 38, 40
aesthetics 5, 23, 25, 37, 44, 48
  appearance 38, 145, 148, 150, 153
  beauty 152
  debates 6
  experience 147
  judgement 150
  moral 43
  practice 146
  qualities 14
Aids to Reflection (Coleridge) 75
ambivalent secularism. *See* theology, antagonism
anachronism 145
Anglicanism 21
anti-Catholicism 11, 12, 118
anti-Catholic Protestants 13
anti-Christian writing 76
Anti-Jacobin Review 6
antinomianism 62, 149
anxiety 6, 8, 20, 22, 23, 59, 60, 62, 97, 129, 136, 138, 172
apocalyptic language 65, 104, 107
Apostle Paul 134, 135, 137, 142, 143
Arata, Stephen 128, 131, 132
Arnold, Matthew 112
art 150, 151
atheism 3
Auerbach, Nina 158
authoritarianism 98
authority 28, 60
autonomy 50, 146

Baldick, Chris 8
Barth, Karl 15, 68
'A Beleaguered City' (Oliphant) 121
beliefs 10, 13, 18, 26, 42, 60, 66, 70, 73, 81, 90, 100, 108, 126, 159, 163
  Calvinist 70
  Christian 11, 17, 75, 76, 78, 83, 109, 112, 159, 165

collective 167
  religious 4, 22, 94, 108, 112, 126, 133
  theological 13, 26, 56, 73, 77, 102, 103, 133
Bible 1, 2, 27, 79, 80, 98, 112
biological determinism 126
biological process 125
Blagdon, F. 6
blasphemy 12
Bloom, Harold 3
Botting, Fred 144
bourgeois masculinity 132
Bretherton, Luke 2
British imperialism 125, 128, 162, 166
Brontë, Charlotte 21, 22, 76, 96, 98–100, 105, 109, 110, 176
Brontë, Emily 21, 22, 75, 76, 78, 83–5, 87, 89, 91, 176
Brown, Callum 127
Brown, Charles Brockden 65
Brown, David 16–18, 20, 26, 57, 59, 72, 177, 178
Brunner, Emil 67, 68
brutality 89
Burke, Edmund 6, 10
Burstein, Miriam Elizabeth 75
Butler, Marilyn 12
Byron, Glennis 129

Calloway, Kutter 177
Calvin, John 20, 21, 58, 59, 70–2
Calvinism 21, 58, 59, 63–6, 79, 80, 93
Calvinistic moralism 87
Calvinistic Presbyterianism 55
Calvinist tradition 59, 60, 70, 99, 131
capitalism 19
Catholicism 7, 8, 23, 118, 154, 155, 160, 161, 171
cause-and-effect relationship 12
Chadwick, Owen 126
Chalk Cliffs at Rugen (painting, Friedrich) 16

Christ   30, 32, 51, 63, 141, 154, 155, 157, 167, 168. *See also* Jesus Christ
Christian
    Calvinist   78
    colonialism   169
    orthodox   17
    practice   176
    theology   127, 157, 164, 171, 176
    tradition   83
    writing   2, 79, 97, 131
Christianity   11, 17, 76, 110, 112, 127, 177
Christmas Carol, A (Dickens)   114, 115
Chronicles   98
Clarke, Micael M.   76, 78
cognition   33
Coleridge, Samuel Taylor   6, 7, 12, 75, 178
communion   155
Conjectures on Original Composition (Young)   38
conservatism   12
corruption   24, 85, 102, 129–131, 133
Covenanter Gothic   20, 55
creation   25, 28–34, 36–9, 41, 44–6, 48, 49, 51, 52, 99, 150
creation ex nihilo   31–2, 53
creativity   25, 33, 49, 52
Crime and Punishment (Dostoyevsky)   144
crimes   65, 66
criminal behaviours   125, 126
criminality   131
Critchley, Simon   42
critical inquiry   129
critical philosophy   15
critical practices   125
culture   9
    forms   114
    identity   144
    moment   130
    production   112
    Scottish   60

Dante, Alighieri   37
Darwinism   160
Darwin, Charles   127, 129
Davis, Stevie   78
Davison, Andrew   4, 24

Davison, Carol Margaret   5
death   91, 92, 95, 96, 101, 116
Decay of Lying, The (Wilde)   150
degeneration   22, 23, 129, 130, 143, 144, 148
    animalistic   133
    discourses   131, 173
    theory   125, 128, 139, 172
Degeneration: A Chapter in Darwinism (Lankester)   125
DeLamotte, Eugenia C.   109
'demonical corpse'   37
Descent of Man and Selection in Relation to Sex, The (Darwin)   125
Desmond, William   178
devil   36, 37, 87, 94, 133
Dickens, Charles   15, 114, 115
didacticism   57
discourse   11, 23, 24, 56, 60
    Calvinist   66, 67, 69, 70
    class   132
    criminological   130, 135, 144
    cultural   12
    Darwinian   131
    evolutionary   130, 134, 135
    Gothic   102
    of internalization   10
    materialist   125, 129, 172, 173
    medical   144, 145
    moral   136, 164
    non-material   163, 164, 172
    non-theological   125
    physiognomic   134
    political   12
    religious   22, 76, 122, 123, 159, 160
    sacred   81
    science   143
    scientific   111, 123, 126, 129, 130, 137, 138, 140, 144, 145
    secular   80, 81, 130
    sociological   12, 135
    theological   12, 13, 20, 63, 67, 72, 73, 113, 129, 158, 159, 161, 166, 171, 172
discursive techniques   143
divided self   131
divine   10, 15, 18, 24, 30, 32, 36–8, 41, 46, 49, 50, 56–8, 60, 67–71, 91, 110, 126, 135, 170, 178, 179
Dostoyevsky, Fyodor   144

doxology   78, 81
Dracula (Stoker)   19, 22, 129, 157–73
Dracula, The Novel and the Legend (Leatherdale)   158
dualism   66, 149

Eagleton, Terry   10, 44, 50, 51
Eco, Umberto   1
Edwards, Amelia B.   115
Edwards, Jonathan   61, 65
ego   38, 129, 141
Elijah (prophet)   68
embodiment   25, 29, 33, 34, 49, 53, 122, 130, 136, 138, 146, 153–5, 162, 163, 171, 172
Empson, William   30
Enlightenment   10, 39, 64
epistemology   20, 28
Epistle to the Romans   135
eschatology   81, 90, 98, 100, 107
ethical judgements   44, 127
ethics   23, 33, 66, 134, 146, 152
Eucharist   154, 155, 157, 160, 167, 168
evangelism   23, 61, 166, 168
Eve   31, 37, 38, 40
evil   20, 23, 26, 27, 44–50, 52, 53, 86, 129, 130, 138, 139, 144, 157, 172, 173
evolution   126, 128
Evolution and Ethics: Delivered in the Sheldonian Theatre, May 18, 1893 (Huxley)   127
Exodus   98, 99

faith   3, 7, 11, 15, 17, 57–9, 71–3, 81, 103, 110, 112, 120, 156, 162, 168, 171, 178, 179
Faith in the Public Square (Williams)   133
Faust (Goethe)   38
fear   15, 113, 114
Fernie, Ewan   45, 52, 149
fiction   4, 5, 13, 15, 75, 112
Fiddes, Paul   18, 58
fin-de-siècle art   146
fin-de-siècle Gothic   125, 126, 128–30, 134, 137, 143, 172, 173. *See also* Gothic
Flowers of Literature (Prevost and Blagdon)   6
folk medicine   159

forgiveness   80, 85, 93
Foucault's Pendulum (1988)   1
Frankenstein (Shelley)   19, 20, 24–30, 32, 34–6, 41, 48, 53, 54, 134
Frankenstein, Victor   25–9, 31–41, 43–53, 134
Frayling, Christopher   157
freedom   90, 104, 127
French Revolution   6
'A Fresh Approach to Wuthering Heights' (Leavis)   77
Freud, Sigmund   10
Friedrich, Caspar David   16
Furgusson, David A.   112

Geary, Robert F.   9, 11
Gelder, Ken   158
Genesis, book of   31, 99
ghost stories   22, 112–16, 118, 121, 123
Gifford Lecture series   112
Gilbert, Sandra   21, 76, 83, 85, 93, 94, 99
Gillies, Bessy   63
Girard, René   23, 168, 170
Gladstone, William Ewart   159
gnostic language   32
God   3, 15–18, 30, 31, 33, 35, 41, 48, 59, 68, 70, 78, 81, 84, 91, 99, 101, 106–9, 126, 127, 141, 170, 178, 179
    as Divine Father   38
    mediation   32
    nature of   19
God in Mystery and Words (Brown)   177
von Goethe, Johann Wolfgang   34, 38
Gothic   56, 66. *See also* fin-de-siècle Gothic
    barbarism   160
    Calvinist   55–60, 67, 68, 70–2
    cathedrals   7
    contemporary   4, 112
    criticism   1, 2, 4–19, 97, 176
    early   12
    English   14
    fiction   4
    form   111
    ideology   118
    literature   2, 4, 9, 11, 19, 20, 24, 27, 176
    nineteenth-century writing   1, 13, 14, 16, 18, 19, 55

novels 1–3, 5–8, 14, 19, 24, 28, 62, 71, 73, 76, 83, 110, 118, 175–9
studies 48, 111, 129, 175, 179
technique 76, 83
tradition 27, 83, 160
Victorian 111
Gothic Body, The (Hurley) 128
Gothic Flame, The (Varma) 7
Gothic Ideology, The (Hoeveler) 9
Gubar, Susan 21, 76, 83, 85, 93, 94, 99
guilt 65, 137

Halberstam, Judith 149, 151, 153
Halsey, Katie 5, 6
Hampson, Peter 2
hedonism 149, 152
hegemony 22, 73, 99
Herbert, Christopher 158, 162
hermeneutics 59, 76, 79–81, 178
Hext, Kate 150
Hoeveler, Diana Long 9, 11–13
Hogg, James 8, 13, 20, 21, 56, 60, 62, 66, 67, 69, 71, 79, 95, 176
Holy Spirit 59
horror 4, 5, 13, 15, 37, 59, 113, 178
Horror Fiction in the Protestant Tradition (Sage) 1, 13
hospitality 2, 77
Hughes, William 175, 176
human
  activity 47
  agency 123
  finitude 149
  relationships 36, 41, 42, 46, 48, 52
  role in creation 31
humanity 15, 32, 43, 44, 47, 50, 66, 78, 82, 110, 125, 126, 128, 129, 143
Hunt, William Holman 123
Hurley, Kelly 126, 128
Huxley, Thomas 127, 129
hyper-Calvinism 62, 98

iconography 16, 23, 157, 159–61, 164, 165, 170, 171
Idea of the Holy, The (Otto) 113
imaginative apologetics 4, 23, 68, 150, 175, 176, 178, 179
imaginative art 17

imaginative engagement 33, 179
Imfeld, Zoë Lehmann 2, 3, 16, 17, 112, 113, 124, 138, 144
immaterial 7, 20, 62, 63, 66, 72, 73, 155
'Imperial Gothic' 158, 159
industrial age 169
infallibility of the elect 69
Inklings 14
Institutes of the Christian Religion (Calvin) 20, 58, 59
interdependence 38, 50, 52
intimacy 39, 52

James, M. R. 121
James, William 163
Jane Eyre (Brontë) 21, 22, 75–7, 96–110
Jasper, David 4, 9
Jesus Christ 15
Job, book of 26, 35, 36, 46, 98
John's gospel 70
justice/injustice 30, 35, 68, 101, 149

Kant, Immanuel 15
Karschay, Stephen 128
Kettle, Arnold 89
Kierkegaard, Søren 113
Killeen, Jarlath 111
King James Bible 3
Kings 98
Knight, Mark 3, 112, 128, 155
knowledge 22, 33, 49–52, 56–8, 64, 72, 90, 113, 123, 134, 162–4, 178

Lang, Andrew 121
Lankester, Edwin Ray 125, 128
Larsen, Timothy 112
Law of God 135, 156
Leatherdale, Clive 158
Leavis, Q. D. 77
Lewis, C. S. 14, 30
Lewis, Matthew 12, 162
liberation 22, 88, 98–100, 109
  model 21
  radical 103
  spiritual 87
Light of the World, The (painting, Hunt) 123
Literature of Terror, The (Punter) 8

Lives (Plutarch)   34
Lk.
    15:11-32   82
Lombroso, Cesare   126, 128, 129, 132

Marsden, Simon   4, 21, 76, 78, 80,
    86, 112
Marsh, Richard   119, 121
Mason, Emma   3, 112, 128, 155
materialism   22, 110, 144, 162, 173
    evolutionary   127
    medical   163
    scientific   129, 134
    secular   134, 154
    vulgar   9
materiality   22, 41, 49, 50, 53, 155
material reality   60, 65, 66, 72, 98, 113,
    115, 134
material world   20, 21, 53, 62, 66, 67, 90
Maturin, Charles   111
Maynard, John   95
Melmoth the Wanderer (Maturin)   7, 111
metaphysics   15-17, 32, 48-51, 112, 116,
    117, 121, 128, 130, 138, 143
Mighall, Robert   8, 128, 137
Milbank, Alison   2, 13-16, 20, 55, 56, 59,
    63, 64, 66, 67, 99, 104, 160, 171, 177
Milbank, John   16, 48
Miller, J. Hillis   78, 84, 94, 95, 113
Millington, Thomas Street   118, 119
Milton, John   25, 26, 29-32, 34-40, 49,
    51, 54, 83
Mishra, Vijay   8
misogyny   132, 173
modernity   3, 10, 130, 136, 158, 159,
    169, 171
Monk, The (Lewis)   6, 12, 162
monsters   25, 26, 28, 33-5, 40, 43, 45,
    48, 178
monstrosity   20, 134
'MOOR EEFFOC' effect   15
morality/immortality   5, 6, 25, 44, 48, 85,
    114, 115, 129, 137, 142, 143, 145,
    167, 175
moral judgement   45, 48, 57, 147
moral language   130
moral law   149
moral relativism   47

More, Hannah   6
Mt.
    7:13   137
    18:22   79
    25   103
    25:31-46   137
    27:51   141

narcissism   145, 152
narratives   10, 19, 47, 49, 50, 57, 64,
    86, 119
    Gothic   59
    process   57
    structure   28
    voice   29, 45
national identity   6
nationalism   12
natural selection   125, 130
nature of being   158
Newman, Beth   28
Newman, John Henry   159
'Nineteenth Century Religion and Literature'
    (Knight and Mason)   112
'No Coward's Soul is Mine' (Brontë)   78
'No Living Voice' (Millington)   118-19
non-theological reader   16, 17
Nordau, Max   128, 139
'The North Mail' (Edwards)   115-17
Num
    14:18   86

Oates, Joyce Carol   145
Old Testament   69, 98
Oliphant, Margaret   121
On Evil (Eagleton)   51
On the Origin of Species (Darwin)   125
'On the Physical Basis of Life' (Huxley)
    127
ontology   16, 25, 34, 35, 39, 45, 47, 48,
    82, 126, 132, 134, 135, 139, 144,
    148, 151, 153, 176
'The Open Door' (Oliphant)   121-3
Ordway, Holly   15
orthodox Christian model   10
Orthodox Church   161
orthodoxy   15-18, 24, 26, 75, 76, 83, 84,
    110, 177
Others   20, 27, 36, 39, 47, 77

Otto, Rudolph   113
Our Vampires, Ourselves (Auerbach)   158

Paley, William   127
Paradise Lost (Milton)   26, 29, 31, 32, 34, 37, 38, 40, 51
Pater, Walter   23, 147, 150
Pearce, Lynne   96
'pernicious doctrines'   6
personhood   25, 27, 39–42, 44, 45, 47, 48, 50, 90, 175
perversion   139, 146, 149, 153
Phil.
   2   101
philosophy   11
   contemporary   52
   liberal   41
   Western   27
physical connection   40–1
Pick, Daniel   158
Pickstock, Catherine   155–6
Picture of Dorian Gray, The (Wilde)   22, 23, 129, 145–57
Plutarch   34
political conditions   5–6
political emancipation   73
political liberalism   20
political radicalism   5
political systems   100
politics model   42
pragmatism   56, 119
Prevost, F.   6
Private Memoirs and Confessions of a Justified Sinner, The (Hogg)   8, 13, 20, 56, 60–4, 68, 69
privation of being   48, 147, 150, 152, 153
privation theory   145–7, 173
Protestantism   7
Protestants   160, 161, 170, 171
Psalms   98
Psychical Research Society   120
psychoanalysis   8, 10, 11, 63, 111, 112, 117, 177
psychodrama   11
public confession   155, 156
Punter, David   8
purification   145, 157, 158, 165
Puritanism   30, 31

Radcliffe, Anne   8
radical evil   45–7
radical orthodox   16
Ramsay, Andrew   65
rationality   10, 72, 112, 120, 122
realism   28, 87, 116
redemption   30, 32, 59, 85, 87, 94, 135, 145, 156, 157
religion   78, 112, 120
   attitudes   3–4
   belief   4
   content   7
   conversion   119
   definition   11
   elements   5, 7, 9, 124, 160
   expression   11, 76, 78, 87, 99
   extremism   60
   institutional forms   75, 78, 81, 90, 94, 96–8, 107, 123
   models   57
   natural   67
   pagan   154
   practice   7, 11, 19, 77–9, 82, 90, 106, 177
   and science   162
   symbol   11
   tensions   77–96
   theme   176
   tradition   81, 160
religiosity   78, 81–3, 85, 90, 92, 94, 97
Renaissance: Studies in Art and Poetry, The (Pater)   150
repentance   66, 129, 139, 142
resurrection   32, 51, 95, 103, 123
Rev.
   21   107
revelation   10, 15, 17, 18, 21, 24, 27, 33, 34, 56–9, 64, 66–72, 81, 98, 117, 141, 179
Ricoeur, Paul   85
'The Rime of the Ancient Mariner' (Coleridge)   7
rituals   9, 11, 96, 154
Roden, Frederick   156
Rom.
   7   137
   8:38-9   89
Roman Catholic Church   7, 161, 170

Romantic era 38, 39
Romantic ideology 33, 38, 48, 49, 53
Romantic Imagination 32, 36, 49, 54
Romantic individualism 39
Romanticism 7, 20, 32, 48, 50, 53
Rousseau, Jean Jacques 41, 42, 47
Ruins of Empires (Volney) 34
Ruskin, John 16, 23

sacrament 168, 170, 171
  of marriage 104, 109
  theology 23, 121
  tradition 154-5, 157
sacramentality 157, 158, 161, 171, 175
sacrifice 23, 30
sacrilege 84, 91, 160, 167, 168
Sage, Victor 1, 5, 12, 13
salvation 20, 69, 79, 90, 101, 102, 135, 137
Samuel 98
Satan 37, 49, 87
scepticism 22, 56
Schleiermacher, Friedrich 21, 91
Schwartz, Regina 31
scientific ideology 161
scientific theory 144
Secular Age, A (Taylor) 3
Secularisation of the European Mind in the Nineteenth Century, The (Chadwick) 126
secularism 22, 123, 125, 127, 130
secularity 130, 173
secularization 3
Sedgwick, Eve Kosofsky 80, 81
Seed, David 38
semiotics 65, 70, 113, 160
sensations 146, 149, 150, 152
'A Set of Chessman' (Marsh) 119-21
sexuality 164, 165
sexual 'wantonness' 165
Shelley, Mary 19, 20, 25-8, 31, 32, 37, 39, 41, 45-9, 53, 83
sin 20, 30, 36, 47, 58, 60, 65, 80, 85, 86, 93, 102, 110, 129, 133, 138, 172
'Sinners in the Hands of Angry God' (Edwards) 61
Smith, Andrew 10
social contract 42, 43, 47, 50

Social Contract, The (Rousseau) 41, 42
social norms 73, 76
Society for Psychical Research 112
Sorrows of Young Werther (Goethe) 34
spiritual condition 37
spiritual freedom 101
spiritualism 8, 118
spirituality 11, 155
spiritual reality 15, 58, 61, 62, 65, 66, 67, 72, 131
St Augustine 48
Stevenson, Robert Louis 66, 130, 135, 137, 138, 144-6
St John of Revelation 105
St John the Evangelist 105
Stoker, Bram 19, 23, 157, 159-61, 169
'The Story of the Goblins Who Stole a Sexton' (Dickens) 114
Strange Case of Dr. Jekyll and Mr. Hyde, The (Stevenson) 22, 23, 66, 128-45
Strictures on the Modern System of Female Education (More) 6
structuralism 9
structuralist theory 60
Styler, Rebecca 176, 177
subjectivity 21-4, 34, 35, 45, 60, 61, 63, 65-7, 98, 103, 108, 113, 123, 126, 129-31, 135-8, 142-5, 156, 158, 172, 175
sublimity 5, 6, 10, 53, 96, 101
suffering 15, 35, 61, 102, 115, 141, 142
Summers, Montague 7, 8, 24
Supernatural in Gothic Fiction, The (Geary) 9
supernaturalism 122, 123, 145, 176, 178
superstition 159, 160-5, 169
Swanson, Kathryn 108
symbolism 11, 13, 123

Taylor, Barry 177
Taylor, Charles 3
teleology 19, 116, 126
testimony 29, 58
theodicy 19, 26, 98
*theologia civilis*r (civil theology) 42
theological anthropology 144
theo-logos (talk of God) 3, 17, 18, 178

theology
    absence in Gothic criticism   5–19
    antagonism   2
    apophatic   57
    Calvinist   23, 56, 57, 60, 61, 63, 67, 70, 72
    Christian   1, 10, 11, 14, 17, 48, 112, 126, 131
    confessional   154
    contemporary   4, 19
    criticism   76, 89, 158
    and culture   177
    debates   3, 4, 22, 71, 112
    Gothic   98, 119, 177
    history and   13, 14, 19
    hospitality   2
    ideas   2, 3, 8, 9, 11, 13, 16, 17, 20–1, 67, 76, 113, 119, 120, 123, 134, 158, 177
    imaginative   14, 48, 77, 177
    institutions   100
    language   2, 15, 26, 28, 45–7, 65, 71, 83, 104, 108, 123, 126, 130, 132, 133, 137, 156, 163–5, 169
    material   20, 126
    methodology   1
    model   76
    modern   165
    narrative   60
    natural   6, 10, 56, 58, 68–70, 117, 127, 177
    orthodox   161, 167
    Pauline   23
    political   22, 77, 97, 175
    practice   24, 78, 80, 108
    Protestant   12, 13
    reasoning   159
    reformed   20, 55
    repressed   177
    social   76, 97
    systematic   20–1, 56–9, 68, 70, 72
    traditions   8, 9, 20, 24, 26, 27, 34, 55–7, 70, 72, 83, 91, 99
Thormählen, Marianne   21, 85, 95, 105, 107, 109, 110
Tolkien, J. R. R.   14
Tradition and Imagination (Brown)   26
tragedy   59, 86, 106
transcendence   33, 37, 45, 46, 52, 53, 141
trauma   46, 47
Trinitarian theology   30, 31
Trinity   16
truth   1, 14, 16, 18, 20, 22, 24, 27, 41, 56, 59, 60, 62, 64, 82, 102, 115, 116

V21 Collective   19
Vanhoozer, Kevin J.   27
Varma, Devandra   7, 8
Victorian age   22, 111, 112, 114, 123
Victorian England   160
Victorian patriarchy   99
Victorian society   112, 114, 121
violence   43, 47, 85, 87, 94, 165, 167, 171, 178
Volney, Constantin-François   34

Walton, Heather   29, 53
Ward, Graham   11, 71
Weber, Max   19
Weir, Thomas   65, 66
Wieland (Brown)   65
Wilde, Oscar   23, 145–8, 150, 153, 154, 156, 157, 160, 176
Williams, Rowan   23, 130, 133
Winnifrith, Tom   90
Wuthering Heights (Brontë)   21, 76–98, 107, 109, 110

Yates, James   65, 66
Young, Edward   38

www.ingramcontent.com/pod-product-compliance
Lightning Source LLC
Chambersburg PA
CBHW070637300426
44111CB00013B/2147